Backcountry Skiing
Utah

Second Edition

Tyson Bradley

FALCONGUIDES ®

GUILFORD, CONNECTICUT
HELENA, MONTANA
AN IMPRINT OF THE GLOBE PEQUOT PRESS

FALCONGUIDES®

Text design by Casey Shain
Photo credits: All photos are by the author unless otherwise noted.
Maps by Trailhead Graphics © Morris Book Publishing, LLC

ISSN: 1545-9748
ISBN-13: 978-0-7627-2821-3

Printed in the United States of America
Second Edition/Fifth Printing

Contents

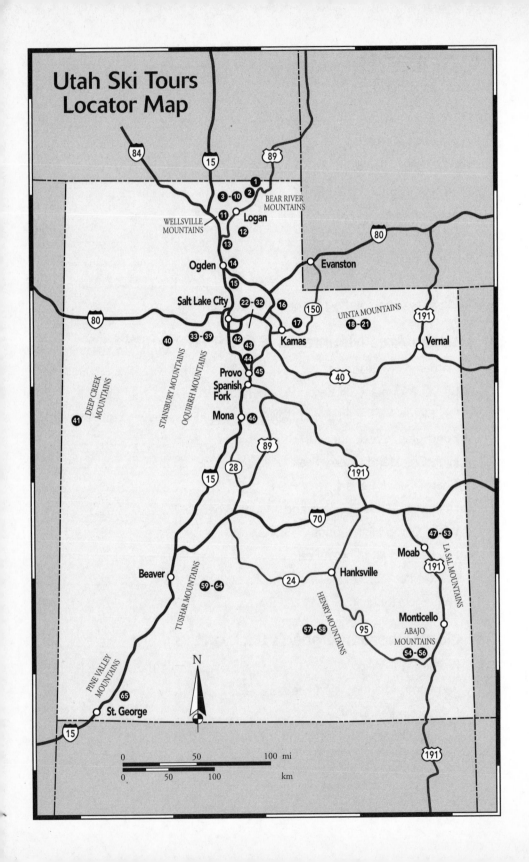

Utah Ski Tours
Locator Map

Where I've indicated access has been granted across
private land, there is no assurance that this will continue
to be true. Proceed at your own risk on private property.

Legend

Interstate Highway	🛣 (90)
State Road	(120)
Local Road	
Downhill Ski Run	
Ascent or Approach	
Cliff Bands	
Parking	**P**
Campground	⛺
Mountain or Peak	△ **Granite Peak 9,028'**
Yurt, Tower, Backcountry Access Point, or Point of Interest	✳
River or Creek	
Lake	
Ridgeline	
Contour Line and Contour Value	*6000*
Chairlift, Tram, or Tow	

Note: A contour line is an imaginary line that connects points of equal elevation. If it were possible to cut level slices on a mountain with a large knife at uniform intervals, the edges of the cut would be the contour lines.

The contour value is the distance from sea level.

The contour interval is the vertical distance between contour lines. Close spacing of contour lines indicates a steep slope, while contour lines spread out indicate a gradual slope.

Foreword

Within a month of my first backcountry tour, I realized that I had made a huge mistake by not starting backcountry skiing earlier in life. Seeing as this revelation took place in Utah, I assumed that the rest of the world was just like this, with easy access, great powder, relatively stable snow, and perfect ski-touring terrain. It was only once I started traveling to other states and continents to ski that it dawned on me—not only is Utah unique, but it has some of the best ski touring on the planet. An average powder day here is a once-in-a-lifetime experience anywhere else; and a great Utah powder day, well, it can redefine your life. While you can get a taste of this at Utah's famous ski resorts, it's merely a teaser for the amazing potential that extends beyond their boundaries.

For better or worse, backcountry skiing requires a long apprenticeship as you discover where and how to get the most for your skiing dollar. This process can take years and can be fraught with frustration and bad experiences. What you really need is a personal guide you can carry in your pack who lets you in on all the tricks of the terrain and steers you in the right direction. Enter this book's author, Tyson Bradley, the Utah backcountry skiing equivalent of Marco Polo. If it can be skied, Tyson has done it. If there's a question about how to do it, Tyson is the guy to ask. He's explored Utah mountain ranges for so long that he's threatening Brigham Young's stature as one of the state's foremost pioneers. With aerial photos, route descriptions, and detailed maps of all of the hidden gems of the Utah backcountry, you can't go wrong.

This is the place. Here's the book. Let the skiing begin!

Andrew McLean
Park City, Utah

Acknowledgments

Many of the individuals who were early influences on my backcountry skiing career might not give me their blessings for writing a guidebook and sharing the secret places and patented techniques they turned me on to. Nonetheless, I would like to extend my appreciation to them, because it was their example and experience that I absorbed and that inspired me to make a life of exploring and writing about mountains.

In particular, I want to thank my parents, Cam and Sky, who led me into the mountains despite all the hassles involved—infinite patience required—to drag three rambunctious boys into the Idaho and Wyoming ranges. Art and Barbara Brown were mentors to my folks (and me) as we progressed from weekend hikes and cross-country day skis to weeklong Wind River backpack trips and winter overnight camping.

Derek Brown and Steve Koerber became partners and highly informal instructors during my teen years. Steve and I lived in Seattle during my university years, and we skied the Cascade volcanoes. These adventures led to off-season ski descent expeditions to South America, Asia, and Alaska. But winters were always spent ski touring in Utah, acquiring the knowledge to write this guidebook.

While I researched ranges outside my Central Wasatch backyard, I met and toured some fine fluff with Al Dymerski in Logan. Dave Medara, director of the Moab Desert Adventures guide service, expedited my research in the La Sal Range and joined me for outstanding corn tours there. Bill Murphy shared a wealth of information and stories from two decades of southern Utah backcountry skiing, and Alec Hornstein added his up-to-date perspective on the Tushar Mountains. Dave Braun, a ski-mountaineering partner on many expeditions, helped me explore the Tushars and Pine Valley Mountains.

Steve Hymas assisted with information about the Powder Mountain area, and Jock Glidden reviewed the North Wasatch section as well. In the Uintas, Bob Merrill and his trusty snowmobile facilitated the research. Ben Dobbin, owner/operator of Castle Peak Yurt, directed me to that area.

The aerial photography was made possible by the expert flying of Jared Higgins and Andy Wallace. Wasatch Powderbird Guides also generously provided images from their collection.

The maps never would have been possible without the software savvy of my father-in-law, Stanislas Faure. Many others also contributed as partners or with bits of beta from different areas, but one frequent ski companion whose support, advice, and computer skills were indispensable is my wife, Julie Faure. Without her blessing and patience, the project would not have come together.

Introduction

Backcountry skiing in Utah is arguably the finest in the world. Great and consistent snow, easy approach climbs, spectacular yet friendly mountains, relatively short drives, and comfortable temperatures are a few of the major selling points. This guide is intended to help skiers of all ability levels enjoy the world of off-piste skiing that begins at ski resort boundaries and trailheads.

Although several guidebooks describe touring in the Wasatch Mountains, this book offers a modern perspective and is the first to include ranges throughout Utah. The Logan Mountains, Oquirrh, Uinta, La Sal, and Tushar Ranges boast incredible skiing that has scarcely been tapped. Tours in these mountains as well as in the Stansbury, Deep Creek, Abajo, Henry, and Pine Valley Mountains are described here. Many snow-covered Utah mountains, including the central Utah plateau ranges, were not included because of their inaccessibility and inconsistent snowpack. This guide focuses on the cream of the Beehive State's corn and powder crop.

Backcountry skiing has evolved from its cross-country roots to a level that involves regular descents of high peaks and steep couloirs. (The latter are described specifically in Andrew McLean's eccentric, amusing, and highly recommended *Chuting Gallery*.) This guide attempts to meet the needs of traditional touring parties, while going a step beyond and describing routes and runs in the alpine terrain where advanced skiing, climbing, and avalanche skills are required.

Despite being generally user-friendly, ski touring in Utah is fraught with many potential dangers and hardships. Increasingly difficult objectives should be attempted in a gradual progression within the comfort zone of all party members. Bear in mind that conditions change radically from year to year and even within a given season.

The Greatest Snow on Earth

Why ski in Utah? Just read the license plates—it has the GREATEST SNOW ON EARTH! Being the highest ranges (after California's Sierra) that Pacific Ocean storms encounter on their eastward march inland, the Bear River, Wasatch, and Tushar Ranges get huge benefits from orographics. This essentially refers to the necessity of clouds to lighten their load of moisture before rising in altitude to cross a mountain range. The Uintas and La Sals are even higher, but they get the leftovers after the more westerly ranges have been pummeled by snow. Storms coming from the northwest are often enhanced by lake effect as they pick up moisture from the warmer surface of the Great Salt Lake and deposit it on the Oquirrh and Wasatch Ranges.

The snow stays cold and dry in Utah partly due to the arid desert environment, but also because of the generally north-facing aspect of many of the steep canyons. Even weeks after a storm, backcountry snow can have a delightful recrystallized surface of shallow powder. Beginners and experts alike find themselves performing better in Utah's "ego snow" than anywhere else they tour.

The southern Utah ranges also benefit from the extended periods of high pressure to develop good corn-snow conditions. Clear, cold nights following hot, sunny days are common in the Tushars, La Sals, Henrys, and Abajos. This pattern enables a stable, supportable crust condition to prevail. In late spring the temperatures throughout most of Utah are often too warm to produce corn snow, but the higher altitude Uintas, with their colder nights, often harbor fine supportable conditions at the 10,000- to 13,000-foot level well into June.

Avalanche Awareness

The biggest mystery and the primary reason that people refrain from backcountry skiing is avalanche hazard. No one can entirely predict avalanches. Yet following basic rules and protocols as well as relying on personal intuition and a healthy dose of respect will normally result in a lifetime of safe and rewarding ski touring. Known slide paths and hazard areas are mentioned in this book, but many, if not most, of the tours described here involve at least some exposure to avalanche potential. Routes described are the most efficient—not necessarily the safest. All users should make their own assessments and be prepared to evaluate every run before skiing.

The most basic essential is an understanding of terrain and where avalanches can happen. Slides occur on slope angles of 25 to 60 degrees. In the Wasatch they occur at angles of 30 to 45 degrees, with the magic number being 38. Remember that slides can continue for great distances onto nearly flat terrain below such pitches. Any terrain feature that breaks over, or rolls from moderate to steep partway down, is likely to fracture at that breakover point. Ridges and other protruding terrain are always safer than gullies, depressions, catch basins, or even smooth headwalls. Trees help anchor the snow.

The other key ingredients in avalanches are the weather and snowpack. Recent deposits of snow weight, whether created by snowfall, wind, or rapid warming of the surface, cause avalanches. Ninety percent of all avalanches are the direct action type, meaning they occur as a direct result of recent loading. Backcountry skiers should wait for twenty-four to forty-eight hours after a significant weather event (snow, wind, heat) before venturing onto avalanche-prone terrain.

Delayed action avalanches are much harder to predict, and anyone doing much ski touring is strongly encouraged to educate him or herself via avalanche courses and books. Several excellent titles and an instructional video are listed in Appendix A. Utah residents are blessed by an abundance of avalanche instruction options relating to the fact that Little Cottonwood Canyon was one of the earliest hotbeds of avalanche research and remains at the cutting edge of snow science. A basic understanding of deep and near-surface faceted snow is crucial to predicting both direct and delayed action slab avalanches.

The Utah Avalanche Center is arguably the premier backcountry forecast center in the United States, having more calls and hits to its Web site than any other center. The forecasts given are especially valid for the relatively limited forecast area of the Wasatch. The La Sal and Logan Avalanche Centers are much smaller operations but give excellent, generally up-to-date information.

To educate yourself about avalanches, take advantage of all available resources and stay in touch with other active ski tourers in the area. Pay attention to weather and snowpack developments from the first storm of the season. Know the underlying strength and probable weak layers before a new storm adds weight. Anyone who has been out recently should have reports of observed avalanche activity or snowpit results, or will be raving about the stability of the pack. Given your own knowledge and input from other sources, make a touring plan based on an expected level of stability. En route to a tour, make as many observations as possible, especially along the approach trail. Look for signs of instability and be ready to upgrade or downgrade the forecast you left home with. Don't let group dynamics override better judgment.

Everyone in a ski-touring party should wear an avalanche beacon and carry a shovel and probe. Beacon searches should be practiced periodically to ensure the users can effectively locate a buried partner. An avalung prolongs life under the snow and provides a secondary line of defense against suffocation, although one-third of avalanche fatalities result from trauma. The best goal is to never get caught in the first place.

To practice avalanche safety, ski slopes one person at a time and regroup regularly in safe areas. Strong skiers should utilize *ski cuts* to trigger sluffs and avalanches on the skier's own terms, rather than Mother Nature's. Every slope should be traversed at the top and again at any subsequent breakover in an attempt to cause a slide. Always ski to an island of safety (rock, tree, or ridge offering protection). Some skiers like to rope up and be on belay for cutting cornices or ski cutting. Bear in mind the quality of the anchor and respect the propensity of cornices to break further back from the edge than ever thought possible. Be conservative. As the saying goes: There are old skiers and bold skiers but no old, bold skiers.

Essential Equipment

Travel light, travel far, but don't forget the essentials. Modern ski-touring gear has become lighter, stronger, and more diverse than it ever was before. Telemark, randonee, and split snowboard are now the three primary modes of crossing snow, although alpine gear with binding inserts have their place. Snowshoes still work and have become popular as a means of hassle-free up and downhill travel on short outings. (Snowshoers may also find many of the tours outlined in this guide appealing and conducive to their craft.) The following is a minimal list of indispensable items and some advice about them.

Transceiver: This market has been flooded out of all proportion to the level of actual demand, and the consumer is the winner! Choose between the user-friendly Tracker, the tried and true Ortovox and Peips models, or the Variovox, marketed in the United States as Barryvox. It has the greatest range and the most technologically advanced digital readout. Some users, however, find it difficult to become proficient with this transceiver. Several other brands claim superiority, including the S.O.S. beacons, but I have less familiarity with them. Whatever you choose, practice with it, keep the batteries fresh, and always wear it on your body in transmit mode.

Shovel: Probably the premier backcountry shovel in the world is made right in Salt Lake City, the Voile Extreme with extendable handle. A model with a built-in saw for cutting snow pits is also available. For maximum diversity, I prefer a saw that cuts wood and ice. Black Diamond and others also produce fine backcountry shovels. Stay away from plastic blades (they don't work in set up avalanche debris) and keep the shovel inside your pack in an accessible location. Exterior shovel compartments seem like a great concept, but they are prone to shovel loss, especially if the backpack is not full.

Probe: Probe ski poles have the obvious advantage of being something you'd carry anyway, but collapsible, tent-pole-style probes are more reliable. They are usually longer when assembled and less likely to become bent or broken before needed. Check your probe periodically (especially at the outset of each touring season) because they ultimately become corroded and unusable. They can be marked for use as snow height measuring sticks when digging snow pits and for quantifying results.

Boots: Telemark, randonee, alpine, or snowboard boots should be comfortable and light. It doesn't hurt to have stiff soles for step-kicking and crampon compatibility. I prefer the Scarpa Terminator 3 for tele and the Denali for randonee, and I use a mountaineering boot, the Inverno, for split-snowboarding. Tape your heels in advance for the first long tour or on any hot day tour with extended flat sections. Soft and comfortable alpine ski boots work well for tours featuring mostly up or downhill travel, rather than significant flats.

Skis: Short, wide, and light is my motto for backcountry skis. They float up in powder, stay above rocks in shallow and faceted snow, enable users to go slow and turn tight in dense trees and narrow chutes, and provide stability at speed. Extremely shaped "parabolic" boards are tricky on hard, steep terrain due to their inability to skid during hockey-stop-style jump turns. They also make skins hard to apply. In corn snow width is not as important, but it makes the crust supportable for a longer period and helps in getting through that variable snow.

Bindings: Select bindings that are lightweight, easily released, and reliable. Voile's classic cable with step-in heel is my favorite for tele, and their split-board binding system is the industry standard. It mates to any four-hole configuration snowboard binding. The Fritchi Diamir has become the most popular randonee, or alpine touring (A/T) binding, owing to its simplicity and reliability. Various alpine ski-binding inserts allow the heels to rise, but none are trouble-free, light, or easy to stow in your pack.

Snowboards: The split-board has vastly increased the number of snowboarders in the backcountry, and whatever minor shortcomings it has in performance compared to a solid board are outweighed by the savings in weight and efficiency. If choosing your own snowboard, you should select a width and flex similar to your resort board but add 10 centimeters of length to enhance flotation in deep snow. Also, you should mount bindings about 1 inch farther back than normal.

Skins: Good adhesive is essential and needs to be touched up or replaced periodically. Longer-haired skins provide better traction in powder but soak up wet spring slush. Hydrophobic skins are better in spring. Snake skins have significant limitations and, like alpine binding inserts, only make sense for skiers doing one tour every few years.

Clothing: Utah winter weather varies from sweltering heat in the midday sun to subzero temperatures in high, windy, shady spots. A light-colored zip turtleneck of synthetic material is the best base layer, and thin long-underwear is usually appropriate on the bottom. In spring a breathable windpant is often all you need. Full side-zip, waterproof pants are advisable (even if only carried as a backup), and a hooded, waterproof shell jacket is a must. A windshirt or fleece and/or light down or synthetic sweater is good to carry for shady lunch breaks. A warm hat and neck gaiter or balaclava are key. Insulated gloves and waterproof mittens should also be carried.

Safety gear: A basic first-aid kit, a repair kit with duct tape, binding screws and driver, epoxy, cord, and possibly a length of rope (minimum 50 feet of 5 millimeters) should be present in a touring party. A compass and altimeter, knife, lighter, headlamp, cell phone, iodine tablets, spare sunglasses, goggles, and sunscreen are basic safety gear. A thermos of hot, sugared tea can revive a bonking partner, and a bivy sack is crucial for dealing with hypothermia or evacuation. Knowing how to make improvised splints and litters greatly improves the margin of safety.

Other: A camera, toilet paper, and spare energy bars or gorp always linger in the top lid of my pack. A light ice ax (or Black Diamond Whippet pole) and crampons (aluminum is sufficient) can improve efficiency and add safety for summit ascents, especially in spring. A 100-foot length of 7 or 8 millimeter (static) rope and a few slings and carabiners are also good for ski mountaineering. A substantial lunch and at least two liters or quarts of water should suffice for most days out. Water bags are great if the tube is kept from freezing.

Route-Finding Tips

Backcountry skiing is similar to normal resort skiing in a general sense only. Off-piste carving requires a revised set of physical and mental skills, although a base of downhill skiing experience certainly makes it easier to become proficient in the backcountry. All manner of terrain presents itself outside resorts, and the hazards are not marked. Also, there is no rescue toboggan nearby to cart one to a medical clinic. Backcountry skiers must always ski in control and look ahead for obstacles, picking a route. This is one of the many satisfying aspects of it—choosing your own line.

The snow is just as variable as the terrain, and learning to pick a good aspect and "read" snow is very important. Generally speaking, northerly and easterly aspects keep snow dry and powdery, whereas southerly through westerly facing slopes get heated by the sun and become crusted. During the shortest days of winter, the sun damages far fewer aspects than in March and April. Altitude also affects snow quality, giving higher areas drier, lighter powder but more wind effects as well.

Conversely, corn snow develops first on the sunnier aspects and lower elevations where midday and afternoon melting are greatest. This snow becomes supportable much sooner in spring than winter, although my best corn skiing in steep Wasatch chutes has been in January and February when slower warming allowed crusts to form without causing wet snow sloughs to clog the gullies with roller balls of debris. Remember that a rock-solid freeze at night is not necessary for producing corn snow. The key factor is sky clarity. Heat escapes into the atmosphere and cools the snow surface during clear nights, but clouds trap the heat. An overcast sky also retards the softening in the morning, resulting either in mushy or rock-hard surface conditions.

The wind's effect on snow is more complicated and devious than that of the sun. It is horrendous when breakable or, if solid, can be nice carving. The worst-case scenario is a wind crust that is variously supportable and breakable with no indication of when and where. Usually, however, an experienced tourer can notice patterns of snow types related to terrain and predictable by appearance. For instance, in gullies the funneling of wind, the venturi effect, creates more and stronger crusts versus the surface snow of surrounding protruding terrain. Often the uppermost portion of a bowl or chute, near the high ridgeline, is wind affected and tricky, but the snow improves dramatically within a few turns.

Typically, wind-crusted snow becomes smooth and chalky, while wind-eroded snow has a rippled or pockmarked look, similar to the spackled walls of a Spanish-style house's interior. Generally, the eroded snow is better, although extremely eroded old snow is known as *saastrugi* and is very tricky to ski due to its firm, yet highly uneven, surface. It is found near the summits of Utah's highest peaks.

How to Use This Guidebook

The goal of this guidebook is to facilitate safe and enjoyable backcountry ski tours all over Utah for skill levels of beginner through expert. The maps show the ascent and descent routes described in the text. They should be used as a supplement to actual topo maps, which include other important information.

Unlike some guidebooks that get you to the general area and then leave the rest to you, I have attempted to explain the safest and most expedient means of accessing the most aesthetic ski runs, the highest peaks, and the best snow quality. If you prefer to discover more on your own, simply ignore the excess details.

This guide also delves into the realm of highly avalanche-prone terrain and mentions routes and runs that a truly risk-averse person would never expose him or herself to. Yet more and more off-piste skiers are entering such terrain, and hopefully with the information given here, this can be done in the safest and most efficient manner.

The ranges covered by this book are generally ordered from north to south and from east to west across Utah. Within each range the tours are either in the same order, northeast to southwest, or in cases where a second tour builds out deeper into the backcountry from the point the first tour ends, they are ordered from inside to out, like concentric circles. For example, in the La Sals, Laurel Highway is the first area most people will visit; then trips into Gold Basin, Mount Mellenthin, etc., which radiate out from the Laurel Ridge, are described subsequently.

Also within each tour description, the easier to reach runs are detailed first. Thus within the greater Little Cottonwood south area, for instance, nearby shots like Scottie's Bowl and Pink Pine Ridge come before far out places like the Coalpit Headwall.

The summary information given is designed to facilitate your choice of tours on any given day. Ratings are strictly based on difficulty of skiing, route finding, and approach. No qualitative ratings are given because perspectives vary, and how could I presume to decide which spots are better? You should use the verbal summary to distinguish the characteristics of one tour from the others. This statewide guidebook is inherently limited to the premier spots within each major range. An exhaustive volume on every tour in Utah would be quadruple the length. Distances given in the summary information are for comparative use and are one way unless otherwise noted. Altitude gain is a better measure of physical difficulty. Even then, the depth of new snow, whether a trail has been broken, and individual fitness are still greater factors in determining which tour is for you.

Hitchhiking is mentioned as a means of linking up many of the one-way or point-to-point tours in this book. It is legal in all the suggested areas, but be careful to hitch in a straightaway or other safe spot for drivers to see you and pull off without causing an accident or traffic jam. Seldom have I heard of any problems with hitching, and it is common practice. Of course, it is done at your own risk.

When to Go Backcountry Skiing in the Utah Ranges

The Utah backcountry turns white every winter to one extent or another. Typically, enough snow exists by late October or early November to ski somewhere and have a reasonably safe adventure. Skiers with excellent skills and a conservative nature can glisse meadow terrain at low speed over 2 feet of light density powder underlain by bushes and rocks without sustaining injury or significant gear thrashing. However, testosterone-crazed youths have blown patellas by dropping their knees in shallow snowpacks, and powder-seeking shredders have become avalanche fatalities due to "pushing the season" by skiing steeps at high speeds when only scant snow exists.

The best time to maximize backcountry skiing fun is midwinter and spring. Alta Ski Resort in the Central Wasatch is probably the first place to offer worthy ski touring in Utah most autumns. An open-skier policy (as opposed to the restrictions imposed at Snowbird), smooth grassy runs, and a consistently bounteous snowpack favor Alta, but similar conditions can exist simultaneously, or even earlier in the season, in low-angle meadows from Logan to Moab to Beaver, Utah.

If an October storm drops 2 feet of snow on Lake Peak or Mount Holly in the Tushars, it's time to dust off skis and skins. A 24-inch snowpack is probably sufficient for many northern Utah locals to enjoy Garden City or Cutler Ridge, and if it pukes white stuff during the Fat-Tire Mountain Bike Festival in Moab, Laurel Highway and the switchbacks below the Geyser Pass trailhead are the first places in the La Sals to try.

December through April are skiable in nearly all Utah ranges most seasons, but areas like the Abajos near Monticello, the Henry Mountains, western Utah's Deep Creeks, and the Pine Valley Mountains outside St. George have inconsistent snowfall, and occasionally no decent skiing develops all year. Steep, rugged, and remote areas in most Utah ranges (such as the entire Southern Wasatch) usually cannot be safely enjoyed until February, and the prime time to ski the high country is typically February/March in the Wasatch and west desert ranges, March/April in southern Utah, and May/June in the Uintas.

Current information on snowpack conditions is available on the Internet via the Avalanche Forecast Center Web sites. Current information on snowpack and weather conditions is available from the avalanche centers in Salt

Al Dymerski and friend tour above Cherry Canyon and the Cache Valley.

Lake City, Moab, and Logan. Phone numbers are listed in the introduction to each chapter. In other areas, use the regional Forest Service of BLM office phone numbers. Guide services also may answer questions about current snow levels and avalanche stability. Watching the winter weather patterns is a great way to stay in tune with where it's snowing. Many seasons seem to favor either southern or northern Utah, but not both. When a zonal flow comes onshore near Mount Shasta, California, Utah as a whole will turn white.

Logan Area Mountains

A Quiet Powder Paradise

The Logan area, including the 45,000-acre Mount Naomi Wilderness, the "world's steepest" Wellsville Range, and the Bear Lake Mountains, offers similar snow and terrain to those of the urban Wasatch Front—without the people. The trailheads are low in altitude (but high in latitude), and the snowpack is slightly less consistent, but the abundance of wildlife and the absence of ski tracks make for a welcome trade-off.

As your drive north through Sardine Canyon above Brigham City, the amazingly situated Cache Valley suddenly presents itself. Hemmed in by the ultra-steep and narrow Wellsville Mountains on the west and the bulky Bear River Range on the east, this is an ideal, fairy-tale habitat for backcountry skiers. Don't be surprised, however, to see a dense haze filling the narrow valley. Inversions are a natural phenomenon in such topography. The color of the fog indicates the smog factor, and here it's usually more gray (natural/cloudy looking) than yellow (polluted looking).

Logan, dominated by stately old churches and Utah State University, is a quiet, friendly town nestled against the Bear River Range at the mouth of Logan Canyon. The canyon boasts dramatic limestone cliffs, similar to American Fork Canyon between Salt Lake City and Provo. Stop at the Forest Service visitor center at the mouth of Logan Canyon to get current avalanche information and a list of the plowed pullouts in the narrow canyon.

The majority of Logan-area ski-touring possibilities are reached from trailheads along the Logan River, although Logan Peak itself can be more easily climbed from Dry Canyon (or Providence Canyon, if you don't mind snowmobiles). The Beaver Mountain and Garden City touring areas are east of the Bear River Range in the Bear Lake Mountains. High and Cherry Creeks are best accessed from the Cache Valley floor north of Logan. The Wellsvilles can be reached from the Sardine Pass area on the south, Pine Canyon to the east, or Mendon on the north.

Several remote areas can be accessed from yurts located in Blind Hollow, the Bunchgrass area, and Hell's Kitchen. These cozy winter retreats facilitate ascents of Mount Elmer, Naomi Peak, and Doubletop Mountain, respectively, and place skiers in the vicinity of countless other enticing runs. Rental arrangements must be made in advance.

Logan Information

Logan Avalanche Center, (435) 797–4146

Logan Ranger District, (435) 755–3620

Utah State University yurt, (435) 797–3264

Powder Ridge Ski Touring, Northern yurts, (435) 752–7853

Beaver Mountain Ski Resort Road and Snow Conditions Hotline, (435) 753–4822

Garden City Meadows

Rating: Easy to moderate.

Gear: Skis or split-board with skins or wax.

Summary: It's a two-hour drive from Salt Lake City, and thirty minutes from Logan, to stunning views of Bear Lake from the safe, friendly powder parks of Garden City Creek. A good area for cross-country skiing is the summer road to Swan Peak. The tour can be done in a few hours and makes a wise choice for the early season given its grassy undersurface and moderate pitch.

Tour 1

Map: USGS 7.5-minute Garden City.

Trailhead: Swan Flats Road, DOT plow shed at milepost 403 of U.S. Highway 89.

Distance: 2 to 4 miles.

Starting altitude: 7,600 feet.

High point: Swan Peak, 9,086 feet.

Access: From Logan, take US 89 through Logan Canyon and past Beaver Mountain Ski Resort to a Department of Transportation (DOT) plow shed just before milepost 403. Or from Garden City, descend a mile west from the Bear Lake Divide on US 89 and pass the SWAN FLATS ROAD sign. Park in the plowed area between the highway and the plow shed.

Description: Skin east by northeast on a (probable) snowmobile track to join the summer road, Swan Flats Road. Follow this north past a spectacular band of limestone bluffs culminating in a sizable natural arch or hole in the cliff. Look up the open (sagebrush) slope just north of all the cliffs—you may see the switchback you can head for as a shortcut. Continue north past the switchback on the road all the way to the point where it crosses the ridge and double back south along it. If avalanche conditions are stable, you could also skin directly up the wide-open, west-southwest-facing, limber pine– and sagebrush–covered slopes to the Bear Lake divide. Here you'll be greeted by two great sights: Bear Lake and a perfect field of powdery meadows dropping gently toward Garden City Creek.

Garden City Meadows and Beaver Mountain Periphery

N 41° 59' N 41° 58' N 41° 57'

W 111°28' W 111°29' W 111°30' W 111°31' W 111°32' W 111°33' W 111°34'

Swan Peak 9,086'

Garden City Canyon

7750
7500
7750
8000
8500
8000
8250
8500
8250
8500
8500
8250

Swan Flats Road

8500
8750

DOT Shed

P *

To Garden City via Bear Lake Divide

8000
7750
7500
7250
7500
7750
8000

89

N

1 mi
km

.5
1
.5
1
.5
0
0

Contour Interval: 250 Feet

7,935'
7750

Long Hollow

P

Beaver Creek

7500
7250
7000
7250
7500
7750

Harry's Dream Lift

Beaver Mtn. Ski Resort

Beaver Mountain 8,860'

8500
8250
8000
8000
7750
7500
7250
8250
7750
8000

89

To Logan 27 miles

Franklin Basin Rd (Joins US 89)

Ski these meadows and skin back up for more laps or continue to the creek, cross it, and skin north along the creek to climb back to the saddle and the road. Alternatively, you can ascend east onto the shoulder of Swan Peak and ski either the west or south aspect back down into Garden City Canyon. There's better snow found by skiing into Swan Creek off the northeast side of Swan Peak. In big-snow years it may be possible to make a one-way tour by skiing all the way down Swan Creek and ending on the shores of Bear Lake.

Swan Flats Road itself can be used as a cross-country tour using waxed or scaled skis. It leads all the way to Swan Peak and stays pretty well packed by snowmobiles. It provides spectacular views of the Bear River Range, upper Logan River, and Franklin Basin. If Swan Peak or Swan Creek drainage is your destination, simply stay on the road and skip the runs into Garden City Creek.

To return to the trailhead from the Garden City Meadows, ski right back down along the southwest-facing approach and enjoy afternoon light for early-season powder or late-season supportable-crust turns on a 1,000-foot, 20- to 25-degree slope.

Beaver Mountain
Ski Resort Periphery

See map on page 14.

Rating: Easy to difficult.

Gear: Alpine skis, snowboard, touring skis, or split-board; skins optional.

Tour 2

Summary: This family resort offers quick and easy access to beginner through expert slopes on north through south aspects.

Map: USGS 7.5-minute Tony Grove Creek.

Trailhead: Beaver Mountain Ski Resort, top of Harry's Dream Lift.

Distance: Drops of up to 1,800 feet over 2 miles or less.

Starting altitude: 7,200 feet.

High point: Beaver Mountain, 8,860 feet.

Beaver Mountain's south ridge backcountry; southeast view.

Access: From Logan, take U.S. Highway 89 through Logan Canyon and turn north to Beaver Mountain Ski Resort at a signed junction 27 miles east of Logan. Buy a lift ticket and check in with the friendly and informative patrol for current conditions. Ride the Harry's Dream Lift for 1,600 vertical feet, and—if you're not too tempted by the enticing glades between mogul runs at the resort—boot or skin 100 vertical feet above the top shack to the summit of Beaver Mountain. Touring outside the resort is generally discouraged by the resort personnel, and backcountry skiers are charged for any ski patrol rescue effort on their behalf. Beaver Mountain Ski Resort (435–753–0921) is open seven days a week, snow conditions permitting.

Description: From the summit of Beaver Mountain, 8,860 feet, your options are almost as limitless as the 360-degree horizon around you. Jutting to the southeast is a rocky buttress that provides the starting point for a south- and east-facing run leading ultimately to US 89, 1,800 feet below. This is the short-hike, alpine-skier special. Small cliff bands bisect the line, creating a series of jumps and drops onto forgiving terrain, a regular huckfest for extreme skiers and snowboarders. You can cut back into the warm and cozy confines of the ski resort at any time by simply traversing hard left. Don't expect any rescue, however, if you make a bad call about conditions or your own abilities. This is strictly out-of-bounds terrain.

For the advanced backcountry skier, a wealth of northeast-facing glades and avalanche slide paths fall from Beaver Peak's long south ridge. You can simply glide down the ridge and then herringbone up. Or if you have skins and freeheels, there's a variety of options. One is to descend a short way on the South Extreme run, then skin up right to the saddle. Another is to drop northwest toward the Logan River and Franklin Basin Road. After 300 feet, traverse skier's left to reach the saddle without skins, or drop as far as your heart desires, then skin back up and south to the saddle. A large burn area here may have lurking widowmakers (leaning dead trees). Avoid windy days.

Off the south ridge, take your choice of easterly drops along ridges or into gullies. This is superb powder skiing but can be avalanche-prone. The last 500 feet of the descent to the highway becomes dense trees and gullies. Traverse as needed to stay on protruding terrain and away from tedious bushwhacking. Beaver Creek can usually be crossed on boulders, but in spring be ready for a challenge. Hitch or have someone run a shuttle back to the resort.

From the west-facing burn glades, another option is to traverse or climb back to skier's right to reach a divide leading to a gentle, pine-covered, northeast-facing run dropping into Sinks Hollow. This is safe terrain in nearly any avalanche conditions; the finish is down a snowmobile track back to the Beaver Mountain access road, less than a mile below the base area.

Finally, from the burn glades you can continue to drop south and west, following the terrain into Logan River Valley and Franklin Basin Road. Skate or pole down the usually snowmobile-compacted road to the parking area (if you stashed a vehicle) or continue another 0.25 mile to US 89 and hitch back to the resort.

Doubletop Mountain, Steam Mill Peak, and Hell's Kitchen Yurt Area

Tour 3

Rating: Easy to difficult.

Gear: Skis or split-board with skins or snowshoes.

Summary: You'll find friendly, rolling meadows, aspens, and good skiing on Steam Mill's northeast aspect. There's an easy approach to the Bear River Divide and Doubletop Mountain.

Maps: USGS 7.5-minute Tony Grove Creek, Naomi Peak.

Trailhead: Franklin Basin Road.

Distance: 3.25 miles to the yurt below Steam Mill Peak.

Starting altitude: 6,750 feet.

High points: Steam Mill Peak, 9,300 feet; Doubletop Mountain 9,873 feet.

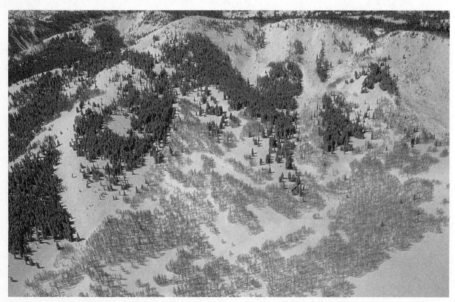

Steam Mill Peak; northeast view.

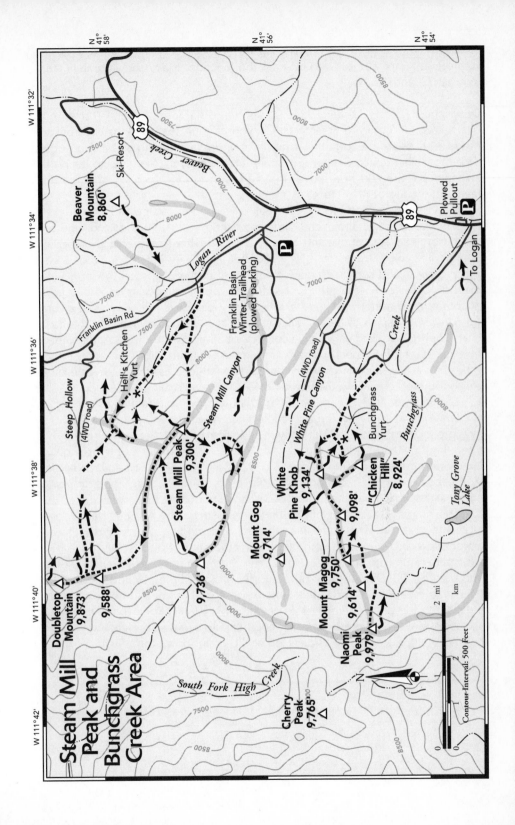

Steam Mill Peak and Bunchgrass Creek Area

N 41° 58'
N 41° 56'
N 41° 54'

W 111° 32'
W 111° 34'
W 111° 36'
W 111° 38'
W 111° 40'
W 111° 42'

Ski Resort

Beaver Mountain
8,860'

Beaver Creek

89

7500

7500

8000

8000

7000

7500

Logan River

Franklin Basin Rd

Steep Hollow (4WD road)

Hell's Kitchen Yurt

Franklin Basin Winter Trailhead (plowed parking)

Steam Mill Canyon

7000

8500

P

P

89

Plowed Pullout

To Logan

Creek

White Pine Canyon (4WD road)

Bunchgrass Yurt

Bunchgrass

8000

Tony Grove Lake

Doubletop Mountain
9,873'

9,588'

Steam Mill Peak
9,300'

9,736'

Mount Gog
9,714'

White Pine Knob
9,134'

"Chicken Hill"
8,924'

9,098'

Mount Magog
9,750'

9,614'

Naomi Peak
9,979'

9000

9000

8500

8000

8500

South Fork High Creek

Cherry Peak
9,765'

9000

7500

8500

N

0   1   2 mi
0   1   2 km

Contour Interval: 500 Feet

Access: From Logan, follow U.S. Highway 89 through Logan Canyon to Franklin Basin Road. Park at a plowed lot near the junction. Many snowmobilers start here to ride into Idaho.

Description: Classic-stride or skate up the nearly flat road, usually on snowmobile tracks, for 1 mile to Steam Mill Canyon. If your destination is the Powder Ridge Yurt, leave the Logan River at the next creek crossing and climb northeast into Hell's Kitchen Canyon. Two miles up the canyon, climb out to the north and look for the yurt in a grove of aspens surrounded by low-angle, south-facing meadows at 8,140 feet.

If a direct ascent to Steam Mill Peak is your goal, escape Hell's Kitchen to the south after only 0.4 mile and climb more steeply up an east-facing tributary gully. Continue east above the gully and ascend the broad east shoulder of Steam Mill Peak to the summit, at 9,300 feet. Fine ski shots in open meadows, aspen groves, and evergreen glades drop northeast and east off the long summit ridge. Farther west, the drops are steeper and rockier as the aspect becomes more easterly. All runs terminate in upper Hell's Kitchen near the yurt.

The south aspect of Steam Mill can be decent skiing and leads to the base of another good skiing area—the south rim of Steam Mill Canyon. An unnamed northeast-facing bowl beckons from the summit of Steam Mill. A return run either down Steam Mill Canyon or along the old four-wheel-drive road that leaves the canyon to drop directly to the Franklin Basin Trailhead makes a nice loop.

Looking east from Steam Mill Peak, the Bear River divide with its bounty of ski terrain draws the eye. The approach is surprisingly friendly: Just stay on the high ground north of Steam Mill Canyon and south of the Steep Hollow cliffs. This open, high plateau leads all the way to Doubletop Mountain, but tempting skiing drops into Steep Hollow along the way. There are steep shots south off point 9,588, the closest significant point to Doubletop. You'll find good runs dropping southeast through northeast, with the east shoulder being the lowest angle.

The dramatic east face of Doubletop is bisected by two cliff bands, one high and one low. There are lines through, depending on snow depth and adventure-skiing quotient. Returning down the south ridge is very benign; a moderate return run into Steep Hollow falls from the pass between Doubletop and point 9,588. Descend the broad upper basin of Steep Hollow for about a mile to a meadow at 8,200 feet where the old four-wheel-drive road ends. Follow it to the Logan River and ski down Franklin Basin Road to the trailhead. To return to the yurt, climb gradually southeast to a wide pass leading into the head of Hell's Kitchen. Drop skier's left and contour down to the yurt.

Bunchgrass Creek and Yurt

See map on page 19.

Rating: Easy to moderate.

Gear: Skis or split-board with skins or snowshoes.

Summary: Friendly, rolling terrain with aspens and meadows. Safe access to Mount Naomi, the Logan area's highest peak.

Maps: USGS 7.5-minute Tony Grove Creek, Naomi Peak.

Trailhead: Bunchgrass Creek.

Distance: 4 miles to the yurt below White Pine Knob.

Starting altitude: 6,300 feet.

High points: White Pine Knob, 9,134 feet; Naomi Peak, 9,979 feet.

Access: From Logan, follow U.S. Highway 89 through Logan Canyon past Tony Grove Road. Park at a plowed pullout on the east side of the highway, between mileposts 393 and 394. This parking area is just south of a bridge over the Logan River.

Description: Either travel south along the highway and find a summer trail along the creek or simply head due west, contouring across a sage-covered meadow to join the creek and trail at the mouth of Bunchgrass Canyon. Follow the creek up the low-angle canyon floor, staying on its south side for about 1.7 miles. The route to Bunchgrass Yurt rises northwestward away from the creek above a broad meadow that offers the first views of the ski terrain above the yurt, White Pine Knob and point 8,924 ("Chicken Hill").

Short runs can be enjoyed lower in Bunchgrass Canyon by switchbacking up into the evergreens south of the creek. An old slide path, currently reforested by aspens, provides a slightly steeper gully run just 0.5 mile from the trailhead. These glades provide some of the best options anywhere in the Logan Mountains for practicing turns on beginner slopes close to the road. Many possibilities for low-angle touring exist along the approach route as it rises gently through sparse aspens.

Tour 4

White Pine Knob and "Chicken Hill" above Bunchgrass Yurt; east view.

To reach Bunchgrass Yurt, simply aim for White Pine Knob, if it's visible. Alternatively, head west by northwest and find the structure on a flat aspen- and subalpine-fir-covered knoll just south of the treeless, historical runout zone from avalanches flowing off the southeast face of White Pine Knob. The yurt is in a safe spot at 8,400 feet, and ski terrain surrounds it.

White Pine Knob, with its open southeast bowl, is very enticing—unless it's sun crusted or loaded up with avalanche potential. The safest and most efficient route is to climb it via the east ridge, which is broad and open and can also be skied. The more aggressive line drops south and east directly toward the yurt and threads between two small rock outcroppings. Watch for a wind pillow and avalanche-prone breakover where the run angles skier's left into the bowl. It's a good line to avoid immediately after a west wind or wind-driven storm has loaded the upper bowl or ridge. A steep, skiable slide path falls toward White Pine Creek from the east ridge at 8,700 feet. Return to the yurt by climbing south through the woods out of White Pine.

"Chicken Hill" is a reliable stash for northerly facing, wind-protected powder. Simply climb west from the yurt and ascend through old-growth spruce and fir to a saddle between "Chicken Hill" and White Pine Knob. Moderate shots drop back to the yurt from the saddle, or climb south and east to the broad summit. Skiable trees and open shots drop north and east all along the summit ridge.

Points west such as point 9,098, Mount Magog, point 9,614, and Naomi

Peak can also be reached via the Bunchgrass Saddle west of Bunchgrass Yurt. Simply continue west over a long flat and ski east off point 9,098, or circumvent it to the north and climb Magog by its northeast ridge. The east face is wide-open skiing from below the summit cliffs. If Naomi Peak—the highest summit in the range—is your goal, traverse below the steepest part of Magog's east bowl and climb 200 feet to cross the south ridge. Ski a short run west, or traverse slightly north and contour past a dry lake bed. A broad, undulating ridge south of White Pine Canyon leads to the innocuous summit and its low-angle east face.

Another alternative is to traverse north from the pass around the base of White Pine Knob and ski into White Pine Creek along the summer trail route. This is a great way to see the impressive, cliff-banded Mount Gog above White Pine Lake at the head of this box canyon. Skiing out along White Pine Creek makes a scenic loop, although it can be a challenge to get across the Logan River and back to your car at the Bunchgrass Trailhead. Most tourers traverse skier's right at 7,600 feet out of White Pine and drop back into Bunchgrass on the summer road.

High Creek and Cherry Peak

Rating: Difficult.

Gear: Skis or split-board with skins.

Summary: This long approach is rewarded by spectacular alpine terrain, huge open shots, and relatively few other tracks. High Canyon's depth and north-facing orientation virtually ensure dry snow, but the terrain presents significant avalanche danger.

Tour 5

Map: USGS 7.5-minute Naomi Peak.

Trailhead: High Creek Campground (or as close to it as you can drive).

Distance: 4 miles to Peak 9,384; 5 miles to Cherry Peak.

Starting altitude: 5,200 to 5,500 feet.

High point: Unnamed peak, 9,384 feet.

Cherry Peak (left) and High Canyon; northeast view.

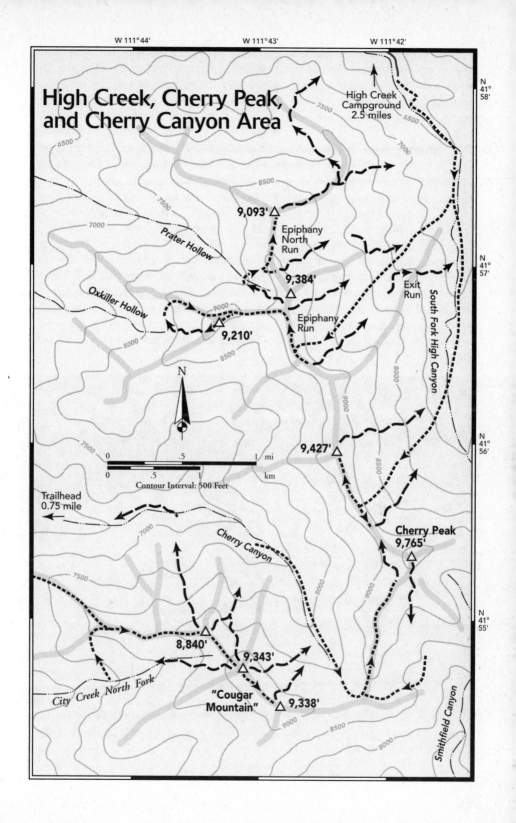

High Creek, Cherry Peak, and Cherry Canyon Area

W 111°44'   W 111°43'   W 111°42'

N 41° 58'
N 41° 57'
N 41° 56'
N 41° 55'

High Creek Campground 2.5 miles

7500
6500
6500
7000
8500

9,093'

Prater Hollow

Epiphany North Run

9,384'

Exit Run

Oxkiller Hollow

7000

9000

9,210'

Epiphany Run

South Fork High Canyon

8000

8500

8000

8500

9000

N

0   .5   1 mi
0   .5   1 km
Contour Interval: 500 Feet

9,427'

Trailhead 0.75 mile

7000

Cherry Canyon

Cherry Peak 9,765'

7500

8000

9000

8,840'

9,343'

City Creek North Fork

"Cougar Mountain"   9,338'

Smithfield Canyon

9000   8500   8000

Access: From Logan, follow U.S. Highway 91 north through Smithfield and Richmond. Two miles north of Richmond, turn right onto High Creek Road. The roadway becomes increasingly snow covered (depending on conditions) as you go deeper into the canyon. Drive as far as you can toward the campground and figure out how to get turned around. Park off the main ruts wherever possible.

Description: Follow the now-closed four-wheel-drive road above High Creek Campground. Pass the junction of the North Fork and the Little Left Hand Fork, and continue up the narrow canyon assessing the safety of crossing below a series of increasingly large avalanche-path runouts. Eventually, you must choose between the unnamed western fork, with its huge and accessible ski terrain, and the main South Fork below the rugged north face of Cherry Peak.

The western fork is home to a run locals refer to as Epiphany, and once you see it you'll realize why. It is amazing. An immense expanse of north- through east-facing ski terrain stretches for 0.5 mile with vertical drops of 2,000 feet all across. Unfortunately, there's no entirely avalanche-safe approach to Epiphany Ridge, although a subridge falling northeast from the summit of Peak 9,384 protrudes between several avalanche paths and could be used to minimize exposure to the wide-open avalanche terrain. A better idea is to visit when ava-

An anonymous backcountry skier and his dogs enjoy perfect powder in High Canyon, Bear River Range.

lanche hazard is low and cut a skin trail up the main slope to the ridge separating High Creek from Cherry Creek.

As you ascend, the outstanding selection of mouthwatering ski lines will undoubtedly become apparent to you. The snow tends to be dry and crustless longest on the far skier's right of the Epiphany Cirque; the most consistently steep skiing is on the skier's left (north) end of the cirque. Another nice 600-foot drop, the Exit Run, can be reached by traversing skier's right from the lower meadows of Epiphany and dropping into the main South Fork. It's an east-facing slide path/meadow with a perfect 30-degree pitch. Simply drop back north along the creek and you'll intersect the approach trail.

From Peak 9,384, it's also possible to drop west into Prater Hollow. This is steep, avalanche-prone terrain with two horizontal cliff bands. There are couloirs splitting through the rocky sections, and the northwest-facing powder is well protected, but be sure to assess the avalanche hazard conservatively. By switchbacking in a northeasterly direction up a sparsely forested slope from Prater Hollow's upper meadows, it's easy to reach a saddle below Peak 9,384 and its unskiable north face. Dropping from here back into the South Fork of High Creek is a great line and creates a loop tour. A well-protected northeast-facing bowl, which starts out at 40 degrees, and a series of more moderate gullies and glades lead down to the creek bottom at 7,700 feet. Then as the canyon takes on a steep V-shape, traverse skier's right through spruce and fir to find open east-facing subridges offering 30-degree skiing through sparse trees and bushes for another 500 feet to the creek and approach trail.

Cherry Canyon and Cherry Peak

See map on page 25.

Rating: Moderate to difficult.

Gear: Skis or split-board with skins.

Summary: A spectacular ridge climb with incomparable views of Cache Valley and great skiing off "Cougar Mountain." A rugged but efficient route exists to Cherry Peak with a descent via High Creek. Good half-day tours are possible.

Map: USGS 7.5-minute Naomi Peak, Richmond.

Trailhead: Cherry Creek Trailhead.

Distance: 6 miles to Bear River divide; 4 miles to Peak 9,384.

Starting altitude: 5,500 to 6,000 feet.

High point: "Cougar Mountain," 9,343 feet; Cherry Peak, 9,765 feet.

Access: From Logan, follow U.S. Highway 91 north through Smithfield to Richmond. Go east at the city center, drive 5 blocks, then turn north and continue out of town on Forest Road 024. After crossing upper High Creek, the main road curves north. Stay right instead and drive into Cherry Canyon as high as possible.

Description: At the road's end, climb south out of the canyon and gain the ridge that forms its south rim. Follow it for 2 miles to Peak 9,343, the northwest summit of what locals call "Cougar Mountain." The west face is open ski terrain with a spectacular view of the valley below. Drop to about 8,200 feet before the canyon tightens up and steepens. Ascend north back to the south rim of Cherry Canyon.

An even shorter tour can be made by skiing northwest off the unnamed point (about 8,840 feet) on the south rim and dropping 2,100 feet to Cherry Creek for a quick return to your car. The run begins in sparse trees, which become dense for a few hundred feet before a slide path opens up and runs to the canyon bottom. This path is one of several reasons it's not wise to trudge slowly *up* Cherry Canyon. Another skiable slide path falls northeast from this same point and intersects the path dropping northwest off "Cougar Mountain."

Longer tours involve skiing east off "Cougar Mountain." The terrain here is mostly open and a bit rocky, with plenty of avalanche potential. Another ski line falls from "Cougar Mountain" just west of the southeast summit (point 9,338). Ski one of these lines early in the day and skin up along the summer trail to the head of Cherry Creek. Then follow the divide to Cherry Peak and make a descending traverse along its west face below the rocky summit and into upper High Creek. This beautiful cirque under Cherry's incredible north cliff requires a full day of slogging from High Creek (see Tour 5, High Creek and Cherry Peak). Cherry Canyon is a more rewarding approach requiring only a short car shuttle.

It's possible to ski right off the shark's fin of Cherry's summit on the south aspect toward Smithfield Canyon, but don't drop below 8,400 feet—the terrain becomes steep with cliff bands and is highly avalanche-prone. Climb southwest to return into Cherry Canyon or come back up the south ridge of Cherry Peak.

"Cougar Mountain" in the foreground and Bear River Divide behind; north-west view.

Utah State University Yurt and Mount Elmer

Rating: Moderate to difficult.

Gear: Skis or split-board with skins or snowshoes.

Tour 7

Summary: This is a beautifully situated yurt with nearby terrain ranging from gentle to expert. Access to the high country of the Bear River Range is greatly eased by packing into the yurt the day before. The yurt is open to any group that includes at least one Utah State University student or faculty member. Contact USU Outdoor Recreation Center (435–797–3264).

Map: USGS 7.5-minute Mount Elmer.

Trailhead: Blind Hollow. Just below Temple Fork, look for a pullout on your right and a trailhead sign on your left.

Mount Elmer behind point 9,238; northeast view.

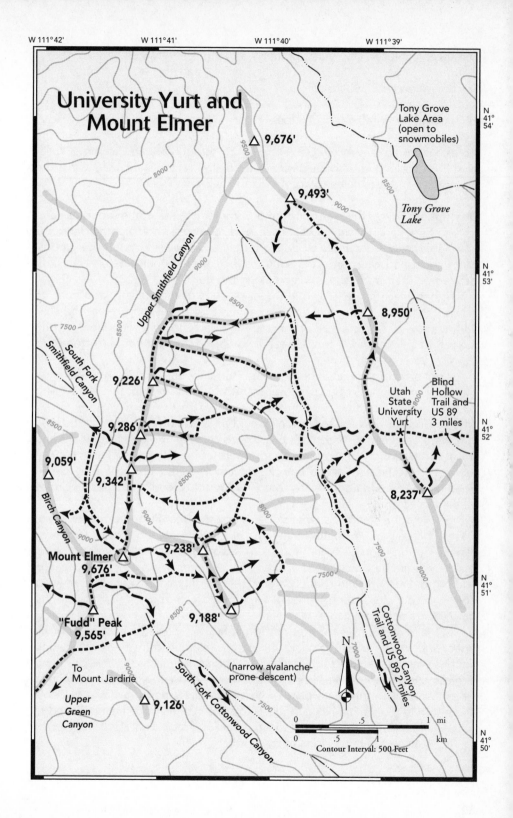

University Yurt and Mount Elmer

N 41° 54'

Tony Grove Lake Area (open to snowmobiles)

Tony Grove Lake

9,676'

9,493'

9,000

8500

N 41° 53'

Upper Smithfield Canyon

8,950'

9,226'

South Fork Smithfield Canyon

9,286'

Utah State University Yurt

Blind Hollow Trail and US 89 3 miles

N 41° 52'

9,059'

9,342'

Birch Canyon

8,237'

Mount Elmer 9,676'

9,238'

N 41° 51'

"Fudd" Peak 9,565'

9,188'

(narrow avalanche-prone descent)

Cottonwood Canyon Trail and US 89 2 miles

N

7000

To Mount Jardine

Upper Green Canyon

9,126'

South Fork Cottonwood Canyon

7500

0   .5   1   mi

0   .5   1   km

Contour Interval: 500 Feet

N 41° 50'

Distance: 4 miles to USU yurt; another 1.5 to 2 miles to Mount Elmer.

Starting altitude: 5,750 feet.

High point: Mount Elmer, 9,676 feet.

Access: From Logan, follow U.S. Highway 89 through Logan Canyon to mile-post 388 and look for a (hopefully) plowed pulloff on the south side. Cross the highway to find the trailhead sign for Blind Hollow.

Description: Follow the creek bottom or summer trail out of the sagebrush and up into Engelmann spruce, Douglas fir, and subalpine fir. Avalanche danger is low in this hollow, due to its moderate terrain and heavily wooded side slopes. Many elk spend winters on the south aspect of the Logan River and its side drainages. Their tracks are common along the trail.

A long, flat meadow fills the upper reaches of the canyon, and here, at about 7,900 feet, you rise out of the canyon to the west and locate the USU yurt. It's found at 8,200 feet in an aspen-ringed meadow with views of the rugged Bear River divide to the west. If you reach the east rim of Cottonwood Canyon, you've gone too far.

Right around the yurt is gentle, open terrain ideal for beginner telemark-ing. Longer, gentle slopes can be reached by heading north on the rising plateau above Cottonwood Canyon. Two miles to the north is Tony Grove Lake, a popular area for snowmobiles and an alternative access route to the yurt. Very early in the season, it's possible to drive all the way to the lake and travel south to the yurt. Fortunately for skiers (at least those who aren't snow-mobilers), the Forest Service has designated the area south of Tony Grove Road a snowmobile-free wildlife area. The Mount Naomi Wilderness includes all the high country west of the yurt.

Enjoying the steeper, deeper slopes along the Bear River divide requires at least a half-day excursion from the yurt. Travel west until the ground falls away toward Cottonwood Canyon. From here, follow the summer trail north along the canyon rim and circle back west to the divide, or ski down into the canyon and climb directly to the divide via one of three prominent, parallel east–west ridges. If your destination is Mount Elmer, follow the pack trail route up the gulch on its northeast flanks.

My favorite route is to ski a northwest-facing, sparsely pined draw or an open, southwest-facing (corn-snow) meadow, starting from the Cottonwood rim due west of the yurt, for 500 vertical feet and then cross the creek. Skin up and climb west by northwest through old-growth timber to gain a well-defined ridge. Ski off its northeast aspect—which is usually wind-protected powder—and return to the skin trail if your goal is to climb higher. Continue up this ridge to the main divide and enjoy a panoramic view obstructed only by Mount Elmer to the south and Mount Naomi to the north.

Upper Cottonwood Canyon; east view.

The range of skiing options in this area is vast. Five east–west gulches offer excellent turning on ideal open glades of 25 to 40 degrees off their northeast aspects. Steeper terrain is available by dropping west off the main divide into upper Smithfield Canyon, although this is serious avalanche terrain. Don't be surprised to find dramatically different conditions here than on the east side. The terrain also steepens and funnels into chutes as you descend the 500 to 800 feet to Summit Creek's South Fork.

Mount Elmer itself can be reached by climbing south along the spectacular and often corniced divide ridge. Impregnable cliffs guard the summit on the northwest, but excellent runs can be had dropping east from just below the summit into the South Fork of Cottonwood Creek. This can be used as an exit route back to the highway, although the creek bottom becomes a very tight and avalanche-prone terrain trap near the confluence with main Cottonwood Creek.

A better option is to climb west to Mount Elmer's long southeast buttress. From this buttress, there are very steep lines dropping northeast toward Cottonwood Creek. Although cut by parallel limestone cliff bands, this is impressive and skiable terrain. The meadows below the cliffs can be climbed directly from Cottonwood Creek. This area provides plenty of space for fresh tracks.

Cottonwood Creek offers a good loop-trip descent option. The trail becomes easier to find as you descend, but the canyon becomes steep walled and narrow. It may be necessary to downhike or leave skins on for the section below the junction of the South Fork. Hitch or hike the 1.5 miles back up the road to Blind Hollow.

A more ambitious loop is to continue south from Mount Elmer along the main divide and drop into Wood Camp. This is a better spring tour because the huge, open bowl above Wood Camp faces south and east. In midwinter powder conditions, however, you can enjoy east and northeast shots by continuing south on the divide toward Beirdneau Peak. Be aware that Wood Camp has been the site of enormous avalanches.

Finally, for those seeking full-on extreme chutes, visit Birch Canyon's upper reaches. Contour around below Mount Elmer's summit cliffs and follow the divide south toward Mount Jardine. Flattop Peak, 9,539 feet, sits northwest of Jardine, and its north face drops extremely steeply into Birch Canyon. Another way to reach Flattop from the Bear River divide is to ski into the south fork of Smithfield Canyon, then climb to its west ridge and ski another west-facing tree shot into Birch Canyon. This terrain is bisected by cliffs down low. Birch and Smithfield Canyons are highly avalanche-prone. Their upper bowls are obviously strafed by giant avalanches on a regular basis. Visit only when the snowpack is very stable.

Wood Camp High Country

Tour 8

Rating: Moderate to difficult.

Gear: Skis or split-board and skins or snowshoes.

Summary: Spectacular skiing with a short, steep approach. Wide-open bowls and steep trees available.

Map: USGS 7.5-minute Mount Elmer.

Trailhead: Wood Camp.

Distance: 3 to 4 miles to Bear River divide.

Starting altitude: 5,450 feet.

High points: Unnamed peak, 8,571 feet; unnamed point 9,065; unnamed point, 9,096 feet; Mount Jardine, 9,565 feet; unnamed point, 8,466 feet; unnamed point, 8,581 feet; Beirdneau Peak, 8,914 feet.

Access: From Logan, follow U.S. Highway 89 through Logan Canyon to milepost 384 and look for a Forest Service sign indicating Wood Camp Trailhead on your left. Parking is within 300 yards of the highway. The huge Wood Camp Cirque fills the horizon looking northwest.

Description: Follow a well-established trail for about 0.5 mile to the junction of Wood Camp Hollow at 5,600 feet. Here you're *already* in the avalanche-runout zone from the epic slide of 1986. The positive side of this is that a climber-friendly swath has been cut through the otherwise dense fir, spruce, and juniper forests. New growth of willows and aspens provide some route-finding obstacles, but you can find a line along the broad valley for about 1 mile until the toe of a subridge leading to Peak 8,571 comes down.

This ridge provides a relatively avalanche-safe approach to the Bear River divide. However, there are several small limestone rock outcroppings that you must climb or circumvent by dropping slightly off the ridge. As you climb, you'll be tempted by protected powder stashes, including a number of short narrow couloirs dropping off to the north. Carry on to the top for the longest prize runs.

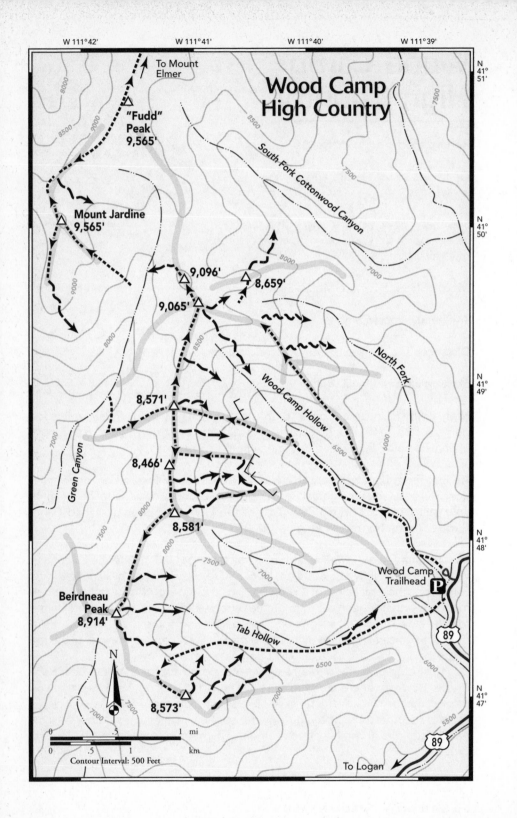

Wood Camp
High Country

W 111°42'   W 111°41'   W 111°40'   W 111°39'

N 41° 51'
N 41° 50'
N 41° 49'
N 41° 48'
N 41° 47'

To Mount
Elmer

"Fudd"
Peak
9,565'

Mount Jardine
9,565'

South Fork Cottonwood Canyon

9,096'
9,065'
8,659'

North Fork

Wood Camp Hollow

8,571'

Green Canyon

8,466'

8,581'

Beirdneau
Peak
8,914'

Wood Camp
Trailhead
P

89

Tab Hollow

8,573'

N

0   .5   1 mi
0   .5   1   km
Contour Interval: 500 Feet

To Logan

89

Wood Camp Hollow and Beirdneau Peak (left); northeast view.

Depending on whether the snow is soft on easterly aspects or corned up on the south, there are many options from here. A relatively easy traverse north leads to the 9,065-foot high point of the Wood Camp Cirque. This point is the start of a spectacular south-facing, spring-snow-type run that drops in a steep, open fall line for 2,200 feet. Good powder shots fall east from this point into the North Fork of Wood Camp Hollow. Point 9,065 can also be reached directly from the valley floor. Either climb the northeast ridge, or if avalanche hazard is low, ascend the southeast bowl.

North of point 9,095 is point 9,096, which has long drops into the South Fork of Cottonwood Creek (see Tour 7, Utah State University and Mount Elmer). Another option is to ski west into the head of Green Canyon and climb to Mount Jardine. Jardine's southeast-facing slopes offer steep, open runs. A reasonable return route to Wood Camp Hollow from Green Canyon can be made by setting a rising traverse heading southeast from the 7,400-foot level in the canyon bottom to a west-facing subridge leading back up to point 8,571. Alternatively, make a one-way traverse trip by planting a vehicle in Green Canyon and doing a bi-canyonal crossing of the Bear River Range.

If midwinter powder-snow conditions are present, great runs lie south from point 8,571. Another continuous subridge dropping from point 8,466 shelters powder on its northeast flank. The line eventually deposits you in a gully, but by sniffing out its shady side, soft-snow turns can be had all the way back to the low-angle valley floor.

Several slide paths cut runs through the trees falling east and northeast off the divide as you continue south to point 8,581. Be careful to stay either left or right of the rocky breakover directly below this point on the divide. Point 8,581 is the southernmost summit in the Wood Camp Cirque, but Beirdneau Peak and its ample east- through north-facing cirque offer possibilities for a loop trip by descending into Tab Hollow, which drops to Logan Canyon only 0.3 mile downstream from Wood Camp.

Beirdneau Peak, 8,914 feet, has beautiful open skiing north and east from its often corniced summit. The long southeast ridge stays above 8,500 feet for 0.75 mile and offers steep and consistent northeast-facing drops of up to 2,300 feet. These are open runs (slide paths) and frequently boast outstanding protected powder conditions. They can be approached from Wood Camp over Beirdneau Peak. A good skin trail rising from upper Tab Hollow to the southeast ridge of Beirdneau could be reused for three or four distinct runs. The two longest shots fall from the end of the ridge 0.2 mile east of the high point. Most skiers return to Wood Camp to go home, but from the bottom of the long shots, it would be much quicker to descend directly down Tab Hollow. There's no trail; brush may be an issue in low snowpack. Also, there's no bridge over the Logan River, meaning a short cruise along the west bank to Wood Camp's bridge is necessary.

Dry Canyon and Logan Peak

Rating: Moderate to difficult.

Gear: Skis or split-board and skins.

Summary: Enjoy quick access from Logan to an efficiently rising trail that takes you to either spectacular open shots off Logan Peak or protected tree and slide paths lower in the canyon.

Tour 9

Map: USGS 7.5-minute Logan Peak.

Trailhead: Dry Canyon Trailhead in the southeastern suburbs of Logan.

Distance: 6 miles to the summit.

Starting altitude: 5,150-plus feet.

High points: Logan Peak, 9,710 feet; north summit of Logan Peak, 9,582 feet;

Dry Canyon; Logan Peak at the top; west view. Skiable slide paths on right; Dymerski's Folly on left.

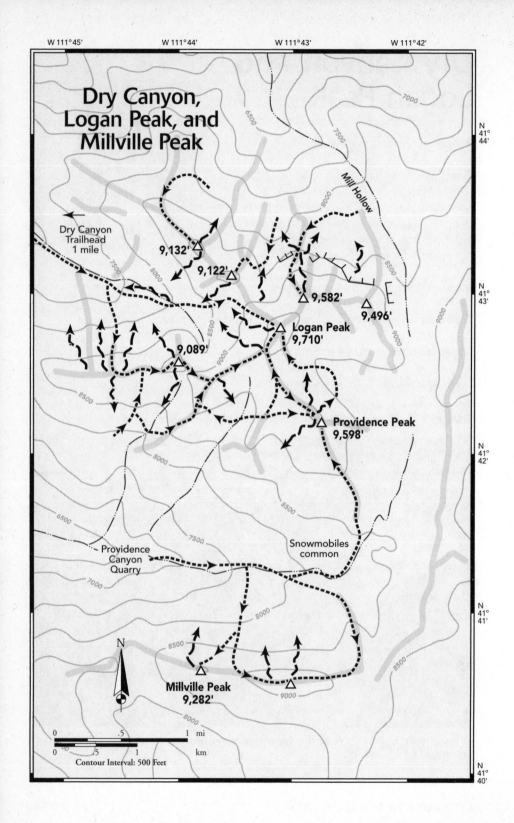

W 111°45'
W 111°44'
W 111°43'
W 111°42'

N 41° 44'
N 41° 43'
N 41° 42'
N 41° 41'
N 41° 40'

7000
8500
7500
8000

Mill Hollow

Dry Canyon
Trailhead
1 mile

7500
8000

9,132'
9,122'

9,582'
9,496'

8500

9000

Logan Peak
9,710'

9,089'

8500

9000

Providence Peak
9,598'

8000

8500

6500

7500

Providence
Canyon
Quarry

7000

Snowmobiles
common

8000

8500

8500

N

8500

Millville Peak
9,282'

9000

8000

0   .5   1 mi
0   .5   1   km

Contour Interval: 500 Feet

unnamed point, 9,122 feet; Little Baldy, 9,089 feet; Providence Peak, 9,598 feet.

Access: Take Center Street east from downtown Logan. It becomes Mountain Road, which makes a right onto Forest Road 25 a few blocks below the Dry Canyon mouth and trailhead. Park at the cul-de-sac above an upscale neighborhood where a wooden sign declares DEVERE AND VELDA HARRIS' NATURE PARK AND PRESERVE. It's often possible to four-wheel-drive for another mile or so up the jeep road into Dry Canyon and park at a pullout or campsite.

Description: In early or late season, you may have to hike to the snow line, but the canyon begins to gain altitude steadily within a mile of the trailhead. The constant uphill grade makes for efficient climbing to the 7,700-foot base of Exit Gully, where the trail switchbacks out of an increasingly narrow gully or terrain trap and into the meadows of upper Dry Canyon.

From here you can see enticing ski terrain left, right, and ahead. An enormous open southwest-facing slope on your left offers more than 1,000 feet of 30- to 35-degree meadows. Easily visible from the Cache Valley, this obvious run is known locally as Dymerski's Folly. Although Al Dymerski skis it, it often has poor snow due to its sun- and wind-exposed aspect. This slope can also avalanche in a big way, as it did on the night of January 11–12, 1997, killing three experienced local ski mountaineers who were camped below it. There's a plaque on a spruce tree honoring them.

Straight up Dry Canyon is 9,710-foot Logan Peak, with a communications and weather station on top. It's most easily reached by climbing up the gut of the canyon, then breaking up and left as it steepens at 8,500 feet. The climb is direct and user-friendly, making an ascent to the summit possible in three to five hours. Many fine tree shots fall from the summit to the northwest back into Dry Canyon. A wide-open alpine bowl drops to the east-southeast; it's typically tracked by snowmobilers coming over from Providence Canyon to the south.

The powderhounds' prize in stable avalanche conditions is the north face. It is unskiable directly off the true summit, unless you'd like to try cliff jumping. From the north summit (9,582 feet), however, there are steep, avalanche-prone chutes dropping to a bench above Mill Hollow. Protected by trees and angled at 35 to 40 degrees, this area often harbors soft powder long after storms have passed, although many of the routes are impassable due to cliffs in low-snow years. Begin with a few hundred feet of skiing near the obvious central chute, then cut left to enjoy the open shoulder or broad subridge. Eventually these shots terminate in an avalanche runout zone at 8,000 feet. Traverse left just above this meadow and finish with another few hundred feet of protected powder in the bowl under Logan Peak's rocky north face. In big-snow years adventurous skiers have dropped from here all the way to Logan Canyon via Mill Hollow for a 5,000-foot odyssey!

Return to Dry Canyon by climbing west and south (quickly) across an avalanche-runout zone and past some rotten limestone outcrops to gain a subridge falling north from point 9,122, near the pass between Logan Peak and Dymerski's Folly. Traverse west along the ridge to ski the southwest shot (Dymerski's) if it's in condition; if not, traverse south to find better snow on the west aspect of Logan Peak.

The most popular terrain in Dry Canyon is the set of north-facing tree shots and slide paths dropping from Little Baldy Peak and the broad ridge between it and Logan Peak. Perfectly angled, well-protected runs abound along this south side of the canyon. They can be accessed by putting in a skin trail from Dry Creek to the 9,000-foot ridge. Huge Engelmann spruce, Douglas fir, and subalpine fir stand watch over 30- to 40-degree glades. The fall lines are increasingly long to the west, culminating in the DB Bowl, a 2,000-foot slide path terminating in a narrow but skiable gully that intersects Dry Creek at 6,900 feet. *DB* are the initials of a local backcountry skier who spends most of his powder days in the misnamed Dry Canyon. (Midseason snowpack is around 300 centimeters at 9,000 feet.)

Thrasher Gully is a 30-degree, 1,200-foot shot so named because of the avalanche-ravaged aspen glade that skiers had to thrash through to get to it after 1996. In that winter a massive slide leveled a five-acre stand of the smooth-barked disaster species and deposited the debris on the opposite side of the gully.

In the right conditions you can make a long drop from the Little Baldy ridge into Welches Hollow and Providence Canyon. Often, however, marginal coverage and sun-damaged south-facing snow limit the attractiveness of this option. Ski as far down as you wish, and then come back up. Providence Peak, with its northeast-facing tree runs down to the lake of the same name, can also be reached within an hour by skinning along the friendly, open ridgetop. (Beware of snowmobile traffic, however; locals call this area the Rodeo Grounds.) Climbing up Providence Canyon and over Providence Peak's bald summit is another route to Logan Peak.

The lower Dry Canyon Trail is basically a friendly outrun for tired skiers at the end of a big day, but in deep snow it can become a bit of a trench. The trail drops continuously, and dense maple bushes and aspen trees hem it in on both sides, preventing speed-killing turns. Locals used to refer to it as Die Canyon for this reason. It's technically closed to motorized vehicles in winter, but ATVs routinely violate the rule.

Millville Peak

See map on page 40.

Rating: Moderate to difficult.

Gear: Skis or split-board with skins.

Summary: From Logan, you'll enjoy quick access to an efficiently rising trail that takes you to consistently good, north-facing powder shots of the peak. This makes an easy partial-day tour when the snow line is high. Snowmobilers dominate the lower canyon and Providence Peak but often leave much of the north face of Millville Peak to skiers while they gallop around in the Rodeo Grounds east of Providence and Logan Peaks.

Map: USGS 7.5-minute Logan Peak.

Tour 10

Providence Canyon with quarry in foreground and Millville Peak above; north-west view.

Trailhead: Providence Canyon Quarry.

Distance: 1.5 miles to the summit from the quarry.

Starting altitude: 5,500 to 6,900 feet.

High point: Millville Peak, 9,282 feet.

Access: Providence Canyon Road rises southeast out of the town of Providence, just south of Logan. Go south from the center on 100 East, which becomes Canyon Road. Drive as high as possible toward the huge old quarry. In mid-winter a snowmobile parking lot is usually plowed at 5,500 feet, but in early or late season, it's often possible to drive much higher.

Description: Ski up the road and canyon bottom, usually on 'bile tracks, or hitch a tow as high as 8,200 feet, where routes divide north and south for Providence and Millville Peaks, respectively. Climb south to the summit ridge and work back west to the top. Alternatively, it's possible to escape the two-stroke stench as soon as the canyon opens up at 7,500 feet. Work up through the woods to the southeast and switchback up the steep final 700 feet to the summit. Use the trail for multiple runs in the glades and avalanche chutes falling due north all along the mile-long summit ridge.

Lower-angle meadow skiing exists below the north face of Millville between the canyon floor and 8,500 feet. This moderate terrain extends all the way to the descending summit ridge east of the peak. The steep shots become longer and more sustained to the west. It's even possible to ski the Waterfall Hollows above the quarry, but most sane tourers will want to traverse skier's right above the quarry cliffs at 7,500 feet rather than descend rugged, narrow gullies directly to the quarry. The optimal "home run" and the longest clean shot in Providence Canyon is an avalanche path that falls from point 9,014 on the summit ridge west of Millville Peak to 7,300 feet in the canyon floor just east of the quarry cliffs.

Wellsville Mountains

Rating: Moderate to difficult.

Gear: Skis or split-board with skins.

Summary: The world's steepest range (as measured by the ratio of width to height) is a great place to ski in stable avalanche conditions. Box Elder Peak and Wellsville Cone boast fine skiing on all aspects, and the place just doesn't get skied out. However, few if any safe havens for storm or weak-snowpack skiing exist here. All approaches are relatively efficient, owing to the continuously steep terrain, but they invariably require traveling in steep, narrow, terrain-trap gullies. The range is well suited to a south-to-north traverse.

Tour 11

Maps: USGS 7.5-minute Honeyville; Wellsville, Mount Pisgah (and Brigham City for the southeast corner).

Trailhead: Rattlesnake Canyon (south), Pine Canyon (east), or Deep Canyon (north).

Distance: 3.5 miles to Wellsville Cone from Rattlesnake or Pine; 3 miles to Mendon Peak from Deep Canyon. Pine and Deep approaches can be shorter in spring or early winter.

Starting altitude: Rattlesnake Canyon, 6,000 feet; Pine and Deep Canyons, 5,000 to 5,400 feet.

High points: Box Elder Peak, 9,372 feet; Wellsville Cone, 9,358 feet; unnamed peak, 8,981 feet.

Access: Rattlesnake Canyon Trailhead is a pullout along U.S. Highway 89/91 just north of Sardine Pass. If you're coming from Logan, drive a short distance up out of Cache Valley toward the pass and park at the first pullout on your right. The highway is divided here by a cement barrier; if you're approaching from the south, you must drive down nearly to the Cache Valley, then make a U-turn where feasible and come back up to park.

Pine Canyon Road is 500 North Street in Wellsville (on Utah State Route 23). Continue straight west as the road becomes dirt and park below a private property gate if it's locked. If not, drive as far as possible up Pine Canyon by making a left at 4,950 feet, where a little-used road continues west.

Deep Canyon Road is Third North Street in Mendon (located 5 miles north of Wellsville on UT 23). Follow the road west to the established trailhead at 5,400 feet, or as high as possible toward it.

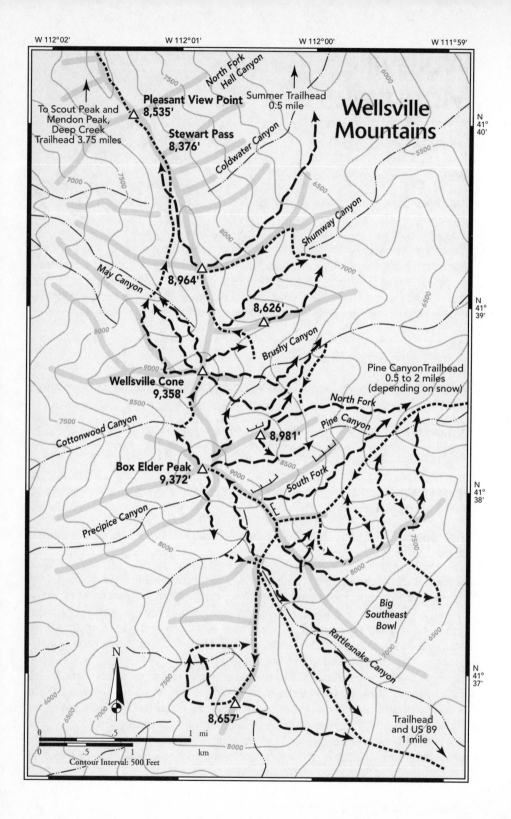

W 112°02'   W 112°01'   W 112°00'   W 111°59'

North Fork
Hell Canyon

Pleasant View Point
8,535'

Summer Trailhead
0.5 mile

Stewart Pass
8,376'

Wellsville
Mountains

To Scout Peak and
Mendon Peak,
Deep Creek
Trailhead 3.75 miles

Coldwater Canyon

Shumway Canyon

N 41° 40'

May Canyon

8,964'

8,626'

Brushy Canyon

Pine Canyon Trailhead
0.5 to 2 miles
(depending on snow)

N 41° 39'

Wellsville Cone
9,358'

North Fork

8,981'

Pine Canyon

Cottonwood Canyon

South Fork

Box Elder Peak
9,372'

N 41° 38'

Precipice Canyon

Big
Southeast
Bowl

Rattlesnake Canyon

N 41° 37'

N

Trailhead
and US 89
1 mile

8,657'

0   .5   1 mi

0   .5   1
km

Contour Interval: 500 Feet

Description: The approach to Box Elder Peak from Rattlesnake Canyon is a good option when a solid melt-freeze crust exists and there's ample snow coverage along Sardine Pass Road. Climb over the fence and follow a road due west, staying south of the creek along a field. Once you're in the canyon, the road disappears, and the best route is climber's left of the gully bottom. Higher up, the gully becomes the most efficient route, but it's narrow and catches avalanches from either side. Pass quickly and at your own discretion. Continue north to a small saddle on the Wellsville divide. Several ski options present themselves.

Just to the south is a nice bowl west of the divide with north-facing runs off point 8,657 and an easy return to the saddle. Alternatively, ski east of this peak for a long east-facing return run into Rattlesnake Canyon.

Moderate south-facing shots off Box Elder Peak are easily reached by making a rising traverse to the northeast from the top of Rattlesnake Canyon along the indistinct Wellsville divide. Many east-facing runs fall into the upper bowls of Pine Canyon. Use these to make a loop tour by descending Pine Canyon, or climb back to the ridge and descend along the approach route down Rattlesnake Canyon, staying above the gully by continually traversing skier's left for southwest-facing shots in open terrain.

Pine Canyon is the most expedient trailhead to ski down to from the superb east aspects of Wellsville Cone, making it a better option than Rattlesnake for the high peaks, despite its lower start. Ascend the road until it terminates in a deep erosion gully and commit to the gully or brave the hellish bushwhack north of it. At 6,500 feet the gully splits, and you can ascend safer terrain between the two ravines. From here, you can view the fine northeast drops into Pine Canyon from its south rim. To reach these shots, contour south at the 8,000-foot level and switchback to the rim. A beautiful, big southeast-facing bowl also drops from this south rim of Pine Canyon. An easy return to the trailhead from the south rim requires good snow coverage or copious bushwhacking down low.

Alternatively, continue up into the South Fork of Pine Canyon and use the subridge north of it to gain the main Wellsville divide. Ski the east-facing shots back into the South Fork, or ascend north and west to Box Elder Peak, passing steep, cornice-guarded couloirs dropping northeast into Pine Canyon proper. Cache Valley, the Great Salt Lake, and the Bear River Range entertain the eye on this low-angle ridge walk.

Box Elder Peak has a great run off its north face dropping into Cottonwood Canyon on the west side of the range. Ski this shot and skin north to Wellsville Cone to complete the quintessential tour of the high peaks. The east aspect of Box Elder is also skiable but rather short. Point 8,981, however, just east of Elder's summit, has impressive terrain dropping northeast for 1,500 feet into either Brushy or Pine Canyons, on the North Fork of Pine.

Wellsville Cone is really the prize ski peak of the "world's steepest range." The southwest terrain is pretty thin and uninviting, but southeast is an open bowl dropping at 35 degrees for 800 feet, and the east ridge is a 1,100-foot gem of a line. It flattens briefly at 8,200 feet, but you can traverse skier's right and pick up another delightful 600 feet of protected northeast-facing meadows.

Pine Canyon and Box Elder Peak (upper right); Big Southeast Bowl is at left; east view.

The northeast face of the cone is a wide-open 900-foot bowl. North of it is Shumway Canyon, with a long shot off point 8,626—though returning to a trailhead may be challenging. The same is true for the stack of steep gulches north to Coldwater Canyon.

The steepest runs off Wellsville Cone are the northwest couloirs. They cut skier's right and left through the summit cliff bands and fall at 40 degrees into May Canyon. A moderate run drops more westerly off the summit to 8,400 feet before bending north into the canyon. Any of these three runs can be skied for 1,300 feet before hitting woods, and they provide the most efficient route for a south-to-north traverse of the Wellsvilles. Climb out to the north and contour along the low-angle western aspect of the divide to Stewart Pass. The divide undulates but remains easily negotiable for another 1.25 miles to Mendon Peak.

To return to Pine Canyon from Wellsville Cone, traverse or climb south out of Brushy Canyon to a prominent col at 8,000 feet. Drop a moderate east-facing shot into a small hanging canyon, then work skier's right and drop into the main fork of Pine. Open, low-angle meadows lead southeast to the approach trail.

Deep Canyon, besides being a good finish for a south–north ridge cruise, can be good for up-and-back ski tours owing to its north-facing orientation. It's 3 miles and 3,300 feet up to Mendon Peak, but north-facing glades and slide paths begin to present themselves above 6,800 feet.

North Wasatch

Ogden's Backyard

The Wasatch Front rises dramatically from the suburbs of Ogden to Mounts Willard, Ben Lomond, and Ogden, and Francis Peak. Most tourers approach these rugged mountains from the east because the western aspect is dry and extremely steep. Ogden Canyon, the North Ogden Divide, and Weber Canyon are the three main canyons yielding access to the gentler east side. The Farmington Canyon Road cuts through the range just north of Bountiful Peak and rises to 7,300 feet, providing direct access to ski terrain from the northeast.

The touring around Powder Mountain is not really in the Wasatch, but rather in the southern end of the Bear River Range. Someday a road from the north will make this area attractive to Cache Valley skiers, but for now it is the backyard of Ogden and Huntsville.

Touring around Snowbasin and Powder Mountain is strictly on the terms of ski resort operators, and therefore it is usually not inviting to many solitude seekers. Other powderhounds, however, prefer the motorized mode of altitude gain and find the resort periphery skiing outstanding. The Mount Willard and Bountiful Peak areas are primary zones for true backcountry skiing. They are excellent areas that have a wide range of skiing, from protected trees and low-angle meadows to high, rugged peaks and massive, open bowls.

Depending on weather patterns, the Ogden area is often the snowiest in Utah. Being closer to the Great Salt Lake than any other good touring area results in more lake-effect precipitation during storms. Be aware of differences in snowfall and wind in the North Wasatch compared to the primary forecast area of the Utah Avalanche Center around Salt Lake City.

North Wasatch Information

Utah Avalanche Center, Ogden, (801) 626–8600

Wasatch-Cache National Forest, Ogden Ranger District, (801) 625–5112

Snowbasin Ski Resort, (801) 399–1135

Powder Mountain Ski Resort, (801) 745–3772

Black Diamond Mountain Shop, (801) 627–5733

Powder Mountain

Rating: Easy to difficult.

Gear: Skis or split-board with skins (and/or wallet).

Summary: This is a touring-friendly ski resort with frequently excellent snow and coverage. When backcountry skiing is open, the main slopes have been avalanche-controlled by ski patrol. Skinless tours via ski lifts, snowcats, snowmobiles, helicopters, and shuttle bus are available, in addition to the traditional thigh power. Incomparable panoramas of the Wasatch and Uinta Mountains can be enjoyed from all high points, especially James Peak.

Tour 12

Maps: USGS 7.5-minute James Peak, Huntsville; Wasatch Ski Touring Map 3 (Ogden).

Trailheads: Powder Mountain, lower lot, main lot, or Powder Ridge condos.

Powder Mountain Road and adjacent backcountry terrain; east view.

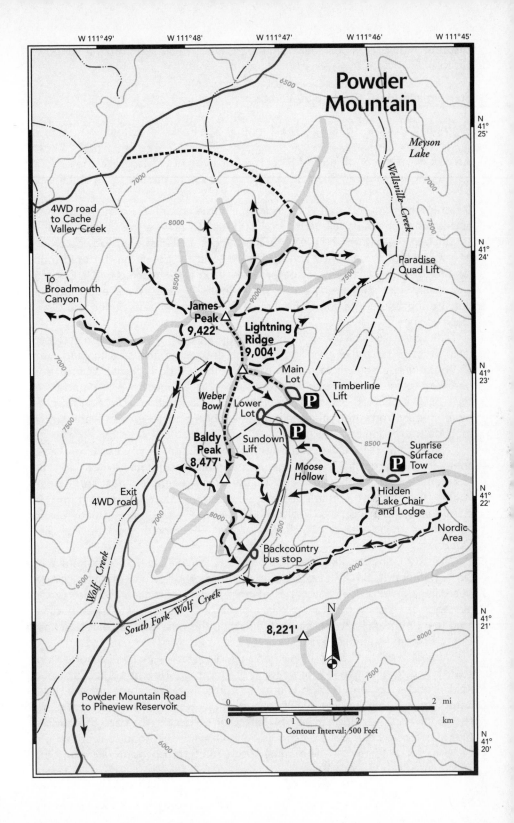

Distance: 1 mile to James Peak from the main lot; 1.25 miles from the Sundown Lift top.

Starting altitude: 7,850 to 8,900 feet.

High points: Lightning Ridge, 9,004 feet; James Peak, 9,422 feet.

Access: From the north end of Pineview Reservoir in Ogden Valley, take 5400 East, Powder Mountain Road. It's well marked, steep, paved, and maintained.

Description: From just south of Sundown Lift (the first lift along the road), east- and south-facing runs fall 1,200 to 1,500 feet to Powder Mountain Road. A shuttle bus, often driven by the venerable Woody, collects joyous powder skiers at a 7,200-foot turnaround. Those who ski to lower points on the road must fend for themselves. Like many other locals, Woody has worked for Dr. Cobabe and family since they founded the resort in 1972. Originally sheep ranchers, they bought the entire James Peak area for 1 cent per acre during the Great Depression.

Lift tickets exclusively for Sundown Lift can be purchased for a reduced rate, compared to the all-area lift ticket. This entitles you to also catch a tow (for $5.00) behind a snowmobile or cat up Lightning Ridge (point 9,004) to the northeast toward James Peak. The southeast bowl, Weber Bowl, is a moderate, open, 600-foot shot. Skinning up Lightning Ridge, either from Sundown or more steeply from the main parking lot, is short and easy even when snow- mobiles aren't running.

James Peak can be climbed from Lightning Ridge, or you can enjoy great shots to the northeast. The angle is generally moderate, except for the Lumberjack Run off the east end of the ridge extending east from point 9,004. This shot got its name from the avalanche-flattened timber found on it. All these shots drop into Wellsville Creek; the return trip is greatly eased by owning an all-area ticket, thanks to the 1999 opening of the Paradise Quad Lift.

West of Lightning Ridge and James Peak is Wolf Creek, a shot known as Don't Mention It, or DMI, because it is private property and has traditionally been illegal to ski. This canyon has plenty of skiing potential, and the current management is showing signs of relaxing their stance. An old four-wheel-drive road that runs parallel to the creek 300 feet up the west bank provides an easy exit to Powder Mountain Road.

James Peak is privately owned and used for heli-skiing on its north side. Tourers have been harassed for heading there without buying a lift ticket, but it holds good snow, and a wide variety of northerly facing shots are available. Returning to a trailhead is difficult. Your best bet is to ski short runs and climb east to the northeast ridge of James Peak, then ski back to the base of Paradise. Alternatively, you can leave a car on Cache Valley Creek Road or Broadmouth Canyon Road (for west-facing runs). Both roads climb northeast from the

Ogden River north of Liberty, Utah. Dropping east off James takes you through amazing terrain often used for inexpensive cat skiing. The Carpe Diem and Y Chute shots fall south and east for 2,500 feet to Paradise Quad.

Yet another fine touring area at Powder Mountain is from Hidden Lake Lodge atop the Hidden Lake Chairlift. It's also possible to drive to this point on the unmarked right turn just before the main lodge on Powder Mountain Road. This point or Sunrise Ridge (0.5 mile east and available by surface lift) is the access point for the excellent cross-country touring area to the east, which is always open due to its low avalanche hazard.

Dropping southwest is allowed whenever touring is opened by patrol. Drops of nearly 2,000 feet are available, along with roadside pickup service by Woody and company along Powder Mountain Road at 7,200 feet. Moose Hollow is the most direct and north-facing shot. It falls west from the 8,900-foot Hidden Lake Lodge into some fine "powder country," as the off-piste goods are known. The line becomes northwest facing and funnels to the road at 7,700 feet.

Ben Lomond and Willard Peak

Rating: Easy to difficult.

Gear: Skis or split-board with skins.

Summary: These are major Wasatch summits, with often incredible skiing and amazing views. The avalanche danger is potentially high but can be mitigated, especially by enjoying the lower terrain southeast of Ben Lomond. Cross-country skiing is excellent on the numerous summer roads of North Fork Park.

Tour 13

Maps: USGS 7.5-minute North Ogden, Mantua; Wasatch Ski Touring Map 3 (Ogden).

Trailheads: North Fork Park, Camp Utaba, or North Ogden Divide.

Distance: 4 miles to either summit from North Fork Road; 3.5 miles to Chilly Peak from North Ogden Divide.

Starting altitude: North Fork Park, 5,400 feet; Camp Utaba, 5,600; North Ogden Divide, 6,184 feet.

High points: Ben Lomond, 9,712 feet; Willard Peak, 9,763 feet; Mount Willard, 9,422 feet.

Access: From the rural community of Liberty, north of Pineview Reservoir in Ogden Valley, go north on 3300 East, staying left on North Fork Road after 1.4 miles. For Ben Lomond, turn left after 1 mile toward North Fork Park and park where the plowing ends above a new residential area. For Cutler Ridge and Willard, continue on the main road and park where the plowing ends at Camp Utaba.

Description: For Ben Lomond, there are two good routes. Cutler Ridge is gained from the Camp Utaba parking spot, and Rodeo Ridge ascends from North Fork Park. Cutler may have better skiing and leaves the road into Cutler Basin soon after it levels off at 6,000 feet, just before a gate. The unmarked Cutler Ridge Trail departs here but may not be visible in winter. The route follows protruding terrain with relatively low avalanche hazard and climbs directly to the Wasatch divide, which you can ascend west to the summit of Ben Lomond.

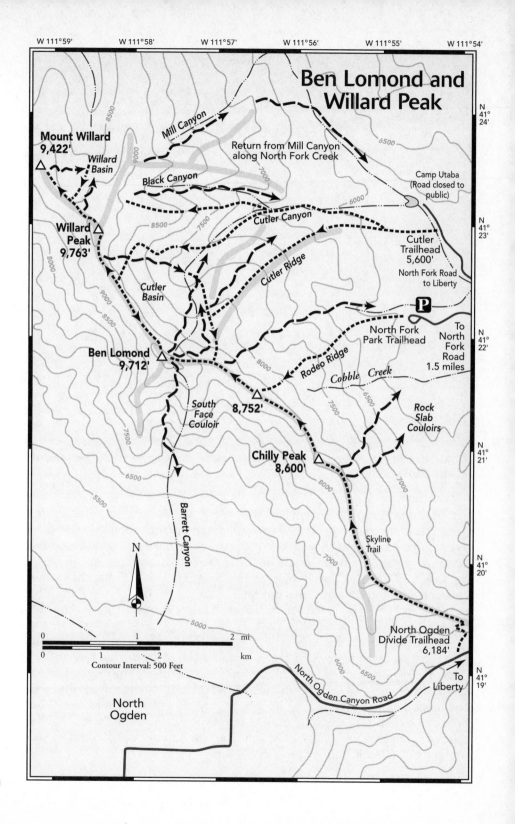

Ben Lomond and Willard Peak

W 111°59'   W 111°58'   W 111°57'   W 111°56'   W 111°55'   W 111°54'

N 41°24'

Mill Canyon

Return from Mill Canyon
along North Fork Creek

Camp Utaba
(Road closed to
public)

Mount Willard
9,422'

Willard
Basin

Black Canyon

N 41°23'

Willard
Peak
9,763'

Cutler Canyon

Cutler
Trailhead
5,600'

North Fork Road
to Liberty

Cutler Ridge

Cutler
Basin

P

North Fork
Park Trailhead

N 41°22'

To
North
Fork
Road
1.5 miles

Rodeo Ridge

Cobble   Creek

Ben Lomond
9,712'

South
Face
Couloir

8,752'

Rock
Slab
Couloirs

N 41°21'

Chilly Peak
8,600'

Barrett Canyon

N

Skyline
Trail

N 41°20'

0   1   2 mi
0   1   2   km
Contour Interval: 500 Feet

North Ogden
Divide Trailhead
6,184'

To
Liberty

N 41°19'

North Ogden Canyon Road

North
Ogden

A touring party minimizes avalanche hazard by following a small ridge toward Willard Peak.

From the horse corrals in North Fork Park, the Rodeo Ridge route rises more steeply than Cutler, but it's more direct. It ascends the same oak- and pine-covered broad ridge feature that the summer trail does, intersecting the Wasatch divide just north of point 8,752. Follow the scenic, broad ridge southwest to join the Cutler route(s). The final 700 feet is avalanche-prone, but wind scouring usually leaves one side of the ridge clear of new drifts. The terrain along both approach routes below the divide is excellent for powder skiing.

For Willard Peak, you can either traverse along the Wasatch divide from Ben Lomond or—if conditions are *very* stable (which they must be to ski in Cutler Basin)—climb directly up Cutler Creek and the basin. The ridges north of Cutler Creek can also be used to ascend Willard, but they're difficult and recommended more for skiing in Mill or Black Canyons. Follow Cutler Creek Road from Camp Utaba, passing various forks but staying the western course into the narrow, avalanche-prone Cutler Canyon. The first ridge is for Mill Canyon, the higher one for Black; straight on is for Willard.

Once you're above the canyon, enter the real avalanche problem, Cutler Basin, where at least three snowmobilers have perished. Immediately skin north, staying close to the few remaining trees on slightly protruding terrain. At 7,900 feet, traverse west below a rocky knob and gain a medial moraine ridge left over from the glacial age. Ascend this small hogback until it disappears below the south-facing cliffs of Willard Peak, then switchback southwest to the Wasatch divide, employing a rocky, transverse bench for what protection it affords. Even in low-hazard conditions, such terrain should be crossed one person at a time.

Gain the summit of Willard Peak from the west, or continue on the scenic divide to Mount Willard and ski into seldom-visited Willard Basin, which is also accessible from Mantua. Willard Peak is skiable from the summit only on the west, and the line cliffs out big time after 1,500 feet. The best run drops into Cutler Basin from just south of the top for a 2,500-foot, moderately steep, southeast-facing corn delight. An early start is necessary to ski this line and ascend back to safety before it heats up. If sloughs are peeling off the cliffs, ascend south in the lower-angle woods east of Cutler Creek to reach Ben Lomond via the east ridge, as described earlier.

Ben Lomond has been skied on its impressive south face into the North Ogden suburbs, but it's a pretty wild line. The west face is even more radical and may be awaiting its first descent. Bring a long rappel rope and a thick helmet! The east ridge makes a relatively conservative descent linking into the Cutler Creek or ridge approach routes.

The proud line off Ben Lomond, and one of the finer in the northern Wasatch, is the northeast face. A series of parallel gullies separate smooth ridgelets falling at perfect powder angles (35 to 40 degrees) for 2,000 feet and rolling on for another 500 feet before funneling into Cutler Canyon. Ski this line when avalanche danger is low.

Another useful trailhead for the Ben/Willard massif is the North Ogden Divide. The skiing above here is mostly of the low-angle variety along the ridgeline leading south to Chilly Peak, 8,600 feet. Climb initially on an excellent summer trail from the trailhead. Along the broad ridge, views are superb of the Great Salt Lake and more. A pair of excellent couloirs drop northeast from Chilly Peak, slicing through the giant rock slabs to reach the Cobble Creek area near Ben Lomond Camp.

Snowbasin Periphery

Rating: Easy to difficult.

Gear: Skis or split-board with skins.

Summary: Very short approaches from lift tops make for user-friendly touring, but much of the terrain is avalanche-prone and difficult to return from. Steep and rugged terrain north and west of the resort offers excellent skiing for expert tourers; moderate areas to the southeast cater to casual backcountry enthusiasts.

Tour 14

Maps: USGS 7.5-minute Ogden, Snowbasin; Wasatch Ski Touring Map 3 (Ogden).

Trailheads: Top of Strawberry Express, Porcupine Chair, Middlebowl Chair, Olympic Tram, or John Paul Express.

Distance: 0.25 mile to DeMoisey Peak from the top of Strawberry Express; 0.2 mile to the ridge from Middlebowl Chair; 0.5 mile to Ogden Peak from Porcupine Chair; 0.15 mile to Allens Peak from Olympic Tram.

Starting altitude: 8,900 to 9,340 feet.

High points: DeMoisey Peak, 9,370 feet; Mount Ogden, 9,570 feet; Allens Peak, 9,465 feet; No Name Peak, 9,070 feet.

Access: Drive south on Utah State Route 226 (Snowbasin Road) from UT 39 just southwest of Huntsville. From the south, use UT 167 from I–84.

Description: Expansion at Snowbasin in the late 1990s brought the Easter Bowl and Strawberry Basin areas (previously the domain of ski tourers) in bounds. These are still good powder stashes, but they get skied up faster now. To reach bona fide backcountry terrain from the resort, it's necessary to go west or south from Strawberry Lift top, north from John Paul Express or Olympic Tram, or west from Middlebowl or Porcupine.

The most important factor in determining where to go is avalanche stability and corresponding access points approved by ski patrol. The resort is obligated to allow access into National Forest lands from the private holdings of Snowbasin. All the lifts that terminate below the Wasatch divide, however, have permit areas extending to the ridge that can be closed to the public due to avalanche hazard that might affect in-bounds skiers—a perfectly reasonable precaution. This type of buffer zone between ski runs and resort boundaries is

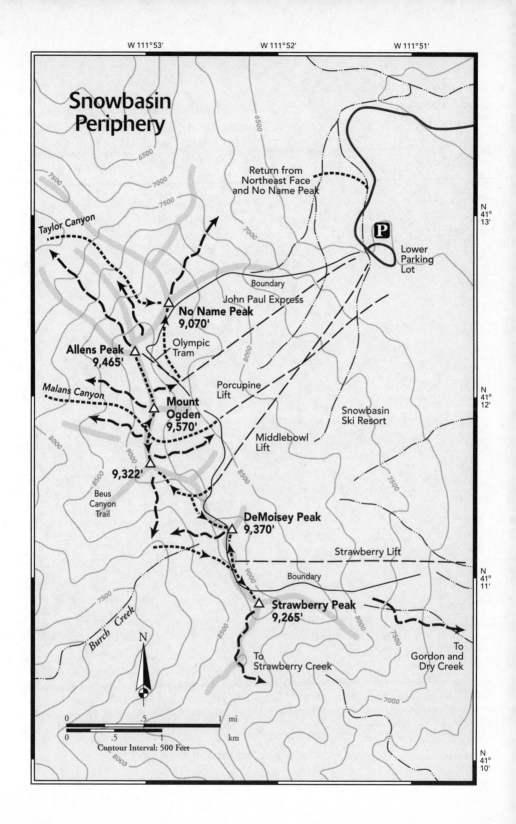

Snowbasin Periphery

W 111°53' W 111°52' W 111°51'

Return from
Northeast Face
and No Name Peak

Taylor Canyon

P

Lower
Parking
Lot

Boundary

John Paul Express

No Name Peak
9,070'

Olympic
Tram

Allens Peak
9,465'

Malans Canyon

Porcupine
Lift

Snowbasin
Ski Resort

Mount
Ogden
9,570'

Middlebowl
Lift

9,322'

Beus
Canyon
Trail

DeMoisey Peak
9,370'

Strawberry Lift

Boundary

Burch Creek

Strawberry Peak
9,265'

N

To
Strawberry Creek

To
Gordon and
Dry Creek

N 41° 13'

N 41° 12'

N 41° 11'

N 41° 10'

6500

7500

7000

7500

6500

7000

8000

8500

9000

8000

8500

9000

7500

7500

8500

8000

7500

7000

8000

0   .5   1 mi

0   .5   1 km

Contour Interval: 500 Feet

Allens Peak and the Banana Chute near Snowbasin Ski Resort.

standard procedure throughout much of the United States. Check in with patrol for current conditions and closures before going touring.

When the snowpack becomes safe, touring to Mount Ogden, DeMoisey Peak, and Allens Peak, among others, is quick and highly rewarding. Short hikes lead to panoramic views and steep bowls and headwalls. Snow is often sun and wind affected by the time enough stability exists to render this terrain safe, but skiing can be a good challenge, especially on the steeps of Mount Ogden. Unfortunately, tourers have had accidents by attempting steep skiing above cliffs when the snow was too firm or their skiing ability was overrated.

Strawberry Express offers access to the Wasatch divide within the resort boundary. This means touring can be done anytime, but it's discouraged when conditions are unfavorable. Strawberry Canyon is accessible by skiing south along the west side of the divide and dropping in, but this is marginal ski terrain with many cliffs. The next canyon south has much friendlier terrain up high and feeds into Strawberry Canyon down low. Make sure there's plenty of snow for this tour, because brush and oak are prevalent in the lower portions and make tough bushwhacking. South of Strawberry Cliffs, a gate is often open, allowing you to ski moderate terrain down to Gordon Canyon. The best escape route for all these tours is the road that traverses north down to Dry Creek and from there to UT 167 (Trapper's Loop). Be aware that this is private property, and no trespassing signs should be respected.

North from Strawberry Bowl along the divide is DeMoisey Peak, 9,370 feet, and some good west-facing shots into upper Burch Creek. South-facing corn-snow skiing is also available in this moderately steep bowl by continuing farther north past DeMoisey. Return to the resort via Strawberry Bowl.

Skiing west to Mount Ogden is best done via Malans and Taylor Canyons or Beus Canyon, but both routes require a great deal of downhiking on the summer trails once you enter the dense brush, usually below 7,500 feet. Trailheads are at 5,000 feet. Unless a rugged adventure is your goal, your best bet is to ski the bowls up high, then return to the resort.

The north face of Allens Peak is easily accessible from the Olympic Tram, although this is often closed due to weather concerns. In this case, if Easter Bowl is open, approach from John Paul Express. One amazing gully, the Banana Chute, drops for 2,800 feet—initially at 40 degrees—into Taylor Canyon. Visible from I–15, this is one of the premier lines in the state of Utah. Perhaps the ideal time to ski it is after the ski resort closes in spring, when conditions are often very stable and the trail down Taylor Canyon is easy to find. A less steep, more bowl-shaped shot falls from the east shoulder of Allens. Returning to the ski resort from these runs is strenuous, and continuing down Taylor Canyon, which is all private property, is long. The easiest option is to ascend the eastern gully to 8,500 feet and then climb east to No Name Peak.

No Name features great moderate skiing off the summit on the east face into Easter Bowl and steep, avalanche-prone gullies on the northeast. The latter area is always open, but should be skied only when the snowpack is very stable. It offers 2,500-foot runs with only a ten-minute traverse across the flats to the lower parking lot and John Paul Express.

Bountiful Peak via Farmington Canyon

Tour 15

Rating: Easy to moderate.

Gear: Skis or split-board and skins.

Summary: A dizzying mountain road accesses friendly ski terrain north of Bountiful Peak and its north ridge. Partial-day tours are very feasible here. Although the open bowls and powdery glades must often be shared with snowmobiles, the steeper, wooded gulches descending north from point 8,735 are more skier- and less 'biler-friendly. The area is great for cross-country skiing, especially along summer roads.

Map: USGS 7.5-minute Bountiful Peak.

Trailhead: Farmington Canyon, at the junction of Skyline Drive and the gate closing Francis Peak Road to public access.

Distance: 2 miles to Wasatch Divide (one way).

Bountiful Peak with Mud, Rice, and Hell Hole drainages on right; north view.

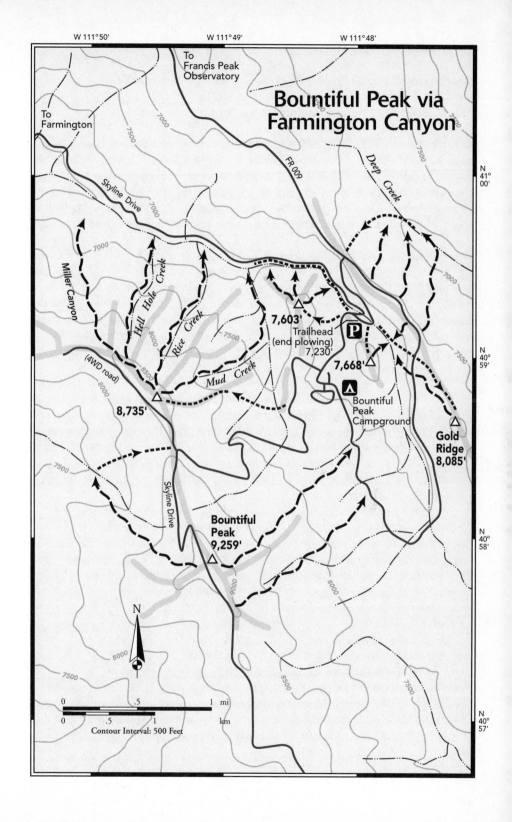

Bountiful Peak via Farmington Canyon

W 111°50'   W 111°49'   W 111°48'

To Francis Peak Observatory

To Farmington

Skyline Drive

FR 009

Deep Creek

Miller Canyon

Hell Hole Creek

Rice Creek

7000

7500

8000

8500

Mud Creek

7,603'

Trailhead (end plowing) 7,230'

7,668'

P

Bountiful Peak Campground

Gold Ridge 8,085'

(4WD road)

8,735'

Skyline Drive

7500

Bountiful Peak 9,259'

8000

8500

9000

N 41° 00'

N 40° 59'

N 40° 58'

N 40° 57'

N

0   .5   1 mi
0   .5   1   km

Contour Interval: 500 Feet

Starting altitude: 7,230 feet.

High points: Bountiful Peak, 9,259 feet; unnamed point, 8,735 feet.

Access: Go east at the Lagoon/Farmington exit off I–15 between Bountiful and Kaysville. Go south on Main Street toward Farmington, then turn east onto 600 North and north onto Skyline Drive (Farmington Canyon Road). A brown recreation sign lists the Farmington Canyon winter regulations, which include no overnight parking along the road. Climb steeply on pavement for a few miles, then switchback even more steeply on improved dirt (four-wheel drive is often helpful). Park at a locked gate where the unplowed Skyline Drive splits to the south. In midwinter snowmobiles frequent this approach road—drive carefully!

Description: Most tours in the Bountiful Peak area begin with a section of travel along the fairly flat and usually snowmobile-packed Skyline Drive past the Bountiful Peak Campground turnoff. However, several short tours involve continuing on up Farmington Creek until Francis Peak Road switchbacks north. Continue along the creek and angle southeast up onto Gold Ridge, or switchback west to point 7,668. Moderate runs fall northwest and northeast all along the 2-mile-long Gold Ridge. Return routes from the northeast-facing runs and upper Deep Creek are via the saddle at the head of Farmington Creek.

In summer, when the road is open to the observatory, tours to Thurston Peak and the east aspect of the rugged Francis Peak massif are quite feasible and highly appealing. The terrain is impressive, but winter access is long from any trailhead. The most spectacular bowls fall east from Thurston near the north end of the Francis Peak massif, about 5 miles north of the observatory. Travel along the ridgetop, however, is not only easy but also beautiful. Cache a vehicle as high as possible along Peterson or Dalton Creeks above the Morgan Valley to do an excellent loop tour.

To reach Bountiful Peak or the tasty powder terrain north of it along the Wasatch divide, skin south along Skyline Drive, staying west past Bountiful Peak Campground as the road switchbacks into a basin of rolling pine glades and finally reaches the divide. Alternatively, leave the road at 7,500 feet and cross the various branches of Right Fork Canyon to access the south rim of Mud Creek. Climb westward to point 8,735, the satellite peak north of Bountiful Peak. From this point, good ski options include northwest, northeast, and east-northeast.

Miller Creek drainage drops from a point several hundred yards west along the descending summit ridge. The fine north-facing run rolls into Hell Hole Creek for 2,000 feet at 25 to 35 degrees through open meadows and sparse pines to Farmington Canyon Road. A similar drop, Rice Creek, falls northeast from point 8,735. Finally, Mud Creek parallels the alternate ascent route and offers a viable east-northeast-facing descent to Farmington Canyon. Do a car shuttle for these runs, or hitchhike the few miles back up the road to the trailhead.

Bountiful Peak itself is best climbed by continuing south and east on Skyline Drive along the broad divide. Stay west, away from the often corniced northeast edge of the ridge. Although the actual summit (9,259 feet) is guarded by cliffs, a point just southeast of it lends itself to skiing. Make a conservative assessment of avalanche stability before skiing this convex, northeast-facing slide path. A more east-facing run also drops from the peak. Return along Francis Peak Road from the base of these runs in Farmington Flats.

Tours as short as one hour can be accomplished from the Skyline Drive Trailhead in Farmington Canyon by climbing to point 7,603. This knoll has good glades falling northwest through northeast back to Farmington Creek. Depart Skyline Drive after only a few hundred yards where it bends south into a small drainage. Cross the gulch and climb northwest to the aspen-covered point. Ski to the creek and cross it to the road, or skin back up along the south bank to your car.

The High Uintas

Wide-open Country
and Rugged Alpine Peaks

The biggest wilderness and the highest mountain range in Utah naturally attracts skiers, both the cross-country and mountaineering-oriented kinds. Although the notoriously dangerous "continental" snowpack and the remote nature of the spectacular peaks have long dissuaded many would-be skiers from the Uinta Mountains, there are ways to enjoy the area in relative safety and with a minimum of slogging.

The Weber River area, and Smith and Morehouse Canyon in particular, offers everything from flat-tracking to steep chutes within a modest drive of Park City (thirty minutes) or Salt Lake City (one hour). Mirror Lake Highway runs right past 12,000-foot peaks, giving access to trailheads as high as 10,715 feet once the road is plowed, usually around Memorial Day. Mounts Agassiz, Bald, and Watson are some of the gems in this area. Normally, late May and June offer plenty of compacted, stable snow for cross-country skiing, beginner and intermediate touring, and expert ski mountaineering. Skiers owning snowmobiles can enjoy Uinta solitude and beauty long before the road is plowed, because it's a veritable snowmobile highway from Soapstone Basin on the west to the northern closure south of Evanston, Wyoming, in winter and spring.

For midwinter touring in the High Uintas, no less than nine backcountry yurts are now being maintained; clusters are located east of Kamas, south of Evanston, and northwest of Vernal. These are typically equipped with sleeping bags, bunks, and woodstoves for cooking, comfort, and camaraderie. They tend to be located in the easily accessible, lower-angle terrain where avalanche danger is relatively low.

For those who relish a challenge and value serenity, the vast eastern Uintas are the place to escape humanity and its trappings. A spring tour to Kings Peak makes an excellent two- or three-day adventure to the roof of Utah. As the high point of the state, however, it might actually have a ski track on it somewhere. To guarantee solitude, take a week or two and ski along Uinta divide from Hayden Pass to Leidy Peak above Vernal during a spell of high pressure in April or May.

The main activity around most of the yurts is cross-country skiing on groomed trails; this is pretty self-explanatory and not described here. The Ridge Yurt in the Lily Lake system has good bowl skiing nearby, however, and the Kamas area yurts also offer downhill skiing. The Castle Peak Yurt–area is described here. Tremendous ski-mountaineering descents exist on Tokewanna, Explorer, LaMotte, Yard, Squaw, Emmons, and many other High Uintas summits, but access is long and visits are few.

The tours are arranged here essentially in chronological order of when they become accessible. Stillman and Castle Peak are midwinter options; the high country opens up later. Kings Peak is best attempted after the road is plowed to the Henrys Fork Trailhead but before the snow melts on the approach/return route—that is, March through May. The Trail Lake area is the first available once plowing begins on Utah State Route 150, then the Mirror Lake area; finally, the road is plowed to the Hayden Pass area, where you can often ski into July.

Uinta Information

Utah Avalanche Center, Park City, (435) 658–5512

Wasatch-Cache National Forest, Kamas Ranger District, (435) 783–4338

Evanston Ranger District, (307) 789–3194

Mountain View Ranger District, (307) 782–6555

Ashley National Forest, Vernal side yurts, (435) 789–1181

Kamas area yurts, Norwegian School, (800) 649–5322

Evanston side yurts, Evanston Parks and Recreation Department, (307) 789–1770

Smith and Morehouse Area

Rating: Moderate to difficult.

Gear: Skis or split-board and skins or wax.

Summary: This is the only public-access trailhead in Weber Canyon and harbors the best snow-and-ski terrain in the western Uintas. 1.5 to 6 miles of flat-tracking on the summer road gives you access to a wide variety of touring options, from steep, avalanche-prone glades and slide paths to low-angle woods and above-timberline High Uintas–type terrain. The Bear Trap Creek and Peak 10,003 areas can be enjoyed in a partial day, whereas Hells Kitchen, point 10,396, and Erickson Basin are full- or multiday outings. Excellent routes for ski traverses start at Yellow Pine Creek, Coop Creek, or Trial Lake on the Mirror Lake Highway and end at the Smith and Morehouse trailhead.

Maps: USGS 7.5-minute Slader Basin, Erickson Basin, Hidden Lake (small portion).

The huge debris pile above Smith and Morehouse Reservoir in the spring of 2002 bears testimony to the avalanche-prone nature of the Uinta snowpack.

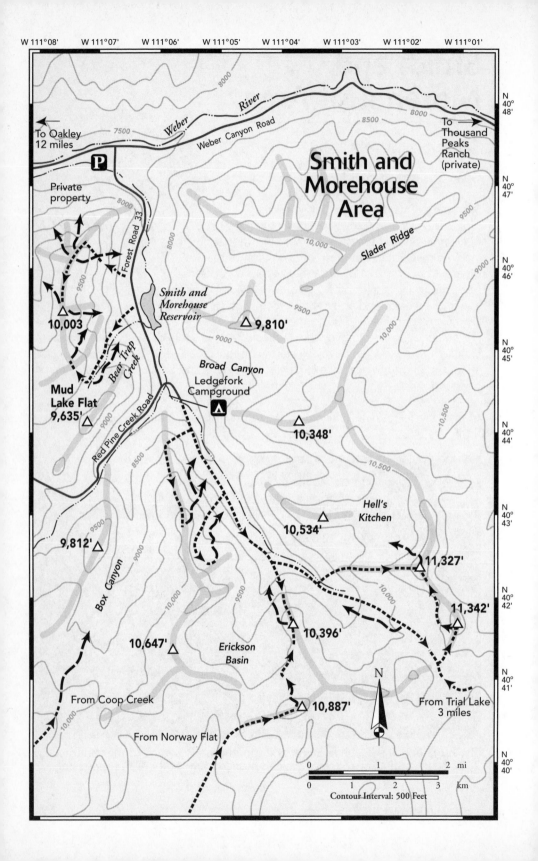

Trailhead: Smith and Morehouse Canyon, at confluence with Weber Canyon.

Distance: 2 to 10 miles (one way).

Starting altitude: 7,300 to 7,400 feet.

High points: Unnamed peak, 10,003 feet; unnamed peak, 10,268 feet; unnamed point, 9,972 feet; unnamed point, 10,369 feet; unnamed point, 10,887 feet; unnamed point, 11,342 feet; unnamed point, 11,327 feet.

Access: From Oakley on Utah State Route 32, drive 12 miles east on paved, plowed Weber Canyon Highway to its junction with Smith and Morehouse Canyon. This is the end of winter maintenance. There's a plowed parking lot popular with snowmobilers. Park in this road-end lot. If there is not enough space, public parking is also available at a large pullout overlooking the Weber River at Stillman Fork. Also here is the gated entrance to Thousand Peaks Ranch, the base for a commercial snowcat skiing operation. It's located on the excellent terrain of Windy Ridge, north of Weber River. (Please note: There is *no trespassing* allowed on Thousand Peaks Ranch.)

Description: A snowmobile would be helpful for covering the miles along Smith and Morehouse Road. Otherwise, simply skate or classic stride up the nearly flat, usually well-compacted road. The closest touring opportunities (the east flanks of Peak 10,003) appear to the west of the road after about 2 miles, where National Forest land begins.

This terrain is steep and avalanche-prone, and the trees are too tight for snowmobiles. Yet skiable glades exist, especially above 8,000 feet. Be extremely careful in route selection and snowpack-stability assessment here. In April 2002 an avalanche left literally thousands of trees in a pile measuring 500 feet long, 300 feet wide, and 10 to 15 feet deep. Although 90 percent of this avalanche and mud-slide deposition was primarily subalpine fir, mature Engelmann spruce and Douglas fir were also among the carnage. The debris pushed to within 75 feet of the road at the south end of Smith and Morehouse Reservoir.

Make an ascending traverse north and west to intersect the northeast ridge of Peak 10,003, and follow this high ground southwest to the glade or ridge of your choice. More moderate skiing falls north and west off this ridge into Shingle Mill Canyon. There is no legal exit, however, down to Weber River Road from this canyon.

Bear Trap Creek offers low-angle, well-anchored terrain, but much of the drainage is dense evergreen timber. Climb west and south from the wide point of the reservoir through relatively young fir trees north of the creek. Intermittent meadows will be encountered en route to the Mud Lake Flat Plateau at 9,400 feet. Ski the low-angle glades.

The Red Pine Creek drainage or the Box Canyon tributary would be a good exit after a traverse from Yellow Pine Creek and the Castle Peak area. South of

Red Pine Creek, above the Ledgefork Campground, is Peak 10,268 and its associated buttresses. The northeastern aspect of this ridge offers 2,000-foot runs in glades and slide paths. The safest ascent routes go up the broad, densely timbered "ridge" dividing Smith and Morehouse Canyon from Red Pine.

About 1.5 miles above Ledgefork is a bowl with open, high, north-facing terrain and slide paths leading down to the canyon floor. Access is steep, densely wooded, and not particularly user-friendly. A similar terrain feature is situated just south of point 9,972 near the confluence of Erickson Creek with Smith and Morehouse.

Located southeast of Erickson Creek, and dividing the creek from Smith and Morehouse, is point 10,396, the most obvious ski peak in the area. Its northwest aspect is a moderately steep, open ramp offering a reasonable ascent and excellent descent, provided stable avalanche conditions.

At the head of Erickson Creek is Erickson Basin, which is actually easier to access from Coop Creek or Norway Flats Roads off UT 150. Point 10,887 presides over the basin and has excellent ski terrain on its broad north face. The best ascent route to the summit is from the west. If point 10,887 is skied on a traverse from the south, point 10,396 can also be toured by means of a short, rising traverse from North Erickson Lake.

Hells Kitchen and points 11,342 and 11,327 harbor impressive west- and northwest-facing high-Uintas-type alpine ski terrain. Point 11,342 is at the head of Smith and Morehouse Canyon and has a shorter approach from the Trial Lake Trailhead on Mirror Lake Highway. It can be skied as part of a traverse from Trial Lake to Smith and Morehouse Reservoir. From Trial Lake (see Tour 19, Trial Lake and Mount Watson Area), follow the summer trail due west through the low saddle north of Haystack Mountain. From there glide on a slight downgrade past Long Lake and its unnamed southwestern neighbor. Skin west and northwest from there, again following the summer trail to the head of Smith and Morehouse Canyon. Ascend north on a broad slope to the summit, or skip the peak and descend directly to Weber River, a 10-mile glide.

Point 11,327 is the southern limit of Hells Kitchen, the immense, high, glacier-carved basin northeast of Smith and Morehouse Creek. Its huge northwest face has lured many skiers, but few have actually made the hefty investment of effort required to ski it. One approach to the summit is to ascend Smith and Morehouse Creek to 9,000 feet, then climb east on the broad, low-angle west ridge. A more efficient option for a fit touring party traveling on a supportable crust is to climb point 11,327 from the flats below point 11,342 via the northeast ridge. Two excellent alpine runs are possible en route from Trial Lake, at 9,800 feet, to Weber Canyon, at 7,400 feet.

Castle Peak Area

Rating: Easy to moderate.

Gear: Skis or split-board with skins or wax; snowmobile.

Summary: Following a one-hour drive from Salt Lake City and a low-angle approach up a wide road with spectacular views of the Wasatch, you'll find a well-appointed yurt and several skiable peaks. This is recommended as a short-day skinless road tour, a single-day loop, or a multiday yurt-based getaway. It's a good introductory tour to the Uinta Range.

Map: USGS 7.5-minute Castle Peak.

Trailhead: Upper Setting Road (optional finish at Yellow Pine Canyon).

Tour 17

Jim Hopkins carves the northwest face of Castle Peak with Mount Timpanogos behind.

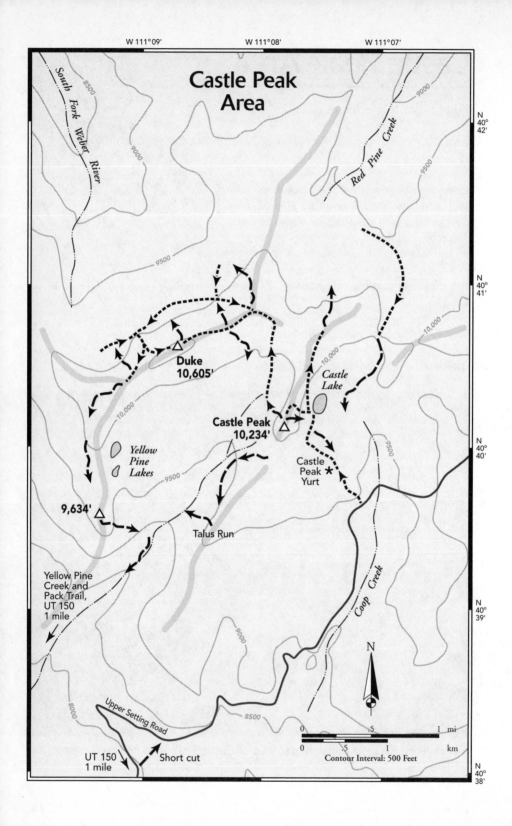

Castle Peak
Area

W 111°09' W 111°08' W 111°07'

N 40° 42'
N 40° 41'
N 40° 40'
N 40° 39'
N 40° 38'

South Fork Weber River

8500
9000
9500

Red Pine Creek

9500
10,000

Duke
10,605'

Castle Lake

10,000

Castle Peak
10,234'

Castle Peak Yurt *

9500

Yellow Pine Lakes

9500

9,634'

Talus Run

Yellow Pine Creek and Pack Trail, UT 150 1 mile

9000

Coop Creek

N

8000

Upper Setting Road

8500

UT 150 1 mile

Short cut

0   .5   1 mi
0   .5   km

Contour Interval: 500 Feet

The Duke, 10,605 feet, near Castle Peak Yurt; north view.

Distance: 6 miles (one way).

Starting altitude: 7,300 feet.

High points: Castle Peak, 10,234 feet; The Duke, 10,605 feet.

Access: From the town of Kamas, just east of U.S. Highway 40, drive 8.5 miles toward Mirror Lake Pass on Utah State Route 150. Approximately 2 miles past the Forest Service's Uinta Wilderness Trail Park fee booth and pullout, park at the junction of Upper Setting Road (Forest Road 034).

Description: Climbing skins or waxed or scaled skis provide sufficient traction, unless there's significant new snow, as the road contours back to the west for about a mile. Here it makes a 180-degree bend and contours east for 2 miles into upper Coop Canyon. A more direct route (skins only) leads up a ridge on the west side of Coop Canyon and bypasses the long switchback.

On a clear day the views back toward the central Wasatch Range, Park City, and Deer Valley are impressive, especially as the eastern aspect of the range catches the morning light. You can easily drive from Park City or Salt Lake City and enjoy this portion of the tour as a half-day outing.

Another 1.5 miles of gradual ascent up the sparsely lodgepole-pined drainage brings Castle Peak into sight to the northwest. Look for an old ski trail or surveyor's tape on a tree. This marks a route climbing west to a knoll at 9,500 feet, where Castle Yurt is situated. Rentals can be arranged. (Please see the Uinta contact numbers at the end of the chapter summary.) From the yurt, travel due west and then climb northwest past a rocky transverse ridge to Castle Lake (about 0.5 mile).

Gain the low-angle north ridge of Castle Peak and ascend to the 10,234-foot summit. Incredible vistas of the Uintas to the east and the Wasatch to the west greet you. The northwest face offers good open skiing, although it's an avalanche-prone slope and it can be wind affected, being high and open.

Run laps on Castle Peak's northwest face, ski back to the yurt off the east face, or work the northwest aspect of Yellow Pine Canyon by traversing skier's left from the base of the summit massif. A series of sparsely treed and open talus slopes offer good powder skiing and drop down into lower Yellow Pine, where a well-used trail, primarily west of the creek, leads back to UT 150 at the toll booth. Hitchhike 2 miles up the highway to retrieve your vehicle.

A more committing but rewarding option is to ascend the Duke, 10,605 feet, by climbing over a series of small north-to-south-trending ridgelets to gain the main Uinta divide. Follow it to the broad summit. The northwest face (Duke's Drop) is an 800-foot slide path, initially angled at 30 degrees but breaking over to 40 as you descend. It offers ample space for multiple runs. Be sure to make a conservative avalanche assessment before skiing this face. Return to Yellow Pine by wrapping around the west side of the Duke and skiing east-facing glades or the steeper southwest face of point 9,634.

Kings Peak— The Roof of Utah

Rating: Difficult.

Gear: Skis or split-board and skins, scales, or wax; ice ax and crampons.

Summary: This tour requires a long approach for a relatively short ski, but the line is good—and it's the highest point in Utah. Go when the road is melted or plowed to the trailhead but while sufficient snow remains for approach and return on skis.

Tour 18

Maps: USGS 7.5-minute Kings Peak, Mount Powell, Gilbert Peak NE; 1:100,000 Kings Peak.

Trailhead: Henrys Fork.

Distance: 12 to 16 miles (one way).

Starting altitude: 9,400 feet.

High point: Kings Peak, 13,528 feet.

Access: Exit I–80 east of Evanston, Wyoming, at the Fort Bridger exit (exit 34) and go 5 miles on the business loop to a four-way stop. Turn south onto Wyoming Highway 414 and drive 3 miles to Mountain View. Go southwest on Wyoming Highway 410 for 7 miles to a 90-degree bend, where a left branch heads south to China Meadows and Henrys Fork. Stick to this primary gravel road for 13 miles, then turn left again, following signs toward Henrys Fork. Drive about 11 miles or as far as possible toward Henrys Fork Campground, making a right off the main road just before it crosses the Henrys Fork River.

Description: An overnight trip is pretty much mandatory for Kings Peak. Even better is two nights; that way you can enjoy a good rest after your summit day, and your long, low-angle ski out on morning crust is relatively fast and painless compared to carrying a load in potentially breakable afternoon slush. (Every March a Wasatch Mountain Club group skate skis in and out of this area in one marathon day.) Approach the Uinta divide by skinning up the Henrys Fork drainage for 8 miles (from the campground) to Henrys Fork Lake. Camp here or ascend a bit higher toward Gunsight Pass, the obvious notch in the divide to the southeast.

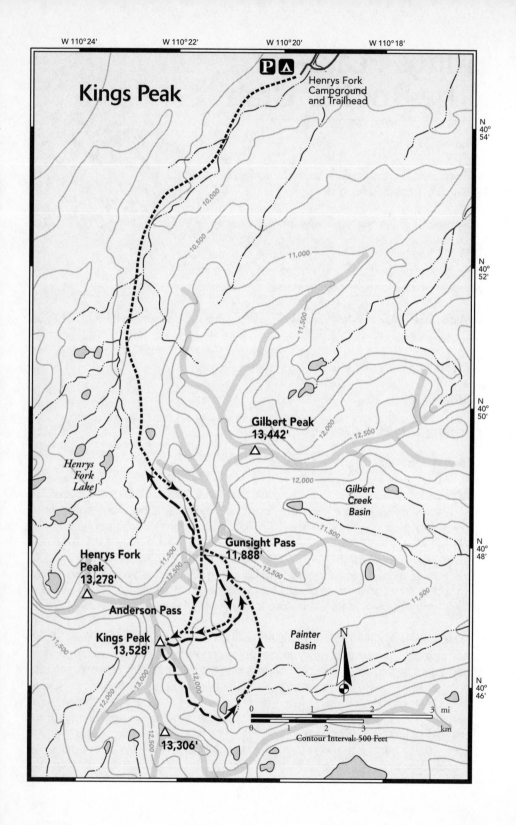

Kings Peak

W 110°24'   W 110°22'   W 110°20'   W 110°18'

P △ Henrys Fork Campground and Trailhead

N 40°54'

10,000

10,500

11,000

N 40°52'

11,500

Gilbert Peak
13,442'
△

12,000

12,500

N 40°50'

Henrys Fork Lake

Gilbert Creek Basin

12,000

11,500

Gunsight Pass
11,888'

N 40°48'

Henrys Fork Peak
13,278'
△

11,500

12,500

12,500

11,500

Anderson Pass

Kings Peak
13,528'
△

Painter Basin

N

11,500

N 40°46'

11,500

12,000

13,000

12,000

12,500

△ 13,306'

0   1   2   3 mi
0   1   2   3 km
Contour Interval: 500 Feet

Ascend to the pass and drop southeast into Painter Basin. Alternatively, if there's sufficient snow and minimal avalanche hazard, you can traverse a steep slope to the southwest from the pass to a plateau north of the Kings Peak massif and contour across it to the east ridge. If you've skied into Painter Basin, traverse skier's right (south) at the 11,500-foot level for about a mile past a series of cliffs. When a view of the summit opens up, climb east on moderate terrain and gain the east ridge above 12,000 feet. Climb it for 1,500 feet to the summit.

Kings Peak has skiing on the southeast and northeast, but the west is very steep and cliff-bound. The southeast is moderately steep (25 to 30 degrees) and flattens out after 900 feet before a series of benches. The northeast is more like 35 degrees. It drops along the standard ascent route for 2,100 feet. Return over Gunsight Pass and back down Henrys Fork.

Trial Lake and Mount Watson Area

Rating: Easy to difficult.

Gear: Skis or split-board with skins, scales, or wax; ice ax and crampons for higher peaks; a snowmobile is useful before the road is plowed to the pass.

Tour 19

Summary: Mount Watson and the twin summits of Notch Mountain offer moderate to extreme skiing within a few miles of Utah State Route 150. The area becomes accessible without snowmobile aid in early to mid-May once plowing on the highway progresses to the Slate Gorge area. The east face of Mount Watson is a proud line with consistent snow coverage.

Maps: USGS 7.5-minute Mirror Lake; 1:100,000 Kings Peak.

Trailhead: Notch Mountain Trailhead at Trial Lake.

Distance: 2.5 miles to Mount Watson or either summit of Notch Mountain.

Starting altitude: 9,730 feet.

High points: Mount Watson, 11,521 feet; Notch Mountain, 11,206 feet; west summit Notch Mountain, 11,258 feet; east summit Notch Mountain, 11,263 feet.

Access: From the town of Kamas, just east of U.S. Highway 40, drive 26 miles east toward Mirror Lake on UT 150. Park at the Trial Lake/Notch Mountain Trailhead where the highway makes a 180-degree bend at 9,700 feet. Or park where plowing ends and skin to Trial Lake along the snowpacked highway.

Description: Given that the prime skiing on Mount Watson is east facing, an early start and/or a very solid freeze is necessary to ski safe and enjoyable corn conditions. Hence, many tourers choose to make a camp in the vicinity of Trial or Wall Lakes, rather than driving from Salt Lake City or Park City at 4:00 A.M. To access the peak, skin northwest from the highway, passing west of Trial Lake and Wall Lakes. The northeast shoulder of Watson provides the friendliest approach to the spectacular, steep east face. The lower-angle, northeast shoulder can be skied instead if the main shot isn't in shape. There's also skiing on

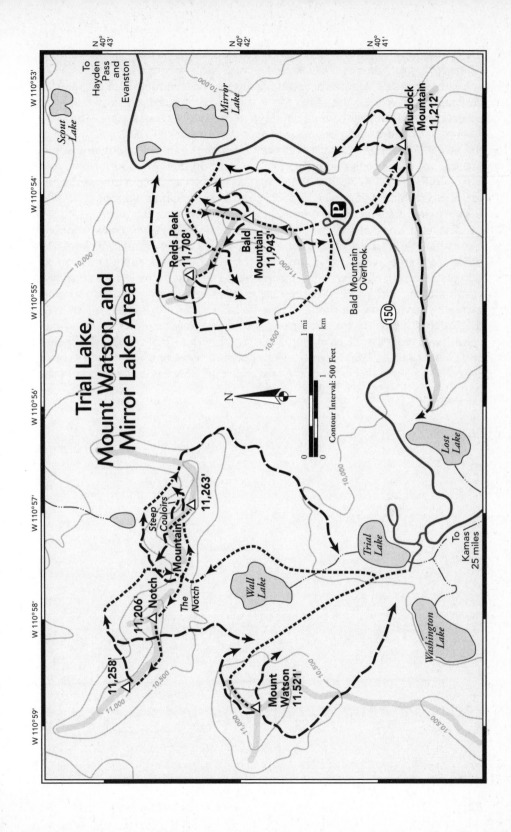

Trial Lake, Mount Watson, and Mirror Lake Area

Scout Lake

To Hayden Pass and Evanston

Mirror Lake

10,000

N 40° 43'

N 40° 42'

N 40° 41'

W 110°53'

W 110°54'

W 110°55'

W 110°56'

W 110°57'

W 110°58'

W 110°59'

Reids Peak 11,708'

Bald Mountain 11,943'

Murdock Mountain 11,212'

P

Bald Mountain Overlook

150

11,000

10,500

10,000

Lost Lake

Trial Lake

To Kamas 25 miles

Wall Lake

Washington Lake

10,500

10,500

11,000

10,500

11,000

Mount Watson 11,521'

The Notch

Notch 11,206'

Steep Couloirs

Mountain

11,263'

11,258'

N

Contour Interval: 500 Feet

1 mi

1

km

0

0

the northwest and southwest aspects, but, like other westerly aspects in the windswept, snow-deprived Uintas, snow coverage is inconsistent.

To reach Notch Mountain, ascend along the Watson route, but stay east of Wall Lake and work up the series of steps to the Notch. From this symmetrical pass, go northwest to the west summit or northeast to the east peak. The west summit has decent skiing on its south aspect from point 11,206 directly above the notch. A steeper shot falls northwest from here, but both north and south aspects are more consistently filled in if skied from the 11,050-foot pass just west of point 11,206. Another good shot falls northeast from the true west summit of Notch Mountain, point 11,258. Reach it by skinning (or booting, as necessary) along the spectacular summit ridge to the west for 0.5 mile.

The east peak of Notch Mountain has some exciting couloirs dropping both west and east off its western summit plateau. The east-facing lines are some of the steepest and most aesthetic shots in the Uintas, cutting through an otherwise vertical 600-foot cliff. The approach climb is up the low-angle southwest shoulder, and good 30-degree skiing falls south from the western summit plateau. The west couloir drops to Lovenia Lake, providing an easy return over the Notch. After skiing the extreme east couloirs, you can either return by traversing west past Ibantik Lake, or make a loop return to Trial Lake by skiing east and climbing to a 10,800-foot gunsight notch. It has a fine east-facing couloir dropping to Notch Lake. From the lake, ski southwest across the broad basin past Star Lake and down to Trial Lake.

Mirror Lake Area

See map on page 81.

Rating: Easy to difficult.

Gear: Skis or split-board and skins, scales, or wax; ice ax and crampons for higher peaks; a snowmobile is useful before the road is plowed to the pass.

Summary: These steep (Bald and Reids) and rounded (Murdock) peaks are very accessible from the highest trailhead in the state and offer everything from gentle meadows to 40-degree headwalls. Prime season begins once Utah State Route 150 is plowed over Bald Mountain Pass, around Memorial Day. Bald and Reid make a good combination tour, and Bald can easily be done in a partial day; it's the major summit closest to a road in the entire Uintas.

Map: USGS 7.5-minute Mirror Lake.

Trailheads: Bald Mountain Trailhead; Mirror Lake.

Distance: 0.6 mile to Murdock Mountain; 0.75 mile to Bald Mountain; 1 mile to Reids Peak.

Starting altitude: Bald Mountain Trailhead, 10,715 feet; Mirror Lake, 10,233 feet.

High points: Bald Mountain, 11,943 feet; Reids Peak, 11,708 feet; Murdock Mountain, 11,212 feet.

Access: Reach the Bald Mountain Trailhead from the town of Kamas, just east of U.S. Highway 40, by driving 28 miles east toward Mirror Lake on UT 150. Park near the Bald Mountain Overlook or at the trailhead, if plowed.

To reach Mirror Lake, continue northeast and down from Bald Mountain Pass for about 1.5 miles and park along the highway near Mirror Lake.

From Evanston, Wyoming, drive south on Wyoming Highway 150 then UT 150 to Mirror Lake. To reach Bald Mountain Trailhead, continue over Bald Mountain Pass to the overlook.

Mirror Lake Highway below Bald Mountain (left) and Reids Peak; northeast view.

Description: Bald Mountain offers moderately steep skiing on its easily accessible south face and steeper, longer, and more committing shots on the northeast and northwest faces, which are also very close to the trailhead. For the south face, simply ascend north to the blunt south ridge and switchback or boot your way up. A cornice may overhang the 500- to 700-foot south face, meaning that it's more feasible to ski from just below the summit ridge. There's usually a cornice-free passage to the summit on the northeast corner of the summit plateau.

Skinning on to the 11,943-foot summit is straightforward—just head north, giving a wide berth to the extremely steep and usually corniced east face. The northeast face is steeper than 35 degrees and has a cliff band at the bottom on the southern end. It's a broad face with a series of skiable shots that become less steep and exposed to skier's left. Rocks may be showing, depending on the coverage. Trend left as you descend to avoid the bottom cliff. The northerly shots can be reached more directly from the Mirror Lake area. Skin northwest from the highway past Emerald Lake and boot up the indistinct north ridge.

Reids Peak can be skied from either the Bald Mountain Trailhead or Mirror Lake. From Mirror, traverse around the north end of the Bald Mountain massif and ascend to the saddle between the two summits. This col can also be easily reached by skiing the northwest ridge of Bald. Stay south of the east ridge to avoid the gnarly north and east faces of Reids and ascend to the 11,708-foot summit. Nearly vertical water-ice gullies ascend to this ridge from the northeast.

The south and west faces of Reids offer good skiing, depending on coverage. Both are quite steep (35 to 40 degrees). To return to UT 150, drop north from either shot into a shallow basin with tarns (small glacial lakes). Skin up along the base of the peak at the 10,500-foot level and ascend gradually south and east below Bald Mountain's south and west faces to the Bald Mountain Overlook. Then glide northeast below Bald's east face to the Mirror Lake Trailhead. This last shot makes a good tour in itself for cross-country skiers and beginners. Ski up the road (if it's not plowed) from Mirror Lake to Bald Mountain Pass and ski the mile-long, 500-foot shot. Climbing the run instead of the road is also feasible and slightly more direct.

Murdock Mountain from the west is another truly benign tour in the area. Its west shoulder is broad and very low angle, and is only a thirty-minute approach from Bald Mountain Pass. Skiing it is a great introductory or kids' tour with low commitment and great scenery. This ridge continues west for 2 miles to Lost Lake with intermittent meadows and woods. Snowmobile parties sometimes tow alpine skiers to Murdock's summit for runs off the north face, and then pick them up in the flats 600 feet below. This face is plenty steep and produces avalanches and sloughs. Do not allow the ease of access to breed avalanche complacency.

Hayden Pass Area

Rating: Easy to difficult.

Gear: Skis or split-board with skins, scales, or wax; ice ax and crampons for higher peaks; a snowmobile is useful before the road is plowed to the pass.

Summary: Steep and rugged alpine peaks in a wilderness setting offer everything from flat-tracking in the meadows to 3,000-foot, 45-degree gullies. Prime season begins once Utah State Route 150 is plowed to the pass, around Memorial Day. This is the gateway to what is by far the biggest range in Utah. A high traverse to the east from here will yield some incredible solitude and amazing skiing.

Tour 21

Map: USGS 7.5-minute Hayden Peak.

Trailhead: Highline Trailhead.

Distance: 1.5 miles to Middle Basin; 2 miles to Mount Agassiz; 5 miles to Spread Eagle Peak.

Starting altitude: 10,350 feet.

High points: Mount Agassiz, 12,428 feet; unnamed point, 11900 feet; Spread Eagle Peak, 12,540 feet; unnamed point, 11,647 feet.

Access: From the town of Kamas, just east of U.S. Highway 40, drive 33 miles east (2 miles past Mirror Lake) on UT 150. Or from I–80 in Evanston, Wyoming, drive south on Wyoming Highway 150 and UT 150. Park at the Highline Trailhead on Hayden Pass.

Description: Ski east for 0.3 mile across the tarns and meadow and climb for 250 feet through timber. For Middle Basin, make an ascending traverse to the northeast below a small cliff band and ascend the Mountaineer's Couloir, the widest obvious gully leading to the col south of Hayden Peak. The steeper, narrower gully north of this is locally known as the Reynolds Wrap Couloir and often has a small rock step in it. From the Hayden col, climb south along the ridge crest toward point 11,820 for the east-facing run, or ski back down the 1,400-foot Mountaineer's Couloir for a short tour.

Alternatively, if an avalanche hazard exists, climb southeast from the tree line and zigzag through the small cliff band to gain a ridge trending northeast.

Hayden Pass Area

Amethyst Lake

Ostler Fork

Ostler Peak
12,718'

Stillwater Fork

Spread Eagle Peak
12,540'

Pass
11,328'

11,647'

Naturalist Basin

A-1 Peak
12,467'

West Basin

Ryder Lake

Middle Basin

Pass
11,410'

Hayden Peak
12,479'

McPheters Lake

Mount Agassiz
12,428'

11,820'

11,900'

12,045'

Highline Trailhead

P Hayden Pass
10,347'

To Evanston

150

Mirror Lake

To Kamas

Bald Mountain
11,943'

N 40° 46'

N 40° 44'

N 40° 42'

W 110° 46'

W 110° 48'

W 110° 50'

W 110° 52'

W 110° 54'

N

2 mi

km

Contour Interval: 500 Feet

0   1   2

The boundary between Summit and Duchesne Counties and the north–south watershed divide is along this ridge and continues east on the high ridge to Agassiz, Spread Eagle, and beyond. Ascend along it by staying left of the crest when it becomes rocky for the final 300 feet. A short tour can be made by skiing northwest-facing tree shots off this ridge from below the rock bands. There are also clean lines dropping south from it.

From just north of point 11,820, a 35-degree, 800-foot headwall drops northeast into Middle Basin. Or ski southwest for a 1,000-foot moderate shot back into Duchesne County. Yet another option is to cut skier's left through a notch south of point 11,820 and ski a beautiful, cliff-lined southeast couloir into Middle Basin. Approach with caution—there is often a cornice overhanging this shot.

Return from Middle Basin by ascending the headwall below point 11,820 and skiing back into Duchesne County as described above. Or traverse southeast in the basin and climb out to Pass 11,410 north of Mount Agassiz. This can be a good northeast-facing run, or you can use it to climb Agassiz via the northwest ridge. Dropping south and west from Pass 11,410 is a relatively moderate draw, occasionally high-marked by snowmobiles violating the wilderness

Skiing northwest off Spread Eagle Peak with the north and southeast faces of Mount Agassiz behind.

boundary. The Snowmobile Gully can be skied from 500 feet higher by ascending the Uinta divide ridge southwest from Pass 11,410 to an unnamed point at 11,900 feet.

Spread Eagle Peak, 12,540 feet, makes a great objective for a full-day outing. Reach it from Middle Basin by traversing above tree line at the base of Mount Agassiz' imposing northeast face. Stay at the 10,600-foot level below a small cliff that boasts 50-foot water-ice smears. Once you're past this northwest-facing quartzite band, skin up onto a bench with small tarns and climb to Pass 11,328 above Naturalist Basin. Ascend the divide northeast to Spread Eagle Peak, cheating to the south side when rock outcroppings (or gendarmes) block passage.

The west-facing gullies off Spread Eagle are impressive, dropping at 35 to 40 degrees for 2,300 feet. Near the bottom, a typical Uintas horizontal rock band poses an impasse in all but a few spots. It may be wise to climb with crampons directly up the line you intend to ski in order to find the diagonal exit gully through the cliffs at the bottom. There's a clean line in most years falling directly from the summit, with a slight jog skier's right at 11,000 feet.

The peak can also be skied on the east face, but it's a long way out of Rock Creek Basin. The northeast is similar to the northwest but not as long and more corniced on top. It provides good access to the nearly 3,000-foot west face of Ostler Peak, which does have several uninterrupted couloirs.

The prime line for most skiers on Spread Eagle is the south face. It drops for 1,200 feet into Naturalist Basin, with a delightful breakover to 35 degrees after 300 feet of low-angle skiing at the start. Skiing west to Blue Lake below Agassiz is relatively painless from the base of this big bowl. Simply glide and skate past Faxon and LeConte Lakes, then either climb Agassiz via the east or south ridge, traverse around the toe of the south ridge and follow the Highline Trail route, or contour at the 10,700-foot level back to your vehicle.

Mount Agassiz has great ski lines on the northwest and southeast; it's sometimes skiable, although not as cleanly, on the southwest as well. Climb it from the west via the Snowmobile Gully and the northwest ridge after contouring at the 10,700-foot level from Hayden Pass Trailhead. From Blue Lake, climb the east or south ridge. It's probably the most efficient major peak to ski from Hayden Pass, since Hayden Peak is more of a paragliding objective.

The southeast face is a consistent 35- to 40-degree shot for 1,600 feet to Blue Lake with only a very short rock band in the middle. It can usually be jumped or schussed. Point 11,647 north of Blue Lake also has beautiful corn skiing all along the ridge between it and Agassiz. The east ridge is steep with a few gendarmes, but they're easily passed on the south. Avoid the massive cornices on the north side of this ridge.

A wavelike cornice parallels the east-facing couloir falling to Blue Lake from the south col below Agassiz. Climb this "Wave Couloir" to gain the south ridge. It's easy to skin up, but it may be more efficient to skin northwest across the south face in order to ski the northwest finger chutes. These shots drop at 35 to 40 degrees to the cliff band that spans the bottom. The key here is to ski the main gut shot and cut right at point 11,200, or enjoy the one just north of it. A diagonal exit gully cuts through the pesky quartzite band below the north gully, but this is tough to see from above. Return to Hayden Pass by traversing at the 10,700-foot level along the western base of the divide ridge. This is also the approach route to the Snowmobile Couloir.

Bob Merrill dropping into the northwest finger chutes on Mount Agassiz.

IV

Central Wasatch

Great Snow, Easy Access, and Amazing Terrain

The Salt Lake City–area mountains, including Mill Creek and Big and Little Cottonwood Canyons, are defined here as the Central Wasatch. This relatively small area is the playground of many avid backcountry skiers. The proximity of this incomparable skiing area to a population of millions accounts for its justifiable reputation as a crowded place. (It's possible to take public buses to and from trailheads!) The vast majority of backcountry users, however, stay close to the most popular trailheads; a motivated touring party can find peace, quiet, and untracked snow any day of the season. Creativity and a willingness to get off the beaten track are important here, but the snow quality and friendly terrain render the tri-canyon area one of the finest ski-touring regions in the world.

Short, avalanche-safe tours with plenty of moderate terrain are mostly found on the north side of Big Cottonwood Canyon (BCC), although White Pine Canyon and Grizzly Gulch in Little Cottonwood Canyon (LCC) have some similar terrain. Extreme descents exist in Wolverine Cirque on Mount Superior and in the high country of the Twin Peaks and Lone Peak Wilderness Areas. Powderhounds maximize their delight with bi-canyonal tours between LCC and BCC in Cardiff, Days, Mineral, Silver, Mill B, and Broads Forks, or between BCC and Mill Creek in the Gobblers Knob/Alexander Basin and Reynolds Peak areas. Aside from the numerous other ski tourers in the most popular (i.e., easiest to access) areas, there is also guided heli-skiing to contend with in much of the multiuse (nonwilderness) terrain. To avoid the helicopter noise and tracks, simply tour in the wilderness areas and/or ski the shared terrain on the days heli-skiing is restricted from the prime tri-canyon area (currently Sunday and Monday). Even within a given drainage, much of the terrain is inaccessible by helicopter, and the Wasatch Powderbird Guides willingly stay out of the Reynolds, Bear Trap, and Willow drainages as well as the lakes district between Alta and Brighton.

The Central Wasatch is a natural place to begin ski touring and to spend a lifetime of winters exploring and perfecting the craft. No place else on Earth, let alone in Utah, can match the ratio of downhill powder-skiing quality gained for effort put forth in this area, and even when the same slope is skied time and again, conditions, partners, and perspective make it new. One of the goals of this book, however, is to offer alternate destinations to the ever-expanding crowd of Salt Lake City–area backcountry tourers.

Central Wasatch Information

Wasatch-Cache National Forest, Salt Lake Ranger District, (801) 943–1794
Utah Avalanche Center, (801) 364–1581
Exum Utah Mountain Adventures, (801) 550–EXUM (3986)
Wasatch Powderbird Guides, (801) 742–2800
Utah Avalanche Center, Park City, (435) 658–5512
Utah Avalanche Center, Alta, (801) 742–0830

Mill D North and Reynolds Peak

Rating: Easy to moderate.

Gear: Skis or split-board and skins; waxed skis or fish scales are appropriate in lower Mill D.

Tour 22

Summary: This is a friendly touring area even when avalanche danger is considerable. Partial- to full-day tours are available. The snow quality is usually very high in wind-protected glades. The obvious lines get skied out soon after (and even during) snowfalls, but nearly all the terrain is skiable, and many nooks and crannies remain fresh.

Maps: USGS 7.5-minute Mount Aire; Alpen Tech Wasatch 1.

Trailhead: Mill D North across Big Cottonwood Canyon Road from Spruces parking lot at the mouth of Days Fork.

Distance: 3.5 miles to Reynolds Peak.

Starting altitude: 7,400 feet.

High points: Unnamed point, 9,990 feet (above The Canyons ski resort Ninety Nine 90 Lift); Reynolds Peak, 9,422 feet; unnamed point, 9,401 feet; Little Water Peak, 9,605 feet.

Access: From I–215 in Salt Lake City, exit at 6200 South and follow the signs toward Brighton at the head of Big Cottonwood Canyon (BCC). Park at the Spruces Campground lot on the right, about 11.5 miles from the mouth of BCC.

Description: Cross BCC Road and follow a summer road as it contours northwest into Mill D Canyon and passes a cluster of cabins. The trail is wide and low angle for 1.5 miles before splitting east to Lake Desolation or west to Dog Lake. Even below this junction, good ski terrain can be found by ascending the first east fork. Low-angle meadows and aspen glades fall northwest from point 9,269, which separates this fork from Bear Trap to the east.

The Lake Desolation area has fine north-facing tree shots falling from its south rim—which can also be approached from Bear Trap or Peak 9,990, a ten-minute walk from the top of The Canyons ski resort Lift Ninety Nine 90. *Powder*

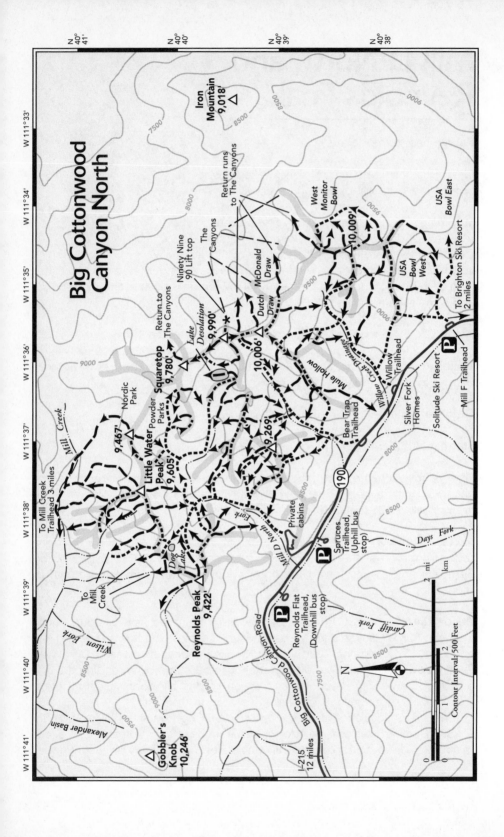

Big Cottonwood Canyon North

Iron Mountain 9,018'

Return runs to The Canyons

West Monitor Bowl

△ 10,009'

USA Bowl East

USA Bowl West

The Canyons

Ninety Nine 90 Lift top

McDonald Draw

Dutch Draw

Return to The Canyons

Lake Desolation 9,990'

Squaretop 9,780' △

Mule Hollow

Willow Creek Divide

Willow Trailhead

Nordic Park

Powder Parks

9,467' △

Little Water Peak 9,605'

△ 10,006'

△ 9,269'

Bear Trap Trailhead

Silver Fork Homes

Solitude Ski Resort

To Brighton Ski Resort 2 miles

Mill F Trailhead

9000

To Mill Creek Trailhead 3 miles

Mill Creek

Mill D North Fork

Private cabins

190

8000

8500

Days Fork

To Mill Creek

Dog Lake

Reynolds Peak 9,422' △

Spruces Trailhead, (Uphill bus stop)

Reynolds Flat Trailhead, (Downhill bus stop)

Big Cottonwood Canyon Road

I-215 12 miles

Cardiff Fork

Wilson Fork

Alexander Basin

Gobbler's Knob 10,246' △

9500

9000

8500

N

Contour Interval: 500 Feet

2 mi

km

Parks refers to the cirque northwest of Lake Desolation. It's a great area for novice skiers with relatively low avalanche hazard and low-angle runs.

Reynolds Peak is at the head of the west fork of Mill D North. Ascend via Dog Lake and the northeast ridge, or climb the east ridge, but be wary of the slide-prone east face. Superb northeast-facing evergreen glades drop from the long east ridge of Reynolds and can be climbed directly by leaving the canyon bottom just east of the Lake "Deso" junction.

Reynolds's northwest face offers fine tree shots into Butler Fork, and the north ridge accesses drop into Big Water Gulch and Mill Creek Canyon. One-way (bi-canyonal) tours into Mill Creek require a vehicle cached at Porter Fork, where the plowing ends 4.5 miles above the toll booth. From Dog Lake, either ski north or ascend east to point 9,401 or Little Water Peak, then ski the north-west-facing woods or northeast-facing open shots into upper Mill Creek.

Bear Trap Fork

Tour 23

See map on page 94.

Rating: Easy to moderate.

Gear: Skis or split-board with skins or snowshoes.

Summary: Enjoy short, safe tours in powdery glades, returning down the same canyon or dropping west into Mill D North for shorter approaches to its eastern branches. Upper Bear Trap is a good spot for early-season and beginner skiing.

Maps: USGS 7.5-minute Park City West; Alpen Tech Wasatch 1.

Trailheads: Bear Trap Fork; park along the south shoulder of Big Cottonwood Canyon Road. Or you can ski into the head of Bear Trap from the top of Ninety Nine 90 Lift at The Canyons ski resort.

Distance: 2 miles to Peak 9,990.

Starting altitude: Bear Trap Fork, 7,600 feet, Ninety Nine 90 Lift, 9,990 feet.

High points: Unnamed point, 9,269 feet; unnamed point, 9,990 feet (above The Canyons ski resort Ninety Nine 90 Lift).

Access: From I–215 in Salt Lake City, exit at 6200 South and follow the signs toward Brighton at the head of Big Cottonwood Canyon (BCC). Park at Bear Trap about 13 miles east from the mouth of BCC. From The Canyons ski resort Lift 9,990, climb a few hundred feet to the Park City/BCC ridgeline.

Description: The trail begins in tight aspen trees and contours into a V-shaped gully that opens up into a beautiful, flat meadow at 8,200 feet. Trails split south and north here, but the main route continues up the gut of the canyon, gaining altitude through thick woods before flattening again at 8,800 feet. Switchback east from here to gain the ridge between Bear Trap and Mule Hollow. Excellent moderate glade and meadow skiing falls north and west back into Bear Trap Fork.

This ridge can also be climbed from the fork at 8,200 feet by ascending northeast through sparse aspen groves. These trees are well spaced for skiing as a short tour or an appetizer before regaining the ridge and continuing up to the evergreen glades. From the junction at 8,200 feet, climb west to drop into Mill D. An indefinite ridge leads to point 9,269 and the low-angle terrain in the southeast fork of Mill D North.

From 8,800 feet in upper Bear Trap, climb northwest to reach the divide above Lake Desolation and some fine aspen glades and meadows for corn- or fresh powder–snow runs back into Bear Trap. This is also the fastest route to the steep north-facing tree shots above Lake Deso. Loop tours descending Mill D North can easily be accomplished with a 1-mile car shuttle up BCC Road.

Peak 9,990 is easily reached from the lift of the same name at The Canyons resort, and it provides downhill access to Lake Desolation and Powder Parks to the west, Beartrap Fork to the south, Squaretop Peak to the north, and Dutch and McDonald Draws to the southeast. These latter three fall east back to The Canyons resort and have been the sites of many avalanche accidents. The Park City side typically has shallower, weaker underlying snow and tends to load quickly in the ridgeline start zones. Do not become a statistic by skiing the high northeast-facing bowls along the BCC/Park City divide when avalanche hazard is moderate or greater.

Willow Creek and USA Bowl

See map on page 94.

Rating: Easy to moderate.

Gear: Skis or split-board with skins or snowshoes.

Tour 24

Summary: You'll find quick and safe access to the Park City/Big Cottonwood Canyon (BCC) ridgeline here and a relatively safe area to ski—even when avalanche hazard is considerable. Signatures in USA Bowl are the envy of skiers at Solitude Mountain Resort.

Maps: USGS 7.5-minute Park City West; Alpen Tech Wasatch 1.

North side of Big Cottonwood Canyon; southwest view. Bear Trap (left), Willow Fork, and USA Bowl.

Trailheads: Willow Creek, Big Cottonwood Canyon; Ninety Nine 90 Lift at The Canyons ski resort.

Distance: 2 miles to Park City/BCC ridge.

Starting altitude: Willow Creek, 8,000 feet.; Ninety Nine 90 Lift, 9,990 feet.

High point: Unnamed point, 10,009 feet.

Access: From I–215 in Salt Lake City, exit at 6200 South and follow the signs toward Brighton at the head of Big Cottonwood Canyon. Park near Willow Creek about 14 miles east of the mouth of BCC. This area needs a better pull-out, but for now just park along the highway wherever it's safe and possible. Or you can park at Solitude Mountain Resort.

Description: Start from 0.5 mile east of where Willow Creek crosses BCC Road, contouring west into the canyon and climbing gradually to Willow Heights flats. From here, the first fork to the east can be ascended to enjoy west-facing evergreen glades or the mostly open south aspect. This drainage provides the shortest route to the twin Monitor Bowls and the south aspect of USA Bowl. The Monitors look very attractive from above, but make a conservative avalanche assessment and drop a cornice or two before skiing these notorious avalanche slopes one person at a time. Return via the low-angle ridge northwest of the bowls.

Stay left (north) at Willow Heights (8,500 feet) in order to ski either the North or upper East Forks. The latter offers great skiing with relatively low avalanche hazard. The north branch is considerably steeper and more avalanche-prone, but its northeast-facing woods often harbor great snow quality, and access into Bear Trap is easy. Mule Hollow, a short subdrainage, can be descended from the top of the North Fork and boasts good southeast-facing aspen runs falling straight to BCC Road.

Gobblers Knob Area

Rating: Easy to difficult.

Gear: Skis or split-board and skins.

Summary: This is some of the premier advanced ski terrain between Big Cottonwood and Mill Creek Canyons. Characterized by long drops and protected powder, Salt Lake City's "backyard" is a popular area despite longer approaches than tours starting farther up Big Cottonwood Canyon (BCC). Butler Fork also has lower shots for partial-day tours.

Tour 25

Maps: USGS 7.5-minute Mount Aire; Alpen Tech Wasatch 1.

Trailheads: Butler Fork in BCC; or Porter Fork in Mill Creek Canyon.

Distance: 3.5 miles to Gobblers Knob from Butler; 4.5 miles from Porter Fork.

Starting altitude: Butler, 7,100 feet; Porter, 5,950 feet.

High points: Gobblers Knob, 10,246 feet; Mount Raymond, 10,241 feet.

Alexander Basin and Central Wasatch from northeast.
PHOTO BY WASATCH POWDERBIRD GUIDES.

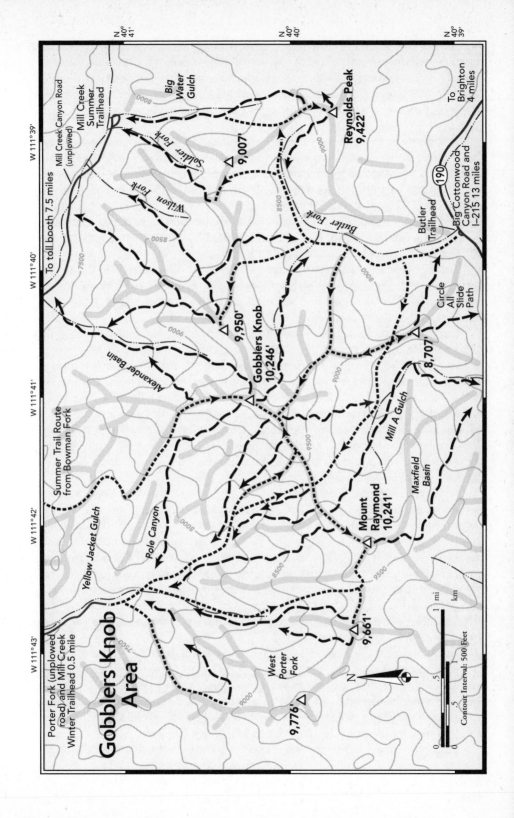

Gobblers Knob Area

Porter Fork (unplowed road) and Mill Creek Winter Trailhead 0.5 mile

Yellow Jacket Gulch

Summer Trail Route from Bowman Fork

Alexander Basin

Pole Canyon

West Porter Fork

9,776'

Mount Raymond 10,241'

9,661'

Maxfield Basin

Mill A Gulch

8,707'

Circle All Slide Path

Gobblers Knob 10,246'

9,950'

9,007'

Butler Fork

Butler Trailhead

Big Cottonwood Canyon Road and I-215 13 miles

To Brighton 4 miles

190

Reynolds Peak 9,422'

Big Water Gulch

Wilson Fork

Soldier Fork

Mill Creek Summer Trailhead

Mill Creek Canyon Road (unplowed)

To toll booth 7.5 miles

W 111°43' W 111°42' W 111°41' W 111°40' W 111°39'

N 40° 41' N 40° 40' N 40° 39'

N

Contour Interval: 500 Feet

1 mi

.5

.5

0

km

0

Access: For the Butler Fork Trailhead, drive 10 miles up BCC Road and park on the plow-widened north shoulder where a Forest Service sign marks Butler Fork. For Porter, exit on 3900 South off I–215 and drive 5 miles past the toll booth in Mill Creek Canyon to the spot where the winter maintenance ends. Many parties cache a vehicle here to make a one-way bi-canyonal tour from Butler.

Description: From Butler, skin up a narrow canyon for 0.25 mile before it opens slightly and the slope angle moderates. After 0.5 mile, turn left for Gobblers via the Raymond saddle and west ridge, or go right into the main East Fork of Butler Creek. This gentle gulch provides a descent route from Reynolds Peak's northwest aspect and offers access into Big Water Gulch, Soldier and Wilson Forks, and Alexander Basin. All these are reached by ascending west along the Mill Creek/BCC divide from the head of Butler.

The upper, northeast-facing portions of Wilson, Alexander, and the drainage between them are highly avalanche-prone. However, by conservative route selection, sticking to ridges and wooded areas, and skiing one at a time, it's possible to tour these areas when the slide hazard is moderate.

Gobblers can be reached via the east ridge by continuing west past Alexander Basin, but most tourers prefer to climb more directly, either along the south ridge (a bit rocky and narrow but avalanche-safe) or, most commonly, via the west ridge and Mill A Basin. Gain the south ridge directly from main Butler Fork or from the saddle atop the west branch, and follow it to the summit. Reach the saddle dividing Butler from Mill A (the next drainage to the west) by switchbacking up through the aspen grove south of the V-shaped West Butler gully. A short tour for competent tree skiers can be enjoyed in this glade; occasionally, given a good snowpack, the south-facing Circle All Slide Path can be skied directly to BCC Road.

For Gobblers/Mount Raymond, descend slightly from the West Butler saddle, skin up an old glacial moraine ridge leading into aspens, and finally switchback up an open slope to the Raymond saddle. To reach the rocky (and essentially unskiable) summit of Mount Raymond (10,241 feet), climb west from the saddle and stick to the ridge. It's possible to drop southwest off the top, but the snow quality is poor. Two prominent chutes fall east from a point just north of the summit, but the more popular runs drop from farther down on the east ridge. These shots can have good snow early in the day and season, but by February they're oriented far enough south to have a sun crust. Good corn skiing often develops here in spring.

Skiing north off the east ridge of Raymond can be excellent, but the terrain all breaks over eventually. Dropping from 9,800 feet—where the east ridge of Raymond is wide and low angle—is a northwest-facing glade that splits at 9,000 feet into slide paths (skier's right) or steep, dense trees (skier's left). Both routes eventually lead to Porter Fork, which usually has ski tracks along the summer trail west of the creek leading out to Mill Creek Canyon.

Gobblers Knob can be reached on skins via the broad west ridge, although the safest and often highest-quality skiing is on the "Corner Pocket," the west edge of the massive northwest face. From the summit, skiing is usually in wind-affected snow; breakovers a few hundred feet down should be carefully evaluated. Avoid the prominent gullies between the main and east summits unless conditions are very stable. The east summit has shorter drops and is reached most directly via Bowman Fork, starting at the Porter Fork Trailhead in Mill Creek Canyon.

From the Porter Fork Trailhead, skin up past homes and go east into Bowman Fork after 0.25 mile, or continue south for the Gobblers area or West Porter Fork. Gobblers is best climbed from Porter via the western flank. Staying close to the fir trees, switchback up to the west ridge and follow it to the summit. Good shots exist in the drainage below Raymond's saddle and along the ascent route.

West Porter Fork offers moderate skiing in mostly wooded terrain. Consider avalanche conditions in the starting zones far above when you're slogging up into Porter Fork. The west fork has four potentially skiable tributary drainages, all with favorable (for snow quality) northeast aspects. Ascend the ridges between side canyons for the safest access. The branch nearest to Mount Raymond is reasonable to ascend, being mostly wooded, but the better skiing is in the adjacent cirque to the west. This is open, avalanche-cleared terrain with good ski runs, and it communicates to Neffs Canyon via the saddle north of point 9,776.

Cardiff, Mineral, and Mill B South Forks

Rating: Easy to difficult.

Gear: Skis or split-board and skins.

Summary: Some of the premier ski terrain in the world lies in these three drainages between Big and Little Cottonwood Canyons. Cardiff Fork (Mill D South on older maps) is characterized by a relatively strong snowpack, long, wide-open shots, and quick access from Alta. It sees abundant skier traffic, whereas its westerly neighbor, Mill B, is exceptionally unpopular with tourers despite its incomparable beauty and heli-free status (because of its inclusion in the Twin Peaks Wilderness Area). Mineral Fork sits between Mill B and Cardiff and has amazing skiing when stable.

Tour 26

Maps: USGS 7.5-minute Dromedary, Mount Aire; Alpen Tech Wasatch 1.

Trailhead: Central Alta Trailhead in Little Cottonwood Canyon (LCC); finish at Reynolds Flat, Mineral Fork, or Mill B South Trailheads in Big Cottonwood Canyon (BCC).

Distance: 1 mile to Cardiff Pass from central Alta; 6 miles to Reynolds Flat.

Starting altitude: 8,650 feet.

Ending altitude: 6,200 feet.

High points: Mount Superior, 11,132 feet; unnamed point, 10,820 feet; Uessler Peak, 10,403.

Access: Go 8 miles up LCC to Alta, pass the lower parking lot, and park near the Alta Lodge. Low-angle tours can be initiated at trailheads in BCC, or vehicles can be cached for a bi-canyonal tour. The Mill B South Trailhead is just below the switchback, or S-turn. The Mineral Trailhead is marked along a straight stretch of road about 7 miles up BCC. Reynolds Flat (an official UTA bus stop) is 11 miles up. It has a large, plowed parking pullout.

Description: Pass Our Lady of the Snows Church and the Alta town offices on an old four-wheel-drive road and cross a low-angle meadow. At 9,000 feet, routes

Big Cottonwood Canyon South

N 40° 38'
N 40° 37'
N 40° 36'

W 111° 36'
W 111° 37'
W 111° 38'
W 111° 39'
W 111° 40'
W 111° 41'
W 111° 42'

To Solitude and Brighton

190

Bear Trap Hollow Trailhead

Silver Fork Homes

Greens Basin

Summer trail (old 4WD road)

Silver Fork

Honeycomb Basin

Solitude Ski Resort

Honeycomb Cliffs 10,479'

Twin Lakes Reservoir

Patsey Marley 10,520'

Davenport Hill 10,120'

Grizzly Gulch

Albion Basin (Alta Ski Resort) 8,700'

Alta Central (Alta Ski Resort) Trailhead 8,650'

Days Fork

Spruces Trailhead (downhill bus stop)

Reed and Benson Ridge

Summer trail (old 4WD road)

Mill D South Fork (Cardiff)

Reynolds Flat Trailhead 0.5 mile (uphill bus stop)

Kessler Peak 10,403'

10,380'

Montreal Hill

Flagstaff Mountain 10,530'

Cardiff Pass

Cardiff Peak 10,277'

Little Superior 10,480'

210

To Salt Lake City 25 miles

Argenta Slide Path

Summer trail (old 4WD road)

Mineral Fork Trailhead 6,400'

190

Big Cottonwood Canyon Road

Mineral Fork

10,634'

Cardiac Ridge/ Bowl

10,820'

Buttress

11,050'

Mount Superior 11,132' (Monte Cristo)

Mill B South Fork

Lake Blanche

To BCC Road 2 miles

N

Contour Interval: 500 Feet

1 mi

1 km

.5

.5

Cardiff Fork and Mount Superior; northeast view. PHOTO BY WASATCH POWDERBIRD GUIDES.

divide to Flagstaff Ridge and Days Fork (north, up a prominent, blunt prow) or west along the telephone-pole line to Cardiff Pass. Nearly all the terrain here is denuded from a combination of avalanches and mining-era logging.

From Cardiff Pass, incredible ski terrain beckons for intermediate through expert skiers. The shots falling north from the 10,000-foot pass are moderately steep initially, then become low angle after 500 feet. Touring out to Reynolds Flat is through meadows and along an old four-wheel-drive road and is easily negotiable for most tourers.

Mount Superior can be climbed by following the undulating east ridge, mostly on foot, from Cardiff Pass. All along the ridge are runs dropping north into upper Cardiff Fork. A wooded ridge descends from the BCC/LCC divide to the old Reed and Benson Mine, providing the lowest-avalanche-hazard route in Cardiff Fork. Little Superior Buttress has skiing possibilities on all aspects, but avalanche danger is significant.

The true summit of Mount Superior (11,132 feet), locally referred to as Monte Cristo, has only two skiable aspects: the extremely risky southeast face and a 40-degree headwall to the northeast. The summit, commonly called Superior, seen from Alta and upper LCC is 11,050 feet; it has become a classic rite of passage for powder skiers on the northeast face and extreme skiers on the southeast. The southeast face, falling at up to 45 degrees for 2,500 feet, is a prize line in powder or corn, but avalanches off the face routinely paste LCC Road. Monte Cristo Chute drops southwest and has a skier's-left traverse after 1,100 feet. The northwest face is often wind scoured but can usually be negotiated into Mill B South.

Cardiac Bowl falls northeast from point 11,050, beginning with two daunting chutes. Cardiac Ridge is a massive slide area falling east-northeast from point 10,820, farther north in Cardiff Fork. Access to Mineral Fork can be made from the pass just north of point 10,820 or via two other saddles farther north on the west rim of Cardiff Fork, where friendly ski terrain exists on the east aspect as well.

The north end of the Cardiff/Mineral Fork ridge is punctuated by 10,403-foot Kessler Peak, with its rugged avalanche chutes on the northwest (Argenta) and east. The lower northeast flank has great powder glades as well. Kessler is most easily ascended via the northeast ridge to 9,200 feet, then head across the dicey north face to the northwest ridge for the remaining 1,000 feet.

Mineral Fork has been the site of humongous avalanches, as proven by the patterns of vegetation. Nonetheless, it has enjoyable northerly-facing shots in its mammoth upper bowl, which can also be entered from Mill B South at the saddle just south of point 10,481. The east-facing shots below 9,000 feet in Mineral Fork are reasonable to ascend from the canyon's mouth in BCC. A sparsely wooded ridge rises from the canyon floor at 7,600 feet, making a safe skinning route to the ski terrain just below the ridge proper. Farther up the east wall of Mineral are steeper, often rocky, avalanche-prone shots commonly skied by Wasatch Powderbird Guides. The exit run down Mineral is on a friendly old four-wheel-drive road with a few steep switchbacks down low.

Mill B South Fork is an enigma in the immensely popular Central Wasatch: It never gets tracked out! Three distinct branches, or cirques, compose the head of this massive drainage. The terrain is rocky; many benches break up the lower terrain. You may be discouraged by the narrow summer trail that exits the canyon, but the chutes and bowls in the central (Monte Cristo) and western (Dromedary) cirques offer acres of outstanding ski terrain that sees only a tiny fraction of the skier days of Cardiff, Mineral, and Broads Forks.

Days Fork

Tour 27

See map on page 105.

Rating: Easy to difficult.

Gear: Skis or split-board and skins.

Summary: This is avalanche-prone but very accessible powder-skiing terrain that's heavily utilized by tourers and heli-skiers alike.

Maps: USGS 7.5-minute Dromedary, Mount Aire; Alpen Tech Wasatch 1.

Trailhead: Central Alta in Little Cottonwood Canyon (LCC); finish at Spruces Campground in Big Cottonwood Canyon (BCC).

Distance: 0.5 mile to BCC/LCC ridge from central Alta; 5 miles to Spruces.

Starting altitude: 8,650 feet.

Ending altitude: 7,350 feet.

High point: Unnamed point, 10,561 feet.

Access: Go 8 miles up LCC to Alta, pass the lower parking lot, and park near the Alta Lodge. Low-angle nordic skiing and short climbs into Greens Basin can be initiated at Spruces Campground Trailhead in BCC, or you can cache vehicles for a bi-canyonal tour. Drive about 12 miles from the mouth of BCC and look for the marked parking lot, which is a downhill UTA bus stop.

Description: Pass Our Lady of the Snows Church and the Alta town offices on an old four-wheel-drive road and cross a low-angle meadow. At 9,000 feet, routes divide to Flagstaff Ridge and Days Fork (north, up a prominent, blunt prow) or west along the telephone-pole line to Cardiff Pass. Flagstaff Ridge is hard to define as a ridge initially; avalanche danger can be minimized by staying close to rock outcrops and stands of trees while you switchback on skins or boot your way up. The ridge protrudes unmistakably above 9,800 feet, and the false summit of Flagstaff Mountain offers inviting access into the upper cirque of Days Fork.

Ascend west to the true summit, 10,530 feet, and ski south into Toledo Bowl, west into Cardiff Fork, northeast into upper Days, or north along the ridge. A 1,300-foot slide path falls from point 10,561. Two other slide paths descend from Reed and Benson Ridge, which divides Cardiff and Days Forks farther north. The northern path has a tourer-friendly, sparsely wooded, east-facing ridge accessing it. The base of this ridge can be reached either from the bottom of higher runs in Days or from Spruces Campground in BCC.

Silver Fork

See map on page 105.

Rating: Easy to difficult.

Gear: Skis or split-board and skins, scales, or wax.

Summary: Smaller terrain features, a rich mining heritage, and a moderate approach make Silver Fork the safest and friendliest ski drainage between Little and Big Cottonwood Canyons.

Maps: USGS 7.5-minute Dromedary, Mount Aire, Brighton; Alpen Tech Wasatch 1.

Trailhead: End of Little Cottonwood Canyon (LCC) Road; finish at Silver Fork Trailhead in Big Cottonwood Canyon (BCC) or at Summit Lift, Solitude Ski Resort.

Distance: 0.5 mile to BCC/LCC ridge from central Alta; 4.5 miles to BCC Road.

Starting altitude: 8,700 feet.

Ending altitude: 7,700 feet.

High points: Honeycomb Cliffs, 10,479 feet; Davenport Hill, 10,120 feet.

Access: Go 9 miles up LCC to the end of winter plowing in Alta. Low-angle Nordic skiing can be enjoyed in Silver Fork. Pick up the trail from Solitude Ski Resort's lower, western parking lot in BCC; you can also cache vehicles for a bicanyonal tour. Drive about 14 miles from the mouth of BCC and park in Solitude's lower lot.

Description: Access to Silver Fork is via Grizzly Gulch, the head of LCC (see Tour 29, Alta/Brighton Periphery), or from Solitude Ski Resort's Summit Lift top. From Grizzly, old four-wheel-drive roads can be used on either the south or north bank of the narrow terrain-trap gully immediately above the trailhead. To travel on the safer south bank, ascend the low-angle summer road, which is superb skating and nordic terrain, until it switches back south at 9,000 feet.

Respect both private yards and avalanche risk when finding a route up toward the mouth of Grizzly Gulch. The old road (often a snowcatted trail) leads up the low-angle canyon to Twin Lakes Pass, from which Mount Wolverine,

Brighton, and Solitude are accessible. To reach Silver Fork at the top of its East Bowl, climb north from Twin Lakes Pass to the Honeycomb Cliffs above Solitude Ski Resort (the ski patrol often allows access from the Summit Lift top) and traverse west, giving a wide berth to the potentially huge cornices overhanging the cliffs.

The East Bowl of Silver Fork, although not a huge, steep slope, has produced more than its share of avalanches. When it's unstable, enter Silver Fork by contouring north and west out of Grizzly Gulch from 9,600 feet to the saddle just east of Davenport Hill, 10,120 feet. Moderately steep gullies drop from the pass, and sparsely wooded glades fall from Davenport, below which the Silver Fork Cabin was located from the mining era until a fire destroyed it in 2000. The structure was so well located that it dodged a century of avalanches; hopefully, it will be rebuilt. Silver Fork can also be gained from Central Alta via Flagstaff Ridge (as outlined in Tour 27, Days Fork) or the more easterly Binx's Ridge. The former is the preferred approach for the popular West Bowl.

A cirque of upper Silver Fork on the rocky east rim north of the East Bowl is known as Flanagans. It holds good, but often very weak, snow in its north-facing trees. Another good tree shot, the Guild Line, is tough to reach but drops north from the north end of the Flanagan Cirque.

Silver Fork, northeast view, with Days Fork immediately to the right.
PHOTO BY WASATCH POWDERBIRD GUIDES.

Most of the skiing in Silver Fork is done on the east-facing meadows that fall gracefully from the 9,700-foot west rim. These are called the Meadow Chutes, and they funnel into avalanche chutes below the dicey, midslope breakovers. Your best approach is either along the west rim from West Bowl or via an aspen-draped, vaguely protruding "ridge" low in Silver Fork separating the meadows from Greens Basin. Whether you're skinning up or skiing down, lower Silver Fork is friendly ski terrain: low angle and wide.

Alta/Brighton Periphery

Rating: Easy to difficult.

Gear: Skis or split-board with skins.

Summary: This spot offers easy access— and it's always open from Supreme Lift in Albion Basin. Partial-day tours are feasible, as are one-way tours to Brighton and Grizzly Gulch. The Dry Fork and Catherine areas are conducive to beginner tours, with low slope angles and short return climbs. Wolverine Cirque and Mount Tuscarora appeal to steep couloir skiers.

Tour 29

Maps: USGS 7.5-minute Brighton; Alpen Tech Wasatch 1 and 2.

Trailheads: Top of Supreme Lift at Alta; Brighton's base, or top of Millicent, Crest Express, or Great Western Express lifts.

Distance: 0.5 to 8 miles (exit at Tibble).

Starting altitude: Supreme Lift at Alta, 10,495 feet; Brighton Base, 8,800 feet; Millicent Lift 9,730 feet; Crest Express, 10,050 feet; Great Western Express, 10,740 feet.

High points: Mount Wolverine, 10,795 feet; Point Supreme, 10,595 feet; Sunset Peak, 10,648 feet; unnamed point 10,321 feet; Patsy Marley, 10,520 feet; Clayton Peak, 10,721 feet; unnamed peak, 10,420 feet.

Access: From I–215 in Salt Lake City, exit at 6200 South and follow the signs to Alta in Little Cottonwood Canyon or Brighton at the head of Big Cottonwood Canyon.

Description: From the top of the Supreme Lift at Alta, beginner through expert terrain is available in Dry Fork to the south, Catherine Pass and Snake Creek to the east, and the Grizzly Gulch and Mount Wolverine areas to the north. Check in with patrol and exit via the Catherine gate for all but the east-facing shots and the Gargoyles area in Dry Fork.

The cat track leading southwest from Supreme top offers access to the pass north of point 10,864. Ski east from the pass into Dry Fork and drop up to 1,000 feet to the creek. Alternatively, stop at the first bench below the open east-facing bowls and ascend south to the Gargoyles, a rocky 10,520-foot buttress.

Alta/Brighton Periphery

Big Cottonwood Canyon Road
I–215
18 miles

190

Silver
Fork

*Silver
Lake*

P

Solitude Summit Lift
Access Point

10,479'

*Twin Lakes
Reservoir*

Return
to
Brighton

N
40°
36'

Grizzly Gulch
(4WD road)

Figure 8
Hill

Brighton Millicent Lift
Top Access Point
* 9,730'

* Brighton Ski Resort
Base Access Point
8,800'

Twin Lakes
Pass

Mount Millicent
10,452'

Return
to
Brighton

Albion
Summer Road

Wolverine
Cirque

Lake Mary

Patsey Marley
10,520'

*Dog
Lake*

Brighton
Crest Express
Lift Top
Access Point
10,050'

Little
Cottonwood
Canyon Road
I–215
17 miles

210

Mount
Wolverine
10,795'

Mount
Tuscarora
10,640'

N
40°
35'

10,321'

Albion Basin
(Alta Ski Resort)

Catherine
Pass

Pioneer Peak
10,620'

Point
Supreme
10,595'

Sunset
Peak
10,648'

Supreme Lift
Top Access Point
* 10,495'

Snake Creek

Supreme Cat Road
Access Point *

To
Wasatch
State Park
4.5 miles

Devils Castle
10,920'

10,864'

*Dry
Fork*

N
40°
34'

To Tibble Fork
Trailhead 5.5 miles

N

Gargoyles
10,520'

0   .5   1 mi

0   .5   1   km

Contour Interval: 500 Feet

N
40°
33'

Gain the summit via the north-facing gullies and ski the same, or drop east to Dry Fork Creek for a 2,000-foot shot. Your route climbing out of Dry Creek is avalanche-prone; stay out of the main gully to minimize hazard.

Another good shot into Dry Creek falls east off the point directly south from behind the patrol shack at Supreme top. This 500-foot east-facing shot can hold powder, but it loads at the top and breaks over in the middle, making it avalanche-prone. To ski into Dry Fork without any climbing, ski a very low-angle run directly south from Supreme top, heading southeast to below Point Supreme.

Point Supreme, 10,595 feet, is a great place for a first backcountry ski run or tour. The summit can be reached by skinning or sidestepping from the standard downhill skier's traverse into the Catherine area. Ski east for 400 feet and return via a shallow, thinly wooded south-facing rib leading to Rocky Point, 10,490 feet, above Catherine Lake. Ski popular 35-degree gullies past rock spires to the lake, or traverse east and climb the ridge to Sunset Peak, 10,648 feet. Good runs fall north along this ascent route.

Sunset's north face offers 700-foot shots falling at 40 degrees initially, but it has been the site of fatal avalanches. Do not be lured by the ease of access on the wrong day. The east face falls into Snake Creek above Wasatch State Park and Heber Valley. The upper 600 feet is moderately steep, but then rock bands bisect the face, requiring a traverse north or south or a return climb to Sunset Peak.

Excellent runs drop into Snake Creek from the ridge dividing it from Dry Fork, but they are slide paths that terminate in a narrow gully. Escape this gully by climbing north for 1,600 feet to Crest Express Lift top at Brighton. The south-facing runs into Snake Creek can be easily accessed from this lift; climb west along the ridge to point 10,321 and on toward Pioneer Peak. North-facing shots into the Dog Lake area at Brighton, Catherine Lake, or Lake Mary are also possible from Crest Express Lift top.

From Catherine Lake, return to Alta by ascending west on a small hogback. Ski west back into the resort, or climb north (usually by booting on the ridge crest) to gain Mount Tuscarora and Mount Wolverine beyond. Tuscarora has steep drops on the north and east, often with corniced entrances. Both aspects lead to the Lake Mary/Martha area and easy returns to Brighton (ski northeast) or Alta (ascend southwest via Catherine Lake).

Wolverine commands a 360-degree panorama worthy of many accolades and offers ski runs from the moderate east bowl to the extreme north-facing cirque west of the summit. The east bowl is less than 25 degrees until a breakover below tree line at 10,200 feet. Return to the summit via the northeast ridge, which can also be accessed from Mount Millicent and Lift at Brighton. Or descend into the Wolverine Cirque and Twin Lakes (defunct) reservoir area via the "Stupid Chute," which falls north from the saddle between Millicent and Wolverine.

The Twin Lakes area has excellent skiing on Figure 8 Hill, directly south of the reservoir. Ski east into Brighton or climb west to Twin Lakes Pass and Grizzly

Gulch to return to Alta. South of Figure 8 Hill is the notorious Wolverine Cirque, site of many accidents and thrills in chutes that drop at up to 55 degrees. The main north-facing chute can be entered by skiing west from Mount Wolverine.

Other attractive chutes drop east all along the ridge leading to Patsey Marley point at the head of Grizzly Gulch. Skiing west off this ridge threatens the summer road and Alta ski resort runs, making it a poor choice when snow is unstable. However, the gut shot (I call it the "Wedding Chute," since I was married in the meadow at its base) drops at 35 degrees for 1,200 glorious feet. Beware of the rocky breakover point midrun. The benign route from Wolverine back to Alta is by skiing along the ridge past the cirque and dropping north off Patsey Marley point near the microwave repeater tower. Despite significant cornices and wind loading at its top, this low-angle, northwest-facing shot rarely slides, and it often basks in great afternoon light.

Great Western Lift at Brighton offers access to the avalanche-prone but impressive east faces of Clayton Peak (10,721 feet) and Peak 10,420. The latter can also be reached from Guardsmans Pass Road, which splits from BCC Road just below Brighton. Simply ascend the wooded ridge leading southeast from the road closure point. Guardsmans Pass is also the return route from Bonanza Flat and the east faces of Clayton and Peak 10,420.

Snowbird Periphery

Rating: Easy to difficult.

Gear: Skis or split-board with skins; ice ax and crampons optional in spring.

Summary: This high alpine ski terrain within a short climb of lift-top access points lends itself to powder and corn skiing during periods of avalanche stability. Multiple runs can be made in a day; a full-day, one-way loop tour is also feasible with a car cached at Tibble. The short access belies the serious nature of Snowbird's peripheral terrain.

Tour 30

Maps: USGS 7.5-minute Dromedary, Brighton; Alpen Tech Wasatch 2.

Trailheads: Snowbird lift tops: Gad 2, Tram, Little Cloud, or Mineral Basin top or base. Finishes at White Pine Trailhead or Tibble Fork Reservoir are recommended.

Distance: 1 to 7 miles, depending on exit point.

Starting altitude: Gad 2, 9,930 feet; Little Cloud Bowl, 10,750 feet; Mineral Base, 9,500 feet; Hidden Peak Tram, 11,000 feet.

Ending altitude: White Pine, 7,700 feet; Tibble, 6,300 feet.

High points: Red Baldy Peak, 11,171 feet; No Name Peak, 10,718 feet; American Fork Twin Peaks, 11,489 feet; East Twin, 11,433 feet; Geek Peak, 11,391 feet.

Access: Reach Snowbird Ski Resort via Utah State Route 210 from Salt Lake City. Public transit is available from many points in the valley. Buy a lift ticket and proceed to the top of Gad 2 Chairlift or the Hidden Peak Tram (one-ride tickets are not available in winter).

Description: Backcountry skiing from Snowbird is always available from the bottom of Mineral Basin Express Chairlift, but all other gates are controlled and opened only when avalanche danger is low. Check in with the friendly and informative ski patrol before exiting the resort. This is required, along with an avalanche transceiver, shovel, and partner. Backcountry access gates are generally open for only part of the day.

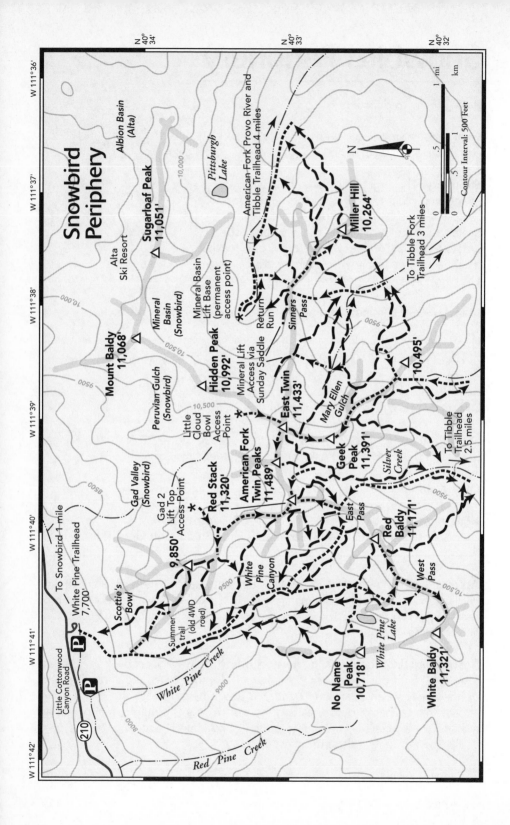

Snowbird Periphery

Sugarloaf Peak △ 11,051'

Alta Ski Resort

Albion Basin (Alta)

Pittsburgh Lake

Mount Baldy 11,068' △

Mineral Basin (Snowbird)

Mineral Basin Lift Base (permanent access point)

Peruvian Gulch (Snowbird)

Hidden Peak △ 10,992'

American Fork Provo River and Tibble Trailhead 4 miles

Return Run

Sinners Pass

Miller Hill △ 10,264'

To Tibble Fork Trailhead 3 miles

Little Cloud Bowl Access Point *

Mineral Lift Access via Sunday Saddle

East Twin △ 11,433'

Mary Ellen Gulch

10,495' △

Gad Valley (Snowbird)

Red Stack * 11,320'

American Fork Twin Peaks △ 11,489'

Geek Peak △ 11,391'

Silver Creek

To Tibble Trailhead 2.5 miles

To Snowbird 1 mile

White Pine Trailhead 7,700'

Gad 2 Lift Top Access Point *

9,850' △

White Pine Canyon

East Pass

Red Baldy △ 11,171'

Scottie's Bowl

Summer trail (old 4WD road)

West Pass

Little Cottonwood Canyon Road

White Pine Creek

No Name Peak 10,718' △

White Pine Lake

White Baldy △ 11,321'

Red Pine Creek

N 40° 34'

N 40° 33'

N 40° 32'

W 111° 36'
W 111° 37'
W 111° 38'
W 111° 39'
W 111° 40'
W 111° 41'
W 111° 42'

Contour Interval: 500 Feet

N

From the Gad 2 Lift top, boot or skin southwest on a minor protrusion to 10,200 feet. For lower drops into Columbine Bowl, Boundary Bowl, Shady Acres, and Scottie's Bowl, traverse west across a steep north face. The Temptation Chutes may lure you back to Gad Valley immediately. These and other shots in Boundary Bowl are short and often sweet.

Continue to the White Pine ridge for longer drops. The traverse intersects the ridge above a good south-facing run called Columbine. It funnels into the small-tree runout zone for the Birthday Chutes, which can be skied into the bottom of White Pine Canyon. Northwest from the ridgetop is Shady Acres, a sheltered, low-angle glade. It funnels into a gully, tight trees, and typically sun-crusted, west-facing slopes below 9,500 feet. These lead to the summer trail (a former four-wheel-drive road), which can easily be followed to the White Pine Trailhead in Little Cottonwood Canyon. Ski north along the ridge to access Scottie's Bowl, as described in Tour 31, Little Cottonwood Canyon South.

Steeper, longer shots can be approached by skipping the traverse at 10,200 feet and continuing to the ridge above. Climb this spectacular, low-angle but exposed ridge until one of the numerous Birthday Chutes beckons. They drop west through north for 500 to 800 feet, starting at 35 to 40 degrees. These have been the sites of many avalanches because they get heavily windloaded.

Continue past the Birthdays to access the Tri-Chutes, a gully run that splits into three narrow chokes at 10,400 feet before continuing to the White Pine Trail. This shot is often wind scoured or "bulletproof" at the top. The western summit of the American Fork Twin Peaks above the Tri-Chutes is called Red Stack, but skiing is nearly always rocky off its top. Traverse below it past the "Tris" to reach Long John Silver, a west-southwest-facing run that becomes good corn skiing in spring. Traverse skier's right (northwest) below the run to intersect the lower Tri-Chutes and return to the White Pine Trailhead.

Upper White Pine Canyon is home to some great ski runs and can be reached from the trailhead on LCC Road, but it's much shorter to come from the Birthdays, Tri-Chutes, or Long John. Ski to the White Pine Trail (an old four-wheel-drive road that contours along the east side of the canyon) and follow it to the open terrain below Red Baldy Peak. This 11,171-foot summit offers impressive, open skiing on its northwest and southwest faces. The northeast aspect has 40-degree chutes skiable only with a deep, strong snowpack. The southeast is steep; cliff bands cross the runs most years. All southerly shots drop into Silver Creek, requiring a lengthy return climb or a car shuttle to Tibble Fork Reservoir (see Tour 43, Box Elder Peak).

No Name Peak (10,718 feet) straddles the Red/White Pine ridge and offers excellent but often rocky skiing on old glacial moraines above the timberline. Reach the peak from the Red Baldy area via White Pine Lake, situated just east of No Name. The summit is best gained via the northwest ridge. Better skiing is located below 10,200 feet, west of the lake. For lower shots in White Pine, see Tour 31.

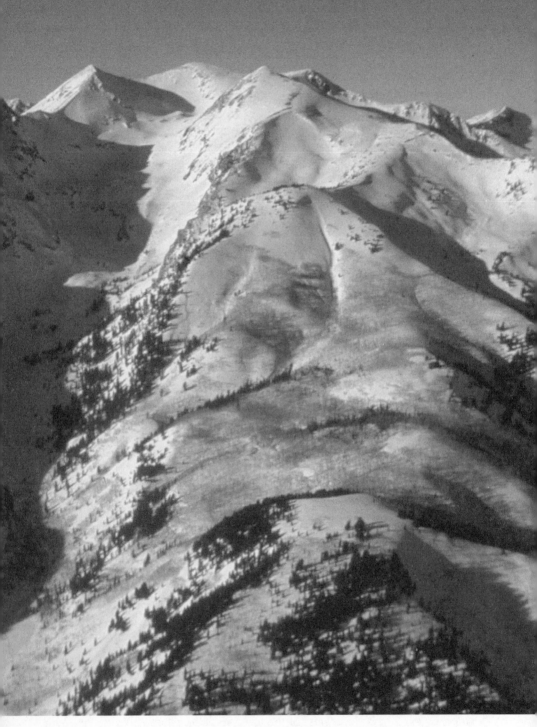

Silver Creek drainage below American Fork Twin Peaks; southwest view.

The pass east of Red Baldy and west of Red Stack is East Pass. It provides the exit from White Pine into Silver Creek. The skiing in this large drainage is primarily south facing and avalanche-prone. In spring corn cycles it skis well, however, and the access from the Tram at Snowbird isn't bad.

When touring "off the Twins" is opened by the patrol, climb a boot trail from a gate above the Road to Provo cat track that runs south from Hidden Peak past Little Cloud Chair into Little Cloud Bowl. This is an exposed trail suitable for ice ax use when snow conditions are firm. It leads directly to the east peak of American Fork Twin Peaks, 11,489 feet. Ski options from here include a low-angle shot falling southwest into Silver Creek and a steep headwall into Mary Ellen Gulch. A short traverse due south accesses point 11,391 (Geek Peak).

A moderate southwest drop into upper Silver Creek flattens at 10,700 feet, and it's possible to traverse skier's left (west) to go through East Pass and into White Pine. Be wary of avalanche potential on the traverse below the southeast face of Red Stack. Also, the southeast side of the pass is steep and can be corniced from the northwest. Steeper but still moderate runs fall into upper Silver Creek from the southeast face of Red Stack and the south aspect of Twin Peaks proper, the highest Wasatch summit north of Timpanogos.

Silver Creek remains conducive to skiing all the way down to 8,300 feet. Then follow the old four-wheel-drive track past the old reservoir flats and down a couple of switchbacks to Tibble Fork Reservoir and Trailhead. Silver Creek can be accessed from the northwest and White Pine via West Pass (between Red and White Baldy) or by skiing south from the western summit ridge of Red Baldy. All forks of Silver Creek are primarily wide-open, avalanche-prone terrain best suited to spring touring.

Another good run into upper Silver Creek is south of Geek Peak. The ridge above 11,000 feet is often scoured and free of snow, but it becomes a friendly, broad, low-angle bowl down to 9,800 feet before breaking over and funneling into a narrow, 35-degree gully. Traverse skier's right or left to find safer, more open skiing below the gully.

Mary Ellen Gulch holds perhaps the greatest array of backcountry ski terrain south of Snowbird now that Mineral Basin is within the resort boundary. Ski the 40-degree headwall southeast from point 11,433, the east summit of Twins, and enjoy the unvegetated, rolling glacial moraine terrain falling gently east. A return to the Mineral Basin Chairlift can be accomplished sans skins by contouring northeast at point 9,900 to Sinners Pass. Sunday Saddle communicates between Mineral and Mary Ellen at 10,400 feet; it can also be gained without skins on a high traverse from Hidden Peak. It's useful for returning from Mary Ellen as well.

Although the high terrain described above is only opened from Snowbird in stable (spring-type) avalanche conditions, Sinners Pass and the Miller Hill area are always available for tours departing from the Mineral Lift base. Ascend moderately steep trees south to Sinners Pass after crossing American Fork Creek below the lift base. Stick to the ridgetop or just west of it, and choose

American Fork Twin Peaks and Miller Hill; southeast view. PHOTO BY WASATCH POWDERBIRD GUIDES.

from several northeast-facing bowls. Except for right off the top of Miller Hill, all this terrain is moderately steep, and the aspen-covered meadows below are very low angled. Still, the low breakovers dropping to American Fork Creek are steep and avalanche-prone. Ski 4 to 5 miles to Tibble Fork Reservoir, or return to the Mineral Lift on the old four-wheel-drive road south of the creek. Remember that the lift closes early to allow for a sweep—usually at 3:00 P.M.

Little Cottonwood Canyon South

Tour 31

Rating: Easy to difficult.

Gear: Skis or split-board with skins; ice ax, crampons, and rope for extreme routes.

Summary: One of the most popular and diverse ski-touring areas in the Salt Lake mountains. Options range from two-hour beginner tours, to 5,000-foot headwalls requiring rappels, to all-day Super Traverse Tours. Most routes finish at separate lower-altitude locations along LCC Road (Utah State Route 210).

Maps: USGS 7.5-minute Dromedary, Draper; Wasatch Touring Map 2.

Trailhead: White Pine.

Distance: 1 to 10-plus miles.

Starting altitude: 7,700 feet.

Ending altitude: 5,300 to 7,700 feet.

High points: Rainbow Peak, 9,947 feet; Pfiefferhorn 11,326 feet; White Baldy, 11,321 feet; Redbird Knob, 10,897 feet; Chipman Peak, 10,954 feet; unnamed point 11,137 feet; North Thunder Mountain, 11,150 feet; South Thunder Mountain, 11,154 feet.

Access: From I–215 in Salt Lake City, exit at 6200 South and follow the signs to Alta and Snowbird in Little Cottonwood Canyon. Look for WHITE PINE TRAILHEAD on Forest Service sign 1 mile west of Snowbird's lowest entrance. The parking lot is plowed after each storm, but it often overflows on busy weekend days. No overnight parking is allowed.

Description: All tours begin with 0.8 mile of low-angle skinning along the old mining road into White Pine Gulch. Tours into Scottie's Bowl turn left (east) and follow the switchbacking mining road to 8,500 feet. It is also possible to continue into upper White Pine Gulch on this deteriorating four-wheel-drive trail; these tours are described in Tour 30, Snowbird Periphery. All other tours cross White Pine Creek and contour west into the Lone Peak Wilderness and Red Pine Gulch.

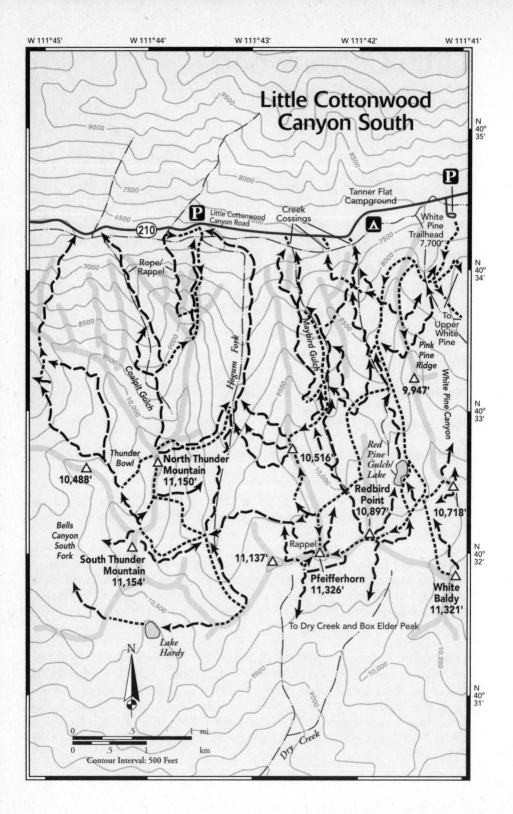

Little Cottonwood Canyon South

Tanner Flat Campground

White Pine Trailhead 7,700'

Little Cottonwood Canyon Road

Creek Cossings

210

Rope/ Rappel

To Upper White Pine

Pink Pine Ridge

9,947'

Maybird Gulch

Hogum Fork

Coalpit Gulch

White Pine Canyon

Red Pine Gulch/ Lake

10,516'

Thunder Bowl

North Thunder Mountain 11,150'

Redbird Point 10,897'

10,488'

10,718'

Bells Canyon South Fork

South Thunder Mountain 11,154'

11,137'

Rappel

Pfeifferhorn 11,326'

White Baldy 11,321'

To Dry Creek and Box Elder Peak

N

Lake Hardy

0   .5   1 mi

0   .5   1   km

Contour Interval: 500 Feet

Dry Creek

Scottie's Bowl makes a good half-day tour and often harbors fine powder due to its northerly aspect and mid-altitude situation. You can reach the bowl by climbing east above the old road after the second switchback. If avalanche danger is present, stay well spread out until your party reaches a northwest-facing ridge. This initial west-facing aspen-covered slope occasionally produces avalanches. It also can provide good skiing if no sun crust has developed on it.

Find a natural bench at 9,200 feet leading east from the ridge to the middle of Scottie's Bowl. The bowl is overhung by cornices on its northwest flank. It may be wise to climb higher on the ridge and drop one of these natural triggers onto the slope before skiing it. Another good bowl sits above Scottie's to the southeast. Exit the area by dropping down the gut of the drainage toward the highway and parking lot below—bushwhacking is involved.

Pink Pine Ridge is the divide separating Red Pine and White Pine Gulches below Rainbow Peak (9,947 feet), the lowest major point along the rugged ridge. It offers 700- to 1,000-foot northeast-facing meadow and tree shots back into White Pine or 2,000-foot northeast-facing shots into the Red Pine and Tanner Flat area along Little Cottonwood Canyon Road. All runs can be approached and skied within two hours from the trailhead. To gain the ridge simply contour northwest along the summer trail toward Red Pine after crossing White Pine Creek. Follow the trail until it rounds the ridge and begins to drop slightly and head southwest. There is a sign here marking the edge of Lone Peak Wilderness. Climb south on the ridge, staying as close to its top as possible until the relatively avalanche-safe, northeast-facing runs present themselves on the left.

Red Pine Gulch can be accessed from Pink Pine Ridge by skiing a west-facing slide path, but snow here is often sun crusted or underlain by wet slide debris. The most expedient approach is to stay on the summer trail as it contours around the ridge and climbs southwest through aspen glades and finally intersects Red Pine Creek at 9,000 feet. This is an idyllic spot for lunch; also, routes divide here for upper Red Pine (left) and Maybird, Hogum, etc. (right).

To climb the Pfeifferhorn (by its standard east-ridge route) or White Baldy, or to enjoy upper Red Pine Gulch, continue south up the canyon. Either skin below west-facing avalanche slopes or dip into the woods to gain a measure of protection from them and climb along the creek to Red Pine Lake at 9,620 feet. Well-protected campsites exist at the south and north ends of the beautiful lake. The classic lake shot is obvious, dropping to the lake's south shore from point 10,897, called Redbird Knob, on the Little Cottonwood/Dry Creek divide. More protected (from both wind and avalanche danger) ski lines drop from upper to lower Red Pine Lake.

A north-facing ridge in the spruce and fir leads to the old terminal glacier moraine below the upper lake. Climb southwest along this moraine ridge to gain the high divide. The divide is broad and friendly, and the views of Box Elder Peak and Utah Lake to the south and west are tremendous. Box Elder can be accessed from here by skiing south and dropping around the toe of

Wishbone Ridge. The west portion of the wishbone, which splits just south of White Baldy, must be circumvented in order to reach the north ridge approach to 11,100-foot Box Elder.

White Baldy (11,321 feet) offers excellent skiing on its northwest and northeast aspects, but the rocky terrain needs lots of snow. From upper Red Pine Lake, climb south through the undulating moraine piles and set a skin trail up the broad northwest face. It's safer to climb along the north or west ridge, but both spines are complicated by exposed rock, sugary snow, and knife-edge character. You can also drop south off the summit into Silver Creek, but cliffs abound. The steep but highly rated northeast run falls from the east summit in White Pine Gulch and is better accessed from the Red Baldy area.

To reach the Pfeifferhorn, continue west along the high divide past Red-bird Knob and either traverse around the upper peak on the south to climb the easier southwest ridge or stay along the knife-edge divide and climb the steep and exposed but straightforward east ridge. Leave skis at the base of it, and after summiting, ski a north-facing shot into upper Maybird to descend most directly. Another entrance into upper Maybird's alpine terrain is via either of the two parallel chutes just west of Redbird Knob, although these runs start at 40 degrees plus.

If steep skiing is the goal, try the northwest couloir off the Pfeifferhorn summit. It is intimidating at 45 degrees and only wide enough for one ski track up top. It cliffs out after 400 feet, and a rappel anchor can be found on skier's right. In big seasons it has been skied sans rappel. Other steep lines drop into Hogum from the saddle west of the Pfeifferhorn. The easiest summit ascent route is on the southwest. Skins can often be used all the way.

The best corn-snow runs return down this southwest face and fall for 3,000 feet to Dry Creek. The exit to Alpine down Dry Creek is pretty straightforward—just stay along the creek bearing skier's left to find an old four-wheel-drive road that's now a trail. The trailhead is another several miles down at 5,700 feet. Great corn runs are also available off Chipman Peak (10,954 feet) southwest of the Pfieff. The easy-traveling terrain south of the divide also makes for quick access into the central cirque of upper Hogum Fork via a low notch between Chipman Peak and point 11,137, the western satellite peak of the Pfeifferhorn.

Not every day is suitable for accessing the high alpine terrain. To enjoy mid-altitude terrain protected from wind and sun crusts, cross Red Pine Creek at 9,000 feet on a summer footbridge and climb southwest through evergreen glades. Good runs can be skied from the 9,500-foot level, where no definite ridge splits Maybird and Red Pine. Ski northeast to Red Pine Creek or north-west for over 1,000 feet to Maybird Creek. These popular tree runs are known as "the Church." To exit Red Pine, simply continue north into aspen glades—be careful crossing the creek since it is a steep V-shaped terrain trap.

The better skiing low in the drainage is on a prominent hogback, or ridge, just west of the creek. It is known as Rocky's Nose, or Signature Ridge, owing to its easy visibility from the highway. Another exit option in times of good avalanche stability is the Red Chute, situated farther west from the nose. It is steep and rocky getting into, but there's good skiing, and it's wide enough for two sets of side-by-side tracks. Use caution crossing Little Cottonwood Creek on snowbridges, logjams, and boulders and bushwhack up to the highway.

In lower Maybird you'll find options include the tube and the aprons. The U-shaped creek bottom, or tube, makes a fine run once it is filled in, but it is a terrain trap to be avoided when heaps of new snow are piled on its steep sides. The aprons actually start much higher and can be accessed by skiing a short run to the creek and skinning southwest again through a beautiful old-growth Englemann spruce glade to the open talus fields at 9,700 feet. To reach lower Hogum Fork, simply continue across the talus and switchback up to the ridge west of the aprons.

The Maybird aprons offer incredible skiing on moderate, open slopes for drops of up to 1,800 feet. They are off fall-line in character, requiring a creative turning style or continual skier's left traverses. The exit is a challenge involving kick-turning in steep, shallow snow with downed timber and boulders. Traverse skier's left from the bottom of the meadows and follow the openings in the dense woods. Above the creek the terrain moderates, and it's not hard to find a crossing spot and hike or ski uphill for 300 feet to the road. Hitchhiking back to the White Pine parking lot is the standard procedure, and restaurant employees heading to work are often sympathetic.

Upper Hogum Fork is normally accessed from the col north of the Pfiefferhorn. Ski a short, 35-degree, west-facing shot into the rolling former glacial basin of upper Hogum's east fork. Skate and glide west and drop a few hundred feet into the head of Hogum Fork, which can also be reached from the south via the col between the Pfiefferhorn and Chipman Peak, as described above.

Ascend west toward the east cirque of Hogum. Gain the north ridge of this cirque and drop into Thunder Bowl. Ski this into Bells Canyon, or traverse right at 9,000 feet and gain the saddle below Perlas Peak (point 9,177), an obvious pyramid-shaped rocky summit between Bells and Little Cottonwood Canyon (LCC). A 3,000-foot, 35- to 40- degree slide path, Coalpit Four, leads to LCC Road. To reach main Coalpit Headwall, a 5,000-foot slide path, make a rising traverse to skier's right (northeast) after skiing the short, moderate Thunder Bowl shot and climb a gully at the north end of the rocky Thunder Ridge. An alternate approach is from mid-Hogum Fork.

Gain the Hogum Hogback (10,516 feet) above the Maybird aprons and ski one of several west- through northwest-facing slide paths. These long shots, known as the Hogum 200, make a great tour in themselves, and the exit down Hogum is not bad. Stay skier's right of the canyon bottom, and expect weak, faceted snow down low. In LCC, reach the road by working skier's left to find the old mill trail and drop down along it to the Lisa Falls/Y Couloir pullout along LCC Road.

For Coalpit via mid-Hogum, ascend west from the base of the Hogum 200 area and switchback up the avalanche run out below the narrow, enclosed Hypodermic Needle couloir. Traverse north to the Coalpit/Hogum ridge below the couloir proper and boot up the aesthetic ridge to North Thunder Mountain. Ski the Hypo and return to the summit on the existing trail, then drop into the Coalpit Headwall. A matching east-facing couloir, the Sliver, falls from the Thunder Ridge about 0.5 mile south of the Hypo.

The headwall may be corniced, and the top is steep and rocky. Enter at an obvious weakness 500 feet to the west and 50 feet lower than Thunder Mountain. The headwall is affected by ski cuts near the top and at the heads of many separate chutes. The slope angle gradually lessens for all 1,900 feet to the woods and first major bench. North Thunder Mountain takes about five hours to reach by any approach and should only be attempted by strong parties in stable weather and avalanche conditions. Good ski shots exist below 9,000 feet in Coalpit Gulch both east and west of the creek. Eventually all paths lead into a narrow, V-shaped gully that is threatened by numerous hanging snowfields. Pass quickly and one at a time on a cool afternoon. A waterfall at 6,900 feet can often be passed on the west, but a rope is advised because many parties choose to rappel 50 feet off a tree.

The Y Couloir and its evil twin, the Y-Not, are best climbed from the bottom when snow has settled for a number of days and temperatures are cool. Park at the Lisa Falls pullout and ski down an old road and cross the Little Cottonwood Creek. Bushwhack briefly then gain the avalanche cone below the Y. A rocky section near the beginning of the enclosed gully is often icy, and crampons and/or an ice tool can be useful. Do not proceed up the Y when sluffs are coming down either naturally or from a party above. The Y-Not is just west and best accessed by staying west at the second significant split in the Y Couloir and traversing over a steep, rocky cleaver at 8,500 feet. An 80-foot overhang near the bottom makes a rope essential for this descent.

Salt Lake Twin Peaks Area

Rating: Moderate to difficult.

Gear: Skis or split-board with skins; crampons and ice ax useful for summit climbs.

Summary: Rising out of the suburbs to a height of 11,330 feet, the Salt Lake Twin Peaks are skiable on five aspects and preside over the incomparable, glacier-carved alpine ski paradise of aptly named Broads Fork. The area is almost entirely open, steep, and avalanche-prone, but its ruggedness and alpine feel make it a favorite of hard-core Utah ski mountaineers.

Tour 32

Maps: USGS 7.5-minute Dromedary; Alpen Tech Wasatch 1.

Trailheads: Mill B South/Broads Fork in Big Cottonwood Canyon (BCC) or Tanner's Slide Path in Little Cottonwood Canyon (LCC).

Distance: 4.5 miles to Twin Peaks from the S-turns.

Starting altitude: Mill B South, 6,200 feet; Tanner's, 7,300 feet.

High points: Salt Lake Twin Peaks, 11,328 feet (west), 11,330 (east); Dromedary Peak, 11,107 feet; O'Sullivan Peak, 11,275 feet.

Access: Mill B South Trailhead is located at the S-turns, about 5 miles up BCC. Tanner's Gulch is located 4.2 miles up LCC.

Description: Ascend the summer hiking trail from the S-turns as it contours west and switchbacks into Broads Fork and crosses the creek. From here skiers can often travel more efficiently by skinning through sparse woods on either side of the trail. After 2.1 miles and 2,100 feet, the terrain becomes entirely open, and the acreage of skiable terrain is mind-boggling. Immediately to the west is the northeast-facing slide path/shallow gully known as Bonkers. Considered by many to be the finest powder run in the Wasatch Range, this 2,400-foot shot frequently gets skied soon after snowfalls. Most people establish a skin trail climber's right of the center, but in places it is essentially up the gut of the run, and no protection from avalanches exists. Make a conservative snow-stability assessment.

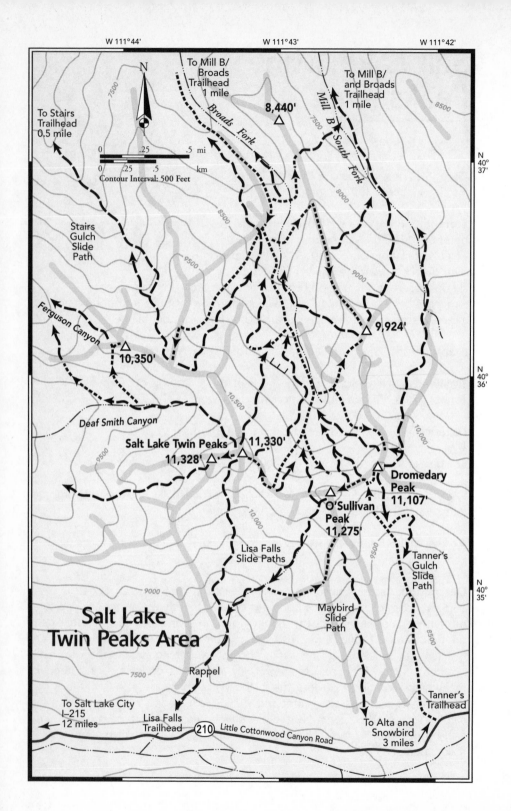

W 111°44'   W 111°43'   W 111°42'

N

To Mill B/
Broads
Trailhead
1 mile

To Mill B/
and Broads
Trailhead
1 mile

To Stairs
Trailhead
0.5 mile

Broads Fork

Mill B South Fork

8,440'

0   .25   .5 mi
0   .25   .5   km
Contour Interval: 500 Feet

N
40°
37'

Stairs
Gulch
Slide
Path

Ferguson Canyon

10,350'

9,924'

Deaf Smith Canyon

N
40°
36'

Salt Lake Twin Peaks   11,330'
11,328'

Dromedary
Peak
11,107'

O'Sullivan
Peak
11,275'

Lisa Falls
Slide Paths

Tanner's
Gulch
Slide
Path

N
40°
35'

Salt Lake
Twin Peaks Area

Maybird
Slide
Path

Rappel

Tanner's
Trailhead

To Salt Lake City
I-215
12 miles

Lisa Falls
Trailhead

210 Little Cottonwood Canyon Road

To Alta and
Snowbird
3 miles

A saddle on climber's right at 10,200 feet is the usual high point of the run, and the steeper skiing above here is considerably more hazardous. It is underlain by talus and rock slab rather than the grass slopes that comprise the lower gut of Bonkers. This saddle is also the access point into Stairs Gulch, an extremely avalanche-prone, narrowing, 4,500-foot gully. It is rare to find good, let alone stable, snow conditions in this slide path, but on a perfect day it is an amazing run. On other days it has been the site of tragedy.

Continuing up Broads Fork past Bonkers means passing under numerous huge slide paths. The smooth quartzite rock slabs of the massive east-facing slopes below the Salt Lake Twin Peaks can release full-depth avalanches during warm spells that deposit boxcar-size chunks of debris in the canyon bottom. The west aspect also has hanging avalanche slopes, but it gets loaded less and doesn't have slab underneath. In stable conditions the giant apron up-canyon from Bonkers provides great intermediate-level skiing. A perfect diving board rock in the upper middle of the run is popular to jump off.

The upper bowls of Broads Fork and the summits of Dromedary, O'Sullivan, and Twin Peaks are more efficiently reached by climbing up Tanner's Gulch from LCC, but a very early start and a melt/freeze weather pattern is required. Many tourers do ascend to the upper reaches of Broads Fork from the Mill B Trailhead. This is prime ski terrain with 100-turn shots left, right, and center. Tanner's Slide Path has no trail, but the route is pretty straightforward. The avalanche potential is extreme. A relatively cool morning following a series of hot, sunny afternoons is the best time to risk it. You should park just above the sign that says NO STOPPING OR STANDING NOV. 1 TO MAY 15 and head west through the bushy deciduous trees to the denuded gully. The snow should be solidly frozen and supportable. Start no later than 6:00 A.M. in order to escape the avalanche catch basin before the sun begins to heat the east-facing rock hanging above.

Climbing skins are often useful in the relatively low-angle lower gully, but boots and crampons can be more efficient when the snow is fully consolidated. At 8,500 feet the gully splits, and the pitch steepens briefly. Take the right branch for 100 feet, then traverse onto the middle ground between the gullies, known as the Heart of Tanner's. This moderate, smooth apron can be great corn skiing and, owing to its wind-protected situation, is one of the first places in LCC to become supportable during a melt/freeze cycle.

Skin or boot up the apron angling left (west) into the upper couloir. This final 1,500 feet can be mushy and breakable even when the lower portions are supportable. The pitch remains 35 degrees and less until the final 200 feet, where northerly winds often create a cornice or steep headwall. Enter Broads Fork via the matching north-facing couloir or a steeper one 200 feet to the west. The snow is typically wind hardened, and tricky skiing can be found in either gully, even when the bowls below are powdery.

The 11,000-plus-foot summits of Dromedary and Sunrise are most easily climbed from Tanner's. To reach them from Broads Fork and the north, ascend the north-facing couloir leading to Tanner's Col. Sunrise can be climbed by following the aesthetic ridge crest west for 500 vertical feet, but Dromedary is a technical ascent unless one descends 200 feet into Tanner's Gulch. From there, traverse east and climb moderate snow slopes. Dromedary has a south-facing gully falling at 45 degrees from a point just west of the summit. Traverse back into Tanner's Couloir or drop directly down the fall line to a narrow keyhole, usually impassable on skis.

The northeast face is skiable in big-snow years, but a horizontal rock band blocks passage into upper Mill B in most seasons. A saddle at the base of Dromedary's impressive summit massif communicates between upper Mill B and upper Broads. The skiing into Broads below this saddle is moderate and unbroken for hundreds of turns. The big west-facing shot in mid-Broads Fork can also be easily reached from the wooded bench on the upper east side of Broads Fork below Dromedary.

Sunrise Peak is really only skiable on the southwest aspect into Lisa Falls Gulch. Fifteen hundred feet of potentially good corn-snow skiing exists before the face funnels into a narrow, typically avalanche debris–choked gully. Finish to Lisa Falls in LCC or skin back up through sparse west-facing trees to access the Maybird slide path. It drops due south at 40 degrees and less to LCC Road.

The Salt Lake Twin Peaks are the domain of serious ski mountaineering. The standard approach involves ascending on skins to the upper west basin of Broads Fork and booting the final 200 feet of 40-degree slope to an obvious saddle between the Twins and Sunrise Peak. Climbing the ridge crest from here is straightforward, except for one 30-foot rock step. This is most easily climbed on the south aspect. In good snow years the east-facing gully system below the East Twin makes a good run. It is much less rocky if entered from the east ridge 400 feet below the summit.

The northeast shot from the East Twin is a 3,000-foot drop often harboring high-quality powder-type snow. It requires skiing a hanging shield of snow above the 100-foot water-ice cliffs and traversing skier's left onto the slabby slopes before reaching the Diving Board apron. This shot begins by skiing north along the summit ridge before accessing a short couloir above the hanging shield.

The northwest couloir line is perhaps the classic one on the Twins. Easily visible from downtown Salt Lake City, it begins as a face before funneling into a gully enclosed on the west by continuous cliffs. It is never more than about 40 degrees and spills onto a broad, low-angle apron in the upper north fork of Deaf Smith Canyon. Deaf Smith is trailless and choked with scrub oak—not an appealing descent! Your better option is to traverse skier's right and climb slightly into Ferguson Canyon. There is reasonable skiing and a trail here, but another option is to ski into BCC via the Power Plant Chutes. It is wise to have climbed and skied these rugged chutes previously, because only a few go through cleanly in normal snow winters.

The southwest aspect of the Twins is a hanging bowl of moderate steepness with usually poor (breakable) snow quality. It leads into the south fork of Deaf Smith and bushwhacking, or one can escape south into LCC via a steep couloir.

Broads Fork (left) and Stairs Gulch with the Salt Lake Twin Peaks and the Lone Peak Wilderness behind; north view. PHOTO BY WASATCH POWDERBIRD GUIDES.

Salt Lake Twin Peaks' Lisa Falls Couloir with Coalpit Headwall, Y Couloir, and Hogum Fork (left) across Little Cottonwood Canyon.

The Lisa Falls Couloir is the longest fall line off the Twins, and it's an adventure run. The upper gully splits the east and west summits and etches a fine white line between acres of vertical red-orange quartzite. Lower, gully winds between granite cliffs and at times large piles of avalanche debris will be encountered. Be sure to complete this descent early in the day. The snow runs out after about 4,000 feet most seasons, and a 100-foot overhanging rappel in a waterfall cools one down. Another shorter rappel leads to moderate down-climbing on surprisingly solid granite until the Lisa Falls slabs are reached. This line is actually the most direct ascent route to the Twins, but it requires rock-climbing.

V

West Desert Ranges

Oquirrhs, Stansburys, and Deep Creeks

Many Utahns and most outsiders are unfamiliar with the 10,000-foot Oquirrh peaks rising within mere miles of 1.6 million humans. Yet by pointing the ski-mobile west (instead of the habitual east) from the Salt Lake Valley, it's possible to ski tour in complete solitude. The only catch is that access is for the most part user-*un*friendly, with rugged four-wheel-drive roads, roadblocks, avalanche-prone approach gullies, and lots of private property. Yet brave these challenges and go the extra mile (or 3) up that old mining road, and you will be pleasantly surprised at what you find.

Farther west and higher, demarcating the Tooele Valley on the west, is the Stansbury Range. Deseret Peak, the crowning glory of this rugged range, makes a rewarding ski tour, but other good touring undoubtedly awaits exploration, especially off Vickory Mountain to the south and Bald Mountain to the east.

Highest and westernmost in Utah is the seldom-skied Deep Creek Range. Like the Stansburys, Oquirrhs, and other Great Basin mountains of Nevada, western Utah, and southern Idaho, this is a basin and range formation. It was formerly an island in Lake Bonneville, the giant ancestor of the current Great Salt Lake. The topography is conducive to skiing, with potentially very long shots, but the snowpack is thin in all but the wettest northern Utah winters.

Although the Oquirrhs stretch some 30 miles from Farnsworth Peak above the Great Salt Lake to Flattop Mountain in the south, the majority of the inter-esting ski terrain is accessed from the communities of Tooele and Ophir. Tooele's Middle Canyon and Ophir Canyon, with its various tributaries, together hold the bulk of the skiable bowls, glades, and chutes in the range, although Pole Canyon west of Lehi provides efficient access to the south end of the range.

Skiing the highest peaks, Flattop and Lowe, is most feasible in corn condi-tions; these areas can be in good shape before corn snow develops in the Wasatch. Powder-oriented tours exist in Picnic Canyon, Halls Canyon (the north aspect of Flattop), Sharp Mountain, and Middle Canyon. The latter area is highly avalanche-prone and should be toured only when the snowpack is strong and mature and temperatures are cool.

West Desert Range Information

Wasatch-Cache National Forest, Salt Lake Ranger District, (801) 943–1794

Bureau of Land Management, Utah State Office, (801) 539–4001

Utah Avalanche Center, (801) 364–1581

Tooele Cirques

Rating: Difficult.

Gear: Skis or split-board with skins or snowshoes.

Summary: This backyard tour for Tooele residents features tremendous high cirques above Middle Canyon. The approach to these is hazardous except in very stable avalanche conditions, but you'll enjoy incredible views of the Wasatch Mountains, the Great Salt Lake, and Tooele Valley.

Tour 33

Map: USGS 7.5-minute Lowe Peak.

Trailhead: Middle Canyon roadblock 4 miles southeast of Tooele.

Distance: 4 miles (one way).

Starting altitude: 5,700 feet.

High points: Unnamed point, 9,747 feet; unnamed point, 9,601 feet.

Access: From Tooele (south of I–80 and west of Salt Lake City), take Vine Street (100 North) east toward the Oquirrh Mountains. It becomes Middle Canyon Road and continues as a paved highway until it's effectively blocked by a berm of concrete and rock. The roadblock is removed in spring when the road melts out, usually in late March. The approach then becomes much shorter.

Description: Snowmobiles or ATVs could be useful for the nearly flat approach up this wide road. It's roughly 2 miles from the roadblock to the intersection with a pair of unnamed side canyons on the south. The one on your right (west) has open ski runs visible up high, but it's heavily vegetated down low. The bigger drainage on your left has a road leading into it that abruptly ends.

If you choose to ascend this latter canyon, be very confident about its avalanche stability. The only feasible trail I've found is directly at the bottom of the narrow terrain trap of a gully that climbs steadily up toward the sizable start zones of the Tooele Cirques. This primarily east- and north-facing basin offers impressive runs of 1,600 feet—fall-line skiing at 30 to 45 degrees.

Climb out of the gully at 7,600 feet and angle for the run of your choice. A good option is to bear left and gain a small subridge dividing Trap Gully from Harkers Canyon (there are several canyons bearing this name in the Oquirrhs).

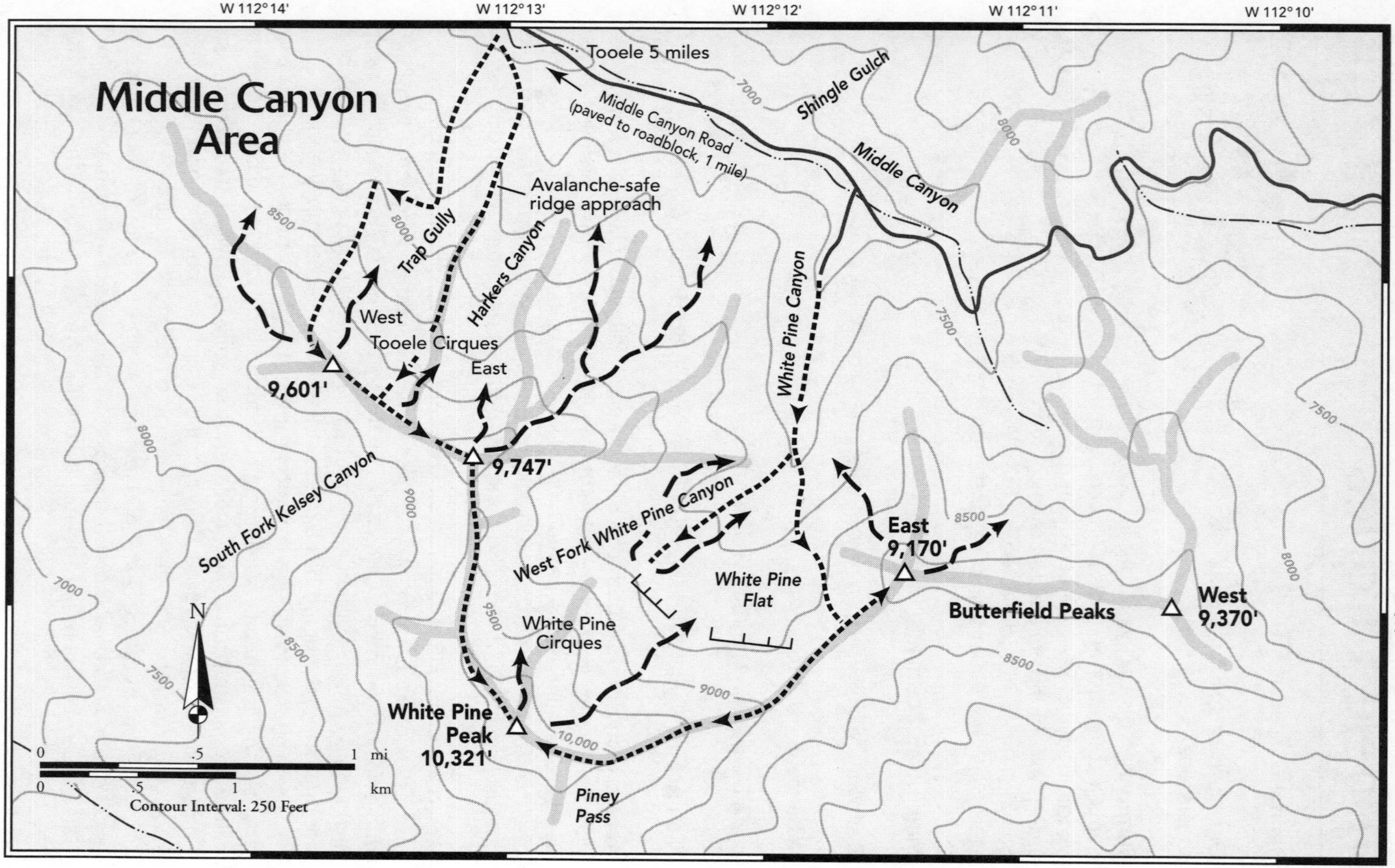

Middle Canyon Area

Tooele 5 miles

Middle Canyon Road
(paved to roadblock, 1 mile)

Shingle Gulch

Middle Canyon

Avalanche-safe
ridge approach

Trap Gully

Halkers Canyon

West Tooele Cirques East

9,601'

9,747'

South Fork Kelseys Canyon

White Pine Canyon

West Fork White Pine Canyon

White Pine Flat

White Pine Cirques

White Pine Peak
10,321'

Piney Pass

East
9,170'

Butterfield Peaks

West
9,370'

N

Contour Interval: 250 Feet

1 mi

km

W 112°14'
W 112°13'
W 112°12'
W 112°11'
W 112°10'

N 40° 29'
N 40° 28'

It may be possible, although considerably longer, to gain this dividing ridge much lower and avoid the terrain trap. Follow the subridge to a saddle between points 9,601 and 9,747. Ski north shots back along your climbing route, or run the ridge south and west to the West Tooele Cirque's high point, 9,601 feet. From here, choose any of a series of steep, open fall-line slide paths that drop back into Trap Gully.

It's also feasible to escape Trap Gully to climber's right at 7,600 feet, finding a friendly ridge that frames the west flank of West Tooele Cirque. It leads to the Settlement/Middle Canyon divide. Easy cruising on this scenic ridge leads to Peak 9,601. The drop from here is pretty amazing. Starting at 40 to 45 degrees, the pitch gradually backs off as the open bowls funnel into a network of deepening gullies. For the sake of both skiing quality and safety, stick to the higher hogbacks between the gullies as long as possible before increasingly tight, postavalanche scrub trees force a drop into one of the gullies.

Alternatively, ascend east and south to point 9,747, the head of Harkers Canyon. Cornices and a small cliff band near the top of this East Tooele Cirque limit entry points to the runs, but excellent skiing options hold (typically) powder snow and fall steeply for 1,000 feet before converging into the lower-angle glades of Harkers Canyon. By edging skier's right as you drop off point 9,747, you can ski another gulch that drops northeast back into Middle Canyon.

Yet another option from the head of East Tooele Cirque is to ski east by northeast along the White Pine/Harkers divide, then head into a more east-facing canyon with open slopes on skier's left. It also falls to the approach road in Middle Canyon. Finally, White Pine Canyon can be reached from point 9,747, but it takes considerably longer than coming directly up that drainage.

If you forego the final drop into Trap Gully and return to your uptrack, a good loop option is to regain the Settlement Canyon divide and drop northwest along it, choosing any one of several open north- and northeast-facing runs. These all converge in the unnamed canyon that drains into Middle Canyon just below Trap Gully.

The exit down any of these steep, narrow gullies is a little easier than the ascent, but once you reach the typically snowmobile-compacted Middle Canyon Road, your car is only a few minutes' skate or classic-stride away.

White Pine Canyon

See map on page 138.

Rating: Moderate to difficult.

Gear: Skis or split-board with skins or snowshoes.

Summary: Gentle approach to serious avalanche terrain or moderate aspen delights.

Map: USGS 7.5-minute Lowe Peak.

Trailhead: Middle Canyon roadblock 4 miles southeast of Tooele.

Distance: 5-plus miles (one way).

Starting altitude: 5,700 feet.

High point: White Pine Peak, 10,321 feet.

Tour 34

Access: From Tooele (south of I–80 and west of Salt Lake City), take Vine Street (100 North) east toward the Oquirrh Mountains. It becomes Middle Canyon Road and continues as a paved highway until it's effectively blocked by a berm of concrete and rock. The roadblock is removed in spring when the road melts out, usually in late March. The approach then becomes much shorter.

Description: Snowmobiles or ATVs could be useful for the 3 miles from the roadblock to the mine dump at the intersection with White Pine Canyon. A crude sign on a tall cottonwood tree announces WHITE PINE. There are picnic tables here and a historic cabin now protected by a chain-link fence.

An old four-wheel-drive road follows the creek for 1.5 miles until a prominent ridge on climber's right marks the entrance into upper White Pine Canyon. Here the drainage opens up broadly to the west and splits into three smaller creek beds. The summer pack trail switchbacks on the gentle ridge between the western and central creeks, making a good route for the West Fork of White Pine Canyon, or Aspen Delight, run. If your goal is to ski from the ridgetops, however, climb to the left at 7,600 feet and gain the high Oquirrh Divide at a pass south of East Butterfield Peak, 9,170 feet. Steep, northwest-facing runs drop back to the canyon floor from this summit, which is only a short climb to the northeast from the saddle. The bald slopes of East Butterfield Peak can also be skied northeast into the head of Middle Canyon, creating a loop route.

White Pine Canyon (left) and Tooele Cirques; north view (late season).

Other options include skiing a gentle tree shot back along your ascent route or climbing the main divide south and west to White Pine Peak, 10,321 feet. This officially unnamed summit is one of the six highest peaks in the Oquirrh Mountains and accesses east- through north-facing slopes that offer impressive runs of 2,000-plus feet, angled at 30 to 45 degrees.

Cornices and cliff bands present serious obstacles to skiing many of the lines off this peak, but the main northeast-facing slide path (whose avalanches deforested White Pine Flat) is a clean run. Another uninterrupted drop falls north from a point just west of the summit into the west branch of White Pine Canyon. Beware the attractive, treeless face between these two gullies, however. It breaks over onto limestone cliff bands at 8,800 feet. These can be passed only on the far western flank.

Below this face and between the slide paths are gently sloping meadows forested by perfectly spaced aspen trees. This Aspen Delight run is a truly excellent intermediate area, wide enough for many laps. It's well protected from avalanches by virtue of being a subtle promontory between deeper runout zones. The only significant hazard to skiing here when slopes above are loaded is the approach up White Pine Canyon. The portion of the climb below East Butterfield Peak should be carefully evaluated and passed one at a time.

Lowe Peak—
Corn Capital

Rating: Moderate to difficult.

Gear: Skis or split-board with skins.

Summary: This is Ophir's quintessential corn-snow tour. Get an early start and ski three runs from southeast through southwest.

Tour 35

Map: USGS 7.5-minute Lowe Peak.

Trailhead: Ophir Canyon.

Distance: 3 to 4 miles (one way).

Starting altitude: 6,800 to 7,000 feet.

High points: Rocky Peak, 10,273; Lowe Peak,10,589 feet.

Access: Reach Ophir by driving south from Tooele on Utah State Route 36, then taking a left onto UT 73 toward Lehi and the Provo area. A signed side road leads into Ophir Canyon and the charming old mining settlement of Ophir at 6,500 feet. Depending on snow depth, vehicle clearance, and four-wheeling skills, you can drive to 7,100 feet. The crux is fording Ophir Creek, first at 6,800 feet just above the junction with Serviceberry Canyon and then in two successive spots.

Description: If you've parked at Serviceberry Canyon or below, you will have forded the modest torrent of Ophir Creek twice already. Otherwise, crossing it will have been a driving adventure (four-wheel-drive recommended), and now you must cross the stream no fewer than four, and possibly up to six, times in the narrow bottom of Ophir Canyon before Picnic Canyon departs to the southeast. There's also a warm spring along here, so the snowpack may be largely melted out. The most expedient solution, given a snow depth of 2 feet or less, is to hike the first 0.5 mile of the tour.

Ophir Canyon becomes friendly above here. The valley floor is fairly broad and forested with well-spaced aspens. Stay in the bottom or slightly south of it for 0.5 mile and past an appealing, unnamed canyon. This small drainage faces northwest and could be a good alternative to Picnic Canyon for a short powder tour. It splits into two distinct slide paths above 8,000 feet.

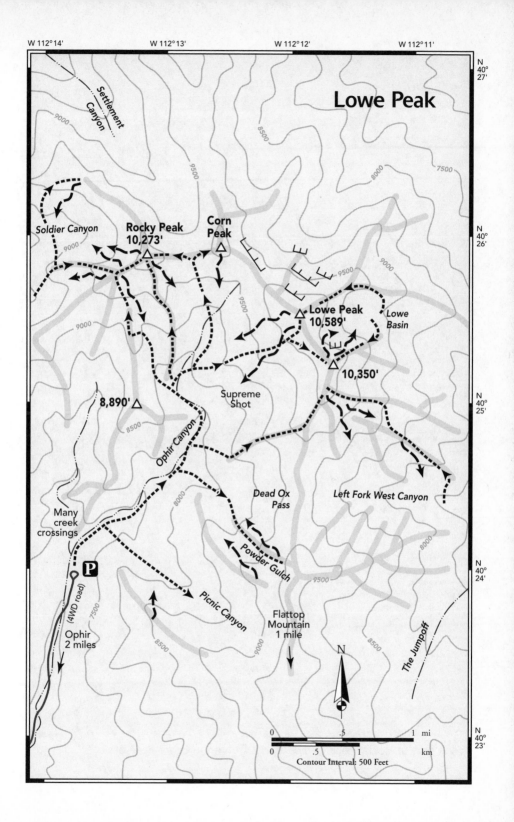

Lowe Peak

W 112°14' W 112°13' W 112°12' W 112°11'

N 40°27'
N 40°26'
N 40°25'
N 40°24'
N 40°23'

Settlement Canyon

Soldier Canyon

Rocky Peak
10,273'

Corn Peak

Lowe Peak
10,589'

Lowe Basin

10,350'

8,890'

Supreme Shot

Ophir Canyon

Many creek crossings

P

(4WD road)

Ophir
2 miles

Picnic Canyon

Dead Ox Pass

Left Fork West Canyon

Powder Gulch

Flattop Mountain
1 mile

The Jumpoff

N

0   .5   1 mi
0   .5   1 km
Contour Interval: 500 Feet

South face of Rocky Peak above Ophir Canyon in Lowe Peak area.

Hundreds of names carved in nearly every aspen tree help you find the way as the canyon turns due north and even runs northeast past a side drainage on the west before arching back to the northwest toward the huge Lowe Peak/Rocky Peak cirque. Here at 8,400 feet is an opening in the aspens; the most direct route to Lowe Peak is to begin climbing up and east through the sparse trees. The route gains a broad ridge and eventually hits the Oquirrh divide just south of the summit.

However, in order to ski the ultimate Oquirrh corn tour, continue up canyon and choose a subridge to ascend. In front of you are three major peaks: Rocky Peak on your left, Corn Peak directly ahead, and Lowe Peak on your right. If it's not yet 10:00 A.M. and snow is good, you may be able to ski all three. Choose a subridge east of Rocky Peak and switchback or boot directly to the ridgeline. Go west to the 10,273-foot summit of Rocky Peak and ski a line southeast past a few small rock outcroppings and all the way back into the canyon bottom at 9,000 feet.

Retrace your steps to the ridge, this time heading east to the unnamed peak with the perfect-looking corn run (Corn Peak). The line faces nearly due south and goes cleanly for better than 1,000 feet. If you're not too tired and the day isn't too hot, climb to the saddle between Corn and Lowe Peaks and climb the ridge southeastward to Lowe. At 10,589 feet, it's the second highest point in the Oquirrhs. Its north face may be skiable in the right year, but it's a complicated maze of horizontal cliff bands—and signs of avalanche activity are everywhere. Getting back on the Oquirrh divide from Mill Canyon below would require technical climbing unless you use the northeast ridge of Lowe Peak, which is narrow but quite reasonable.

A better bet for powder skiing off Lowe Peak is to travel southeast along the divide to the subpeak, 10,350 feet. It has steep north-facing runs, falling directly from the summit, on either side of one obvious cliff band. Ski into Lowe Basin and return to the divide via the northeast ridge of either Peak 10,350 or Lowe Peak.

The corn-snow skiing off the immense southwest face, however, is much more user-friendly. The summit is marked by a fallen communications tower. (But don't despair; a new one has been erected just north of the high point.) The longest drop is accessed from a point slightly south of the summit, but scouring along the ridgetop may require a lower entrance. If this is your last run of the day, it makes sense to ski the more southerly of the three main shots off the top—but the two northerly ones are also beautiful runs, dropping uninterrupted straight to Ophir Creek. All three exceed 2,000 feet of vertical drop, but the southern Supreme Shot is good for 2,600 (400 turns—plus!). It initially parallels the subridge, which you can use as an ascent route. After a few hundred feet, it fades left and over a small cornice feature. A few steeper turns give way to endless carving in an open bowl that leads eventually into aspens and all the way to Ophir Canyon at about 8,000 feet. Ski it in one continuous motion, if you can, and your legs will burn *sooo* good.

Picnic Canyon

Rating: Easy to moderate.

Gear: Skis or split-board with skins.

Summary: This is a short, user-friendly tour with outstanding snow quality and a classic old cabin at the base of a 1,200-foot, open fall-line run.

Map: USGS 7.5-minute Lowe Peak.

Trailhead: Ophir Canyon.

Distance: 1.5 to 3 miles (one way).

Starting altitude: 6,800 to 7,100 feet.

High point: Unnamed point, 9,925 feet.

Tour 36

Access: Reach Ophir by driving south from Tooele on Utah State Route 36, then taking a left onto UT 73 toward Lehi and the Provo area. A signed side road leads into Ophir Canyon and the charming old mining settlement of Ophir at 6,500 feet. Drive as far up Ophir Canyon as possible, or park at the creek ford below Serviceberry Canyon and ski up the road to Picnic Canyon.

Description: If you've parked at Serviceberry Canyon or below, you will have forded the modest torrent of Ophir Creek twice already. Otherwise, crossing it will have been a driving adventure (four-wheel-drive recommended), and now you must cross the stream no fewer than four, and possibly up to six, times in the narrow bottom of Ophir Canyon before Picnic Canyon departs to the southeast. There's also a warm spring along here, so the snowpack may be largely melted out. The most expedient solution, given a snow depth of 2 feet or less, is to hike the first 0.5 mile of the tour.

Picnic Canyon is a wide meadow at the bottom. The summer trail stays left, but skiers can set a track wherever the vegetation is least obtrusive. Right up the middle is likely best, except where a stand of scrubby maples forces you to the right (south) side at about 7,800 feet.

Here you'll notice an open run paralleling the first significant subridge on Picnic Canyon's south slope. A few hundred yards up is the slide path falling from point 8,970, on the canyon's south rim. Try to assess the snow quality and quantity on these runs, because they're easy to reach on your way home.

Picnic Creek narrows into a terrain-trap-type gully at 8,400 feet. It's wise to

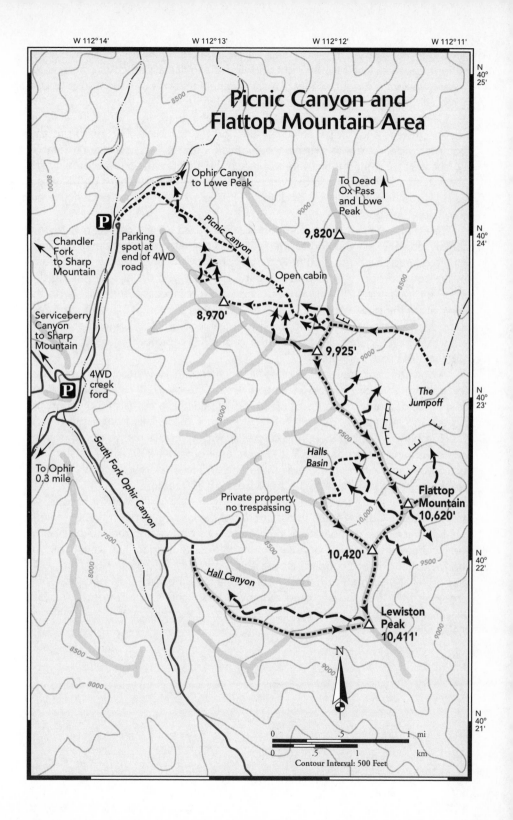

Picnic Canyon and Flattop Mountain Area

W 112°14' W 112°13' W 112°12' W 112°11'

N 40°25'
N 40°24'
N 40°23'
N 40°22'
N 40°21'

8500

8000

9000

Ophir Canyon to Lowe Peak

To Dead Ox Pass and Lowe Peak

Picnic Canyon

9,820'△

Chandler Fork to Sharp Mountain

Parking spot at end of 4WD road

Open cabin

Serviceberry Canyon to Sharp Mountain

8,970'△

9,925'△

4WD creek ford

8500

9000

The Jumpoff

Halls Basin

Flattop Mountain 10,620'△

To Ophir 0.3 mile

South Fork Ophir Canyon

9500

Private property, no trespassing

10,000

10,420'△

7500

9500

Hall Canyon

8500

8000

Lewiston Peak 10,411'△

8500

8000

9000

N

0   .5   1 mi
0   .5   1 km

Contour Interval: 500 Feet

climb out of it to the left (north) and follow a parallel gully for about 300 vertical feet. Break out of it to the right and find the idyllic aspen-covered meadow (it's an avalanche runout) where a rustic log cabin stands. If you choose to use it, respect its historic character and leave it clean.

On a clear day the "cabin 200" shot is obvious from the cabin. It faces west-northwest and drops on a fall line for 1,200 feet (200 turns) from the Oquirrh divide. Assess this shot conservatively with respect to avalanche stability, because there's no really safe approach. Still, given reasonable stability, it's a sweet line. Gain the divide by switchbacking through the aspens on the west-facing slope north of the run or directly up it, staying close to the dense evergreens on the south.

The high point of Picnic Canyon is point 9,925, which commands a view directly down Ophir Canyon to the town and the Tooele Valley beyond. Once you've gained the ridge, you may be tempted by the spectacular, open, east-facing bowls dropping into upper West Canyon. If you travel south along the Oquirrh divide for 0.25 to 0.5 mile, it's possible to access the powdery northeast part of the bowl for shots of 800 to 1,000 feet angled at 30 to 35 degrees. A moderately steep east-facing subridge rises out of West Canyon and intersects the main Oquirrh divide atop the cabin 200 shot. It's the safest climbing route out of West Canyon.

Along the main divide, it's possible to ski south to Flattop Mountain and link up with Tour 37, Flattop Mountain Area. Otherwise, if you want to return down Picnic Canyon, a series of north-facing ski lines is accessible by contouring up and left as you descend. The highest of these falls from a prominent dead limber pine and is steep (40 degrees), with sparse pines. To get to it, contour south and west from the 9,200-foot level of cabin 200. Another shot lies just down-canyon from the dead limber line and faces northeast. Both of these terminate in the small avalanche trees below 8,800 feet.

A summer pack trail crosses Picnic Canyon at this level and provides an easy traverse route to regain the south rim of the canyon at point 8,970. I found this trail through a combination of altimeter use and game tracks. Apparently, the local coyote and deer population use this contouring trail as well. In all but the lowest snowpack conditions, the shots off point 8,970 offer 800 to 1,000 feet of fall-line skiing. From the bottom, it's a straightforward ski back to Ophir Creek and the trailheads. Skiing directly down Picnic Canyon from the cabin area is also feasible, especially in the northern of the two parallel gullies above 8,400 feet.

Flattop Mountain Area

See map on page 147.

Rating: Moderate to difficult.

Gear: Skis or split-board and skins.

Summary: Ophir, Utah, is similar to Ophir, Colorado: an old mining community set high in spectacular ski country. The difference? Utah's Ophir is unknown.

Tour 37

Map: USGS 7.5-minute Lowe Peak.

Trailhead: South Fork Ophir Canyon.

Distance: 4 miles (one way).

Starting altitude: 6,700 feet.

High points: Flattop Mountain, 10,620 feet; Lewiston Peak, 10,411 feet.

Access: Reach Ophir by driving south from Tooele on Utah State Route 36, then taking a left onto UT 73 toward Lehi and the Provo area. A signed side road leads into Ophir Canyon and the charming old mining settlement of Ophir at 6,500 feet. Continue to a picnic area among big cottonwoods. Park here or cross the creek on the four-wheel-drive road into the South Fork of Ophir Creek and park as high as you can drive. If you get to 7,500 feet, stay left at this junction.

Description: Flattop Mountain, 10,620 feet, is the highest in the Oquirrh Range. To reach it, ascend Picnic Canyon to its head at point 9,925 as described in Tour 36, Picnic Canyon. Then ski south on the broad Oquirrh divide to Halls Pass, directly below Flattop. Climb through sparse spruce and pines on the west aspect of the ridge to the summit. Halls Basin is a picturesque meadow directly below the northwest face of Flattop, which is a tremendous ski run.

Most of the 1,600-foot drop is angled at 30 degrees or less, but in the middle is a breakover where avalanches have obviously broken loose and cleared vegetation. This can be avoided by traversing skier's right. The skiing is in open glades with well-protected northwest-facing (typically) powder snow. It's a mostly avalanche-safe slope (except for the breakover); I've found excellent conditions here even after a week of no storms and warm temperatures. The best ascent route out of Halls Basin is to climb east to the Oquirrh divide at Halls Pass and then follow your existing trail back to Flattop, or take a left and return to Picnic Canyon. Another option is to ski northeast off the pass (or off one of the points farther northwest along the divide) into West Canyon and the Jumpoff area. Regain the divide via the subridge north of point 9,925 as described in Tour 36.

The summit of Flattop, like many other Oquirrh peaks, is marked by a communications station. There's also a pipe and a mailbox for summit registry. Skiing options include south, east, and north, as well as the northwest-facing Halls Drop. Dropping south is a gigantic, wide-open 35-degree bowl falling into Pole Canyon. Nice east-facing shots of Lewiston Peak also drop into this broad drainage.

The east face drops from the east summit of Flattop (about 1 mile distant) into Fivemile and Fourmile Canyons above Cedar Fort on UT 73. The north aspect of Flattop, although intriguing, is cut by cliff bands. The only reasonable line is along a broad subridge between the east and west summits. It holds good snow in winter and is more than 40 degrees in steepness (plenty of avalanche potential here). This run and one dropping northeast from Halls Pass terminate in the basin called the Jumpoff at the head of West Canyon's Left Fork. West Canyon is closed to public access at its mouth because the road crosses the Camp Williams Military Reservation. Regain the divide from the Jumpoff area and via the subridge north of point 9,925 as decribed in Tour 36.

To return to your vehicle above the hamlet of Ophir, you have two good options (besides retracing your route along the divide, as mentioned above). One is to follow the summer pack trail north out of Halls Basin and contour past three small west-facing gullies until you reach Picnic Canyon at point 8,970. See Tour 36 for powdery descents from here.

I prefer returning to the summit of Flattop and skiing along the broad Oquirrh divide south toward Lewiston Peak. You can either climb Lewiston or, if you're pressed for time, drop directly into the northwest-facing gulch below it. It offers fine skiing up high but funnels into a tight gully below 9,000 feet. The gully holds good snow, but depth can be an issue, with downed logs and rocks in the creekbed. The gully terminates in a low-angle meadow with old-growth aspen trees just above the South Fork of Ophir Canyon Road. This road leads back to Ophir Creek at the 6,700-foot picnic area just 0.6 mile above Ophir. If you parked here, this return route makes a great loop. If not, you'll have to ski or hike a couple of miles up the summer four-wheel-drive road to its terminus at 7,100 feet.

Pole Canyon— Corn Haven

Tour 38

Rating: Moderate to difficult.

Gear: Skis or split-board with skins.

Summary: South-facing Pole Canyon accesses Lewiston Peak, 10,411 feet, and the tremendous south-facing Flattop Bowl south of the Oquirrhs' highest summit. A four-wheel-drive vehicle is essential for the approach road.

Map: USGS 7.5-minute Mercur.

Trailhead: Ophir Canyon.

Distance: 3 to 4 miles (one way).

Starting altitude: 6,800 to 7,000 feet.

High points: Flattop Mountain, 10,620 feet; "Saddletop Mountain," 9,415 feet; Lewiston Peak, 10,411 feet; Lewiston South, 9,861 feet.

Access: From Utah State Route 73 at Cedar Fort (west of Lehi), drive west on Center Street to 100 West. Find the four-wheel-drive road that climbs toward the Oquirrhs from the southwest edge of Cedar Fort. Follow the main jeep track west and up into cedars, junipers, and piñon pines. Immediately above town, the road becomes a rutted jumble of loose cobbles. A high-clearance four-wheel-drive is essential, unless you want to hike or bike a few rough miles to the trailhead.

Description: An unlocked steel gate marks the high driving point for most winters. Beyond this, the road descends slightly across a snowy east-facing slope and crosses the (dry) creek. It may be necessary to hike again, because the next 0.5 mile is west facing, but the total time to snow line is only twenty minutes. After the subsequent crossing, it's usually possible to keep your boards on.

Here travel is through deciduous bushes and trees. A burn area borders the jeep road on the west. An hour's climb above the steel gate, roads split off first to your left, then right, then left again. These lead to cabins with corrals and a camp (the second left). Up to your right (northeast) is a big southwest-facing corn bowl dropping from point 9,415, or "Saddletop Mountain."

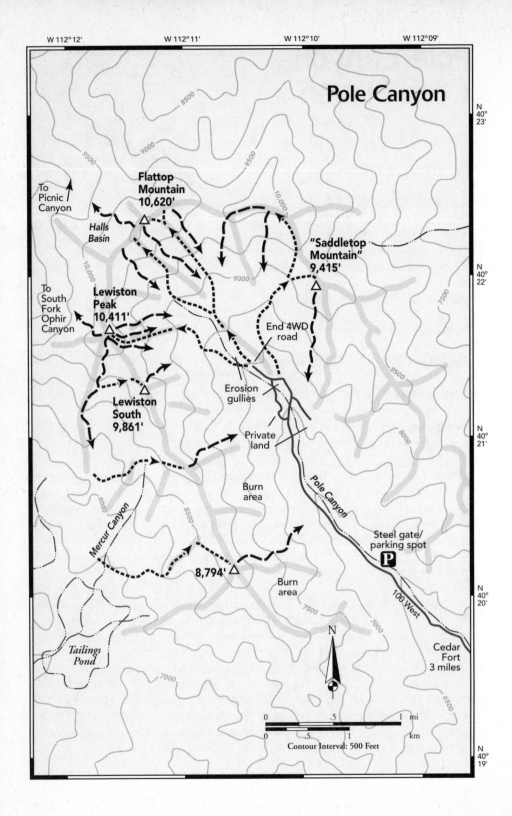

Pole Canyon

W 112°12' W 112°11' W 112°10' W 112°09'

N 40° 23'
N 40° 22'
N 40° 21'
N 40° 20'
N 40° 19'

To Picnic Canyon

Halls Basin

Flattop Mountain 10,620'

"Saddletop Mountain" 9,415'

To South Fork Ophir Canyon

Lewiston Peak 10,411'

End 4WD road

Erosion gullies

Lewiston South 9,861'

Private land

Burn area

Mercur Canyon

Burn area

8,794'

Pole Canyon

Steel gate/ parking spot

P

100 West

Cedar Fort 3 miles

Tailings Pond

N

0   .5   1 mi
0   .5   1 km
Contour Interval: 500 Feet

Flattop Mountain and Pole Canyon–Corn Haven; southwest view from Lewiston Peak.

The jeep track angles down and west across the Pole Canyon floor after coming around the top of an erosion gully. All slopes except Saddletop are accessed from the left (west) gulch of upper Pole Canyon. A central hogback (small, blunt ridge) divides the canyon here. Contour along its west flank as the jeep trail terminates at a heavily graffiti-affected aspen grove. The cleanest approach to Flattop Mountain and its upper bowls is to stay east of the aspens and a pair of treacherous erosion gullies that form up. Gain the subridge above a flat avalanche-runout zone off both Lewiston Peak and the southwest face of Flattop. This southeast-facing subridge leads directly up toward the high point of Flattop and eventually fades into the 30- to 35-degree upper bowl. Wide-open 1,500-foot runs face south and southeast in this huge cirque. The bowl develops supportable sun crust earlier than other south aspects during stable weather cycles. A good second or third corn run can often be enjoyed by climbing to Saddletop and descending its big, open southwest face. This line drops to the approach route lower than the higher shots in Flattop Bowl.

Cold snow runs off Lewiston Peak can also be skied from Pole Canyon. At the graffiti cove, climb west from the main trail and the canyon bottom. Cross a small erosion gully and stay west of it through aspen groves on a sidehill.

This slope becomes the south side of the Lewiston Fork of Pole Canyon. The peak can be reached either by continuing to the high divide climber's left of the gulch or by crossing the gulch to the east ridge of Lewiston Peak. A beautiful northeast-facing ramp drops off this ridge toward the base of Flattop from a point 200 feet below the summit. Above this run the ridge becomes avalanche-prone, first due to bluntness and later because it's a knife edge and you're forced to the south side.

Lewiston Peak is one of the steeper summits in the Oquirrh Range. It can be skied on at least four aspects off the summit. Northwest into the South Fork of Ophir Canyon is a forested run or a tightening gully if you go skier's right to the more west-facing portion. It's only 25 to 30 degrees in steepness and leads into the South Fork of Ophir Canyon (described in Tours 36, Picnic Canyon, and 37, Flattop Mountain Area). South leads toward the mining area of Mercur—an ecological disaster. This drop has 3,000 feet of consistent fall line down to a tailings pond at 7,400 feet. From here contour and climb east to point 8,794 on the southwest rim of Pole Canyon. A northeast-facing glade in the burn area drops 1,600 feet to the approach road. Alternatively, climb to Peak 9,861 (Lewiston South) and ski longer, east-facing shots into Pole Canyon.

The southeast bowl of Lewiston starts out at 40 degrees and gradually moderates in steepness as it falls uninterrupted for well over 1,000 feet. This is the obvious line that you see while approaching up Pole Canyon; it has plenty of avalanche history and potential. The steepest shot off "Lewy" is the northeast, which falls at 40 to 45 degrees initially and holds good, protected powder. After 500 feet, it breaks over in the center; traversing skier's right keeps you out of steep chutes and small cliffs. The run mellows in a delightful apron that runs for another 300 to 500 feet down to the avalanche-runout zone below Flattop.

Simply follow the approach route to exit below the runout area.

Sharp Mountain

Rating: Easy to difficult.

Gear: Skis or split-board with skins.

Summary: This is the closest tour to Ophir, and one with a tremendous view of the Tooele Valley and the Oquirrh and Stansbury Mountains. It makes a reasonable partial-day tour with terrain for all abilities, and it is a bit of a catch basin for snowfall.

Maps: USGS 7.5-minute Stockton, Lowe Peak.

Trailheads: Ophir Canyon or Serviceberry Canyon.

Distance: 1 to 3 miles (one way).

Starting altitude: 6,800-plus feet.

High points: Sharp Mountain, 10,006 feet; Chandler Peak, 8,776 feet.

Access: Reach Ophir by driving south from Tooele on Utah State Route 36, then taking a left onto UT 73 toward Lehi and the Provo area. Ophir Canyon Road is marked and climbs east into limestone-walled Ophir Canyon and the charming old mining settlement of Ophir at 6,500 feet. Depending upon snow depth, vehicle clearance, and four-wheeling skills, you can usually drive to the junction with Serviceberry Canyon Road. Here also is the first of the main road's three fords of Ophir Creek.

Description: Follow the switchbacking jeep road northwest for 1,500 feet of gradual climbing, being careful to avoid a spur that branches south at 7,200 feet. You'll notice increasingly appealing fir and spruce glades south of the road and between the switchbacks. These are the easiest-access ski runs in the Oquirrhs. Above 8,300 feet, the canyon opens up. The jeep road goes north to the small Chandler Saddle, which leads into Chandler Fork and some excellent north-facing ski runs. The left-hand branch of the canyon climbs southwest to a higher saddle on the north–south divide between Ophir Canyon and Dry Canyon to the west. Below the divide, aspen glades between 8,000 and 8,500 feet face northeast and offer low-angle skiing back into the gully bottom. Given that the return run is on the wide jeep road, this area makes a fine beginner tour.

Steeper and longer runs fall northeast from the south rim of Serviceberry

Sharp Mountain

N 40° 24'

N 40° 23'

W 112°14'

W 112°15'

W 112°16'

Ophir Canyon to Lowe Peak

8000

7500

7000

7500

8000

brushy

Chandler Fork

Chandler Peak 8,776'

Chandler Saddle

Serviceberry Canyon

4WD creek ford and parking spot

South Fork Ophir Canyon

Ophir 0.8 mile

Soldier Canyon

8500

8500

9500

9000

Sharp Mountain 10,006'

Dry Canyon

8500

9500

9000

Bald Mountain 9,556'

N

1 mi

km

.5

.5

.5

Contour Interval: 500 Feet

Canyon. The ridge descends gradually to the east and offers open and wooded drops of 1,000 feet and more back down to the approach road. The skiing here is wind-protected powder, the slope angles are 25 to 35 degrees, and one skin trail could access a number of different runs. No place else in the Oquirrh Range offers better skiing with such a minimal approach.

The twin summits of Sharp Mountain can be climbed from either the saddle to their south or Chandler Saddle to the east, which is the quicker route. Ascend a rounded ridge directly west from the saddle. It leads to a lower-angle basin above. Stay south of the basin on a corniced, broad ridge and continue to the south summit. A sizable southeast-facing slope descends back into Serviceberry Canyon from Sharp Mountain. Three wide ravines comprise this bowl. These runs are treeless; signs of avalanche activity are often present. Assess whether they have recent loading before dropping in.

If the snow in the bowl is sun damaged, another option is to ski a northeast shot into Chandler Fork, approximately parallel to your approach route from Chandler Saddle. Stay skier's left (or right) of a narrowing gully in the middle. Up high the skier's right line is under a threatening cornice and may be heavily wind loaded. The run finishes in sparse aspens and spruces. Ski these directly into the V of Chandler Fork and stay skier's right above the creekbed until the terrain forces you down. Avoid the terrain trap of lower Chandler Fork.

Alternatively, skin up after skiing 1,200 feet off the summit and angle up to the Chandler/Serviceberry divide and Chandler Peak, 8,776 feet. This summit can also be reached in ten minutes from the Chandler Saddle. From here you can ski due north back to upper Chandler Fork, northeast for 1,000 feet into the lower creek bottom, or east for 1,500 feet to Ophir Canyon. All these lines have sparse trees and open meadows. The finish in Chandler Canyon involves a little bushwhacking through dense oaks, but the return to your car along Ophir Creek is very easy via the snowpacked road.

Other runs off Sharp Mountain include the west face into Dry Canyon and the north face. This west bowl is cut by a small rock band but otherwise offers moderately steep corn-snow terrain with a commanding view. The north face falls from Sharp Mountain, the north summit. This line is initially moderate and open, but it breaks over after 500 feet and becomes a pair of steep chutes through denser trees. Ski all the way out Soldier Canyon, stop short and skin up the south fork of Soldier Creek, or simply traverse skier's right up high and back into Chandler Fork.

North and west of Sharp Mountain is a broad, very low-angle open ridge that drops gradually toward Soldier Creek. It can be reached by descending northwest from the summit of Sharp Mountain to a saddle, then climbing a short distance west from there. Miles of open meadows with very shallow slope angles make this ridge inviting beginner terrain—but unfortunately, getting to it or off it requires more advanced skills.

Deseret Peak

Rating: Intermediate to difficult.

Gear: Skis or split-board and skins; ice ax and crampons in spring.

Summary: The crowning glory of Tooele Valley and the highest peak in the Stansbury Mountains is a surprisingly friendly ski peak. Well-protected glades offer fine powder skiing below, while classic couloirs beckon ski mountaineers to the Stansbury divide.

Maps: USGS 7.5-minute North Willow Canyon; Alpen Tech Stansbury ski-touring map.

Trailhead: Mill Fork at South Willow Canyon Road end (or the highest drivable point).

Distance: 6 to 10 miles (one way).

Starting altitude: 6,000 to 7,500 feet.

Deseret Peak above South Willow Canyon; east view (late season).

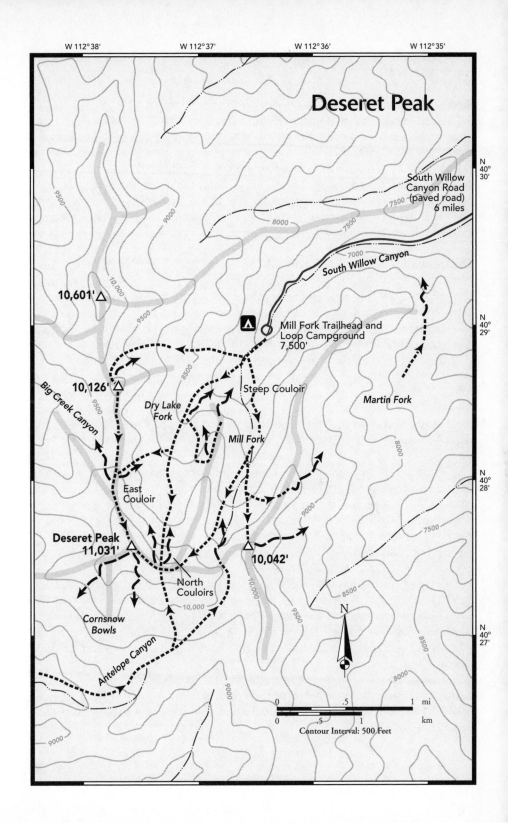

Deseret Peak

W 112°38' W 112°37' W 112°36' W 112°35'

N 40°30'

South Willow
Canyon Road
(paved road)
6 miles

South Willow Canyon

Mill Fork Trailhead and
Loop Campground
7,500'

N 40°29'

10,601' △

10,126' △

Big Creek Canyon

Dry Lake
Fork

Steep Couloir

Mill Fork

Martin Fork

N 40°28'

East
Couloir

Deseret Peak
11,031' △

10,042' △

North
Couloirs

N 40°27'

Cornsnow
Bowls

Antelope Canyon

N

0   .5   1 mi
0   .5   1 km
Contour Interval: 500 Feet

High points: Deseret Peak, 11,031 feet; unnamed point, 10,042 feet; unnamed point, 10,126 feet.

Access: Take exit 88 (Burmester Road) south off I–80 about 40 miles west of Salt Lake City. Drive 6 miles south to Grantsville. Turn right onto Main Street and after about a mile, go south onto West 400. Follow this paved road south for 5 miles past the Grantsville Reservoir. Turn right at a Forest Service sign marked SOUTH WILLOW ROAD. The road is well maintained and paved (with potholes) up to a final cattle guard at 5,900 feet. Above here, the grade increases; the road climbs past a guard station, a narrow section of limestone cliffs with a few established climbing routes, and a series of four campgrounds. At the highest campground, Loop Campground, the road ends.

Description: Skin up the Mill Fork Trail to about 8,000 feet, then turn right up a creek drainage toward the east-facing couloir of Dry Lake Fork (directly beneath the mighty northeast face of Deseret Peak). To gain the high divide from this basin requires the use of one of the two major couloirs, the north-facing or the east-facing one. A more avalanche-safe approach to the divide can be found at the head of Mill Fork itself, i.e., staying left (south) at the previous junction.

The east-facing couloir is enclosed between 9,700 and 10,350 feet, with a maximum incline of 40 degrees. It's well protected from sun, but the venturi effect (funneling of wind) often leaves a crust on its surface snow. It's wide enough for at least two ski tracks side by side. A summer trail near the ridge crest leads to the summit over moderate, wind-scoured northwest-facing terrain. A descent of Big Creek Canyon on the west could easily be done from here.

The north-facing twin couloirs are slightly more appealing as a summit approach. The maximum angle is 35 degrees, and the enclosure is wide enough for five to ten ski tracks abreast. There's no protected route to the couloir base. The skier's-right couloir holds much less snow. The aesthetics of the bigger north-facing couloir are classic. Acres of sheer, white quartzite cliffs stretch north across Deseret Peak's imposing northeast face, and the line can be skied for 1,300 feet to Dry Lake.

Excellent wind- and sun-protected powder often lurks between 8,000 and 9,500 feet in Dry Lake Fork. The wooded ridge between Mill Fork and Dry Lake Fork can be crossed to make a loop. A pair of steep couloirs define the north end of this subridge. The great selling points of both these forks are their north and northeast aspects. They couldn't have a better orientation for snow quality.

A separate tour can be made by switchbacking north from the trailhead at Loop Campground and climbing into Pockets Fork below the horn of Peak 10,126. The route wraps around the rocky pinnacle, providing a shady northeast-facing run back down.

Granite Canyon, Deep Creek Range

Rating: Difficult.

Gear: Skis or split-board with skins; ice ax and crampons may be useful in spring.

Summary: On the far western fringes of Utah stands a high range of rarely visited peaks that are home to some impressively long ski lines, as well as some great granite formations. Snow coverage may only rarely be good, but other people and tracks are even more rare.

Tour 41

Map: USGS 7.5-minute Ibapah Peak.

Trailhead: Granite Canyon.

Distance: 3 to 5 miles (one way, depending on road conditions).

Starting altitude: 6,000 to 6,800 feet.

High points: Red Mountain, 11,588 feet; unnamed point, 11,441 feet; Ibapah Peak, 12,087 feet.

Access: From Wendover, drive south on U.S. Highway 93 in Nevada to Gold Hill Road and turn east toward Ibapah and the Goshute Indian Reservation. Three miles north of Ibapah, turn east toward Callao on Deep Creek Mountains Road. Climb over a pass at the north end of the range and continue south past Callao to Granite Creek Road, an increasingly rugged thoroughfare that becomes a four-wheel-drive track once it enters the granite-tower-lined canyon. Excellent camping sites exist along the road near the canyon mouth, and the possibilities for rock-climbing are astounding, although the granite is crumbly.

Description: Sometimes it isn't possible to drive to the end of the road, but in May 2000 I began hiking in tennis shoes from just below a very steep and loose section near the current end of the road (a sign at 6,870 feet reads CLOSED TO MOTOR VEHICLES). Above here, the old road initially passes through a wide, low-angle meadow rimmed by spires of coarse, crumbling granite. Climb gradually along the road until you see open talus fields rising on your left at 7,400 feet. Directly above here is a 4,000-foot slide path/ski run that faces northeast. It's possible to find good skiing below 9,000 feet in this meadow by simply skinning directly up, making a short day.

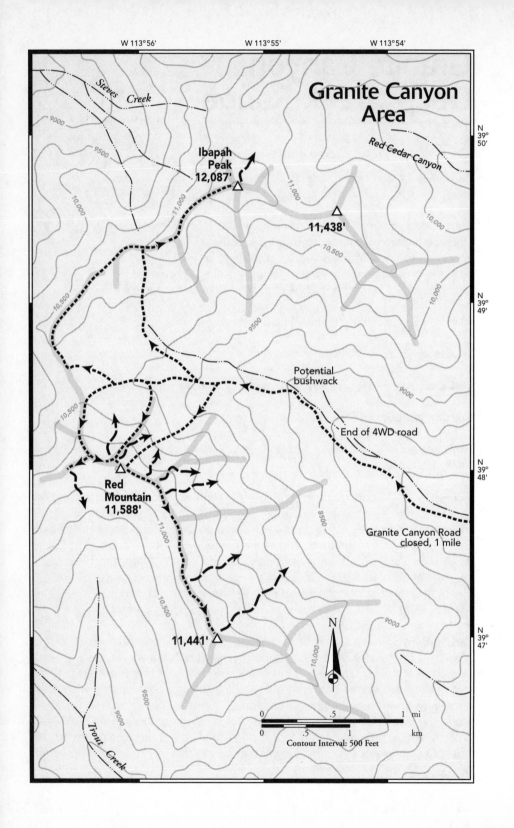

Steves Creek

Granite Canyon
Area

Red Cedar Canyon

N
39°
50'

Ibapah
Peak
12,087'

9000

9500

10,000

11,000

10,500

11,438'

10,000

N
39°
49'

9500

10,500

Potential
bushwack

9000

10,500

End of 4WD road

Red
Mountain
11,588'

N
39°
48'

8500

11,000

Granite Canyon Road
closed, 1 mile

10,500

9000

11,441'

N

10,000

N
39°
47'

9500

9000

Trout Creek

0   .5   1 mi

0   .5   1   km

Contour Interval: 500 Feet

If you want to ski from the high ridge, however, a better route is to continue up Granite Canyon along the summer pack trail heading toward the pass between Red Mountain and Ibapah Peak. Switchback through dense timber on the south side of the main creek where the canyon bottom becomes a narrow V-shape between 8,400 and 8,700 feet. It's difficult to stay on the trail here, and many a ski tourer has had to bushwhack for a few hundred vertical feet. Above here, the trail stays just north of the historical runout zone for massive avalanches cascading from the northeast face of Red Mountain. Continue along the trail to the pass; in avalanche-safe conditions you can also take the most direct access to the high ridge, up the deforested runout zone.

The north face of Red Mountain has several blunt and ill-defined ribs leading to its summit. The friendliest one for ski touring is on the northwest, but the more efficient mode of travel may be booting up the northeast spur from a meadow at 10,000 feet on the pack trail. The bald summit of Red Mountain, 11,588 feet, affords fine views south into Trout Creek and north to Ibapah.

The broad north face of Red offers open skiing at 35 to 40 degrees for 1,500 feet. These slopes are nearly always snow covered and skiable, assuming avalanche stability. Come back up your trail after skiing it, and traverse south and east along the high ridge to ski the 3,000- to 4,000-foot shots. These runs have more north aspect in them as you go farther south along the ridge toward point 11,441. Sparse trees lead to open gullies and finally to broad aprons as you drop uninterrupted to the road. When they're snow covered, these are some of the longest continuous fall lines in the entire state of Utah.

It's also possible to make a loop trip by climbing north and east from the pass to Ibapah and skiing its relatively short and moderate north face into Red Cedar Creek. This may be the easiest approach to the highest point in the Deep Creeks, but the exit down Cedar Creek is rugged, and there's no road or trail. From the bottom of Red Cedar Canyon, it's a few miles south to your car at Granite Creek. Stashing a mountain bike or second vehicle may be useful.

VI

Southern Wasatch

Big Relief, Small Crowds

Defined as the area from Lone Peak south to Mount Nebo, the southern end of the Wasatch Range includes the highest peaks and biggest massifs in the range. Most of the touring here is mountaineering oriented, with long ascents best undertaken in periods of stable snow and weather. Mount Nebo is often done as an overnight tour, but all these peaks can be skied in one long day from the greater Salt Lake metro area.

The Timpanogos, Box Elder, and South Fork Provo River areas include touring suitable for powder skiing, as well as high summit routes better for spring snow. Be aware, however, of differences between the snowpack of these Provo- area mountains and that of the Salt Lake mountains. The Utah Avalanche Center often refers to the Provo-area mountains and avalanche activity near Sundance Ski Resort in its forecasts. Take this information into account as you make conservative assessments of, and route selections in, these high, rugged mountains.

Santaquin and the Provo Peak area have terrain similar to the Cascade and Timpanogos massifs, but they are omitted from this guidebook because the difficult access is compounded by private property holdings. Both summits are best approached from the west: Santaquin above the ever-expanding neighborhoods of Spanish Fork and Provo Peak via Rock Canyon behind the Brigham Young University campus in Provo.

Southern Wasatch Information

Uinta National Forest, Provo Office, (801) 342–5100

Utah Avalanche Center, Provo, (801) 378–4333

Utah Avalanche Center, Park City, (435) 658–5512

Lone Peak Area

Tour 42

Rating: Moderate to difficult.

Gear: Skis or split-board with skins; ice ax, crampons, and rope are useful for a summit traverse.

Summary: Lone Peak's moderate south face is perhaps *the* classic corn descent in the Wasatch, and the east face is one of the steepest shots in the state. The Crows Feet run, highly visible from Salt Lake City, is best accessed via Lone Peak and Big Willow Cirque.

Maps: USGS 7.5-minute Draper, Dromedary Peak; Wasatch Touring Map 2.

Trailheads: Water tank or Hamangog jeep road above Alpine.

Distance: 3.5 miles to Lone Peak from water tank in Alpine.

Starting altitude: 5,800 to 7,000 feet.

High points: Bighorn Peak, 10,877 feet; Lone Peak, 11,253 feet.

Access: From the town of Alpine (located north of American Fork Canyon), go east on 200 North for 2 blocks and turn north onto 200 East. It will become Grove Drive. Go left on Oakridge Drive and left again on Alpine Cove. Finally, go right on Aspen Drive and continue to a water tank. Four-wheel-drive enthusiasts may want to challenge the deeply rutted road toward the First Hamangog, but turnaround spots are few, and the driving is white-knuckle.

Description: Walk or skin on the jeep road across a meadow and up a series of switchbacks, ignoring a left-hand branch. At 7,000 feet the road ends in a small, flat oak grove. Pick up the summer trail route here, climbing north and slightly west to end-run a ridge of evergreens. Drop just slightly and enter a beautiful meadow, Second Hamangog. The south face of Lone Peak stretches above for 3,000 feet to the summit. To reach the Lone Peak Cirque (known more for rock-climbing than skiing), traverse west above 9,000 feet and cut around the Question Mark Wall, located just west of the summit.

For the main south shot, climb either east or west of the small rib that splits the south face into two distinct shots, and continue above it to the east ridge. Follow it to the summit. The south face drops uninterrupted at 25 to 30

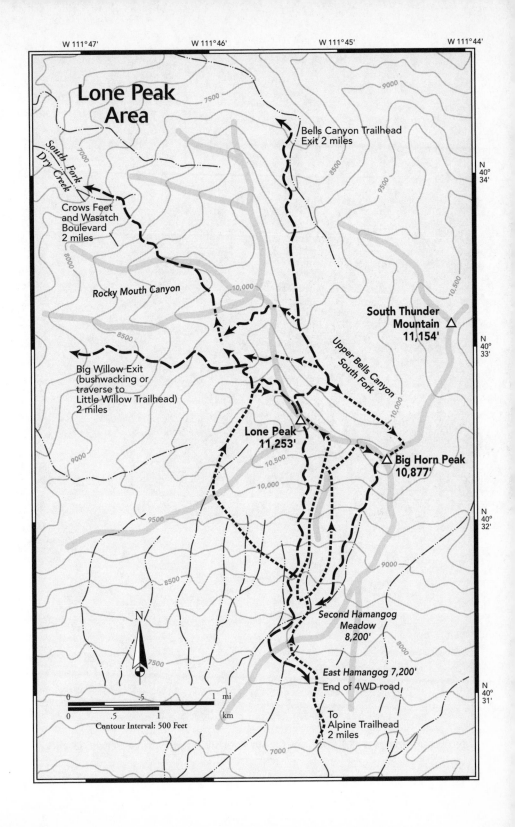

Lone Peak
Area

South Fork Dry Creek

Crows Feet
and Wasatch
Boulevard
2 miles

Rocky Mouth Canyon

Bells Canyon Trailhead
Exit 2 miles

South Thunder
Mountain △
11,154'

Big Willow Exit
(bushwacking or
traverse to
Little Willow Trailhead)
2 miles

Upper Bells Canyon
South Fork

Lone Peak
11,253'

△ Big Horn Peak
10,877'

N

Second Hamangog
Meadow
8,200'

East Hamangog 7,200'
End of 4WD road

To
Alpine Trailhead
2 miles

0   .5   1   mi

0   .5   1
                        km

Contour Interval: 500 Feet

W 111°47'   W 111°46'   W 111°45'   W 111°44'

N
40°
34'

N
40°
33'

N
40°
32'

N
40°
31'

Dave Braun enjoys the 3,600-foot Crows Feet slide path above Sandy, Utah.

degrees. The east portion is bounded on the east by Big Horn Peak, with its southwest-facing granite cliffs. Big Horn has steep skiing off the top on its southwest face and makes a good option for a second corn run in the area. Return via the approach route.

The east face of Lone Peak drops at 45 degrees for 1,000 feet and funnels into two chutes that usually go cleanly through rock bands at the bottom. It's possible to ski and climb southeast to the Dry Creek/Bells Canyon ridge east of Big Horn Peak and ski back to the Second Hamangog. Another option is to make a one-way tour to the Draper area by skiing directly down Bells Canyon or making a side trip into Big Willow and possibly finishing in the Crows Feet.

Big Willow Cirque is accessed from Bells by contouring west from 9,600 feet and crossing the dividing ridge at a low saddle between points 10,561 and 10,292. Ski west down a low-angle draw, then traverse south into the cirque. Two big north-facing aprons offer spectacular skiing in the granite-walled cirque. These aprons can also be skied from the north summit of Lone Peak. Traversing from the south summit to the north, although only 200 feet in distance, is a mountaineering feat along a knife-edge ridge with major exposure. A rope is recommended. The north summit and Big Willow Cirque can also be reached by ascending north through the Lone Peak Cirque.

To reach Big Willow, ski the low-angle, northwest-facing triangle of snow that drops from the north summit, then traverse west to the saddle between Lone Peak and Big Willow Cirques and drop into one of several 40-plus-degree gullies dropping to the aprons below. Watch for wind loading or other signs of instability, because this western end of the range gets less snow and more wind than the center. Big Willow has excellent skiing dropping west below the aprons, but it becomes horrendous bushwhacking for a section between 6,000 and 7,000 feet. The best escape at this altitude is to traverse south into Little Willow Canyon, where a trail exists.

To reach the Crows Feet from Big Willow Cirque, climb north from 9,700 feet below the aprons and drop over the little ridge into Rocky Mouth Canyon. Ski a friendly little 400-foot north-facing shot, then traverse the low-angle north side of this gulch without skins to reach the 3,600-foot slide path known as the Crows Feet. Give it good ski cuts, especially where it breaks over after 300 feet, and ski with good avalanche procedures. Look for a trail on the south-facing side of this small canyon where the snow runs out, or you'll bushwhack down to the fancy homes above Wasatch Boulevard. There is a two-sided tin shelter along Wasatch where the trail comes out to the road.

Box Elder Peak Area

Rating: Difficult.

Gear: Skis or split-board with skins.

Summary: An incredible ski peak standing quite alone between Little Cottonwood and American Fork Canyons. Cross-country skiing is possible near Tibble Fork Reservoir.

Tour 43

Maps: USGS 7.5-minute Timpanogos Cave, Dromedary Peak; Wasatch Touring Map 2.

Trailheads: Dry Creek above Alpine, Tibble Fork Reservoir, or White Pine in Little Cottonwood Canyon.

Distance: 3.5 miles from Tibble or Dry Creek; 6 miles from White Pine.

Starting altitude: Dry Creek, 5,800 feet; Tibble, 6,300 feet; White Pine, 7,700 feet.

High point: Box Elder Peak, 11,100 feet.

Access: To reach Dry Creek from the town of Alpine (located north of American Fork Canyon), go east on 200 North for 2 blocks and turn north onto 200 East. It will become Grove Drive. Stay right on Grove and cross the creek. Continue another 0.25 mile to the trailhead.

To reach Tibble Fork Reservoir, take Utah State Route 92 east from Alpine into American Fork Canyon. Turn left (north) onto UT 44 in the canyon and drive to the reservoir, where a parking lot is maintained.

White Pine is in Little Cottonwood Canyon. From I–215 in Salt Lake City, exit at 6200 South and follow signs to Alta and Snowbird in Little Cottonwood Canyon. Look for WHITE PINE TRAILHEAD on a Forest Service sign 1 mile west of Snowbird's lowest entrance. The parking lot is plowed after each storm, but it often overflows on busy weekend days. No overnight parking is allowed.

Description: Dry Creek is the most popular trailhead for this area; it's a shorter drive than Tibble and closer to the appealing northwest cirque and west-facing runs. Ascend the trail (an old four-wheel-drive road) to 8,200 feet, where the avalanche runout from the northwest cirque is visible to the south. Ascend the northwest spur of the north ridge, and then follow the main ridge to the summit. Along the way, the north-facing Shotgun Chutes will beckon. They fall from

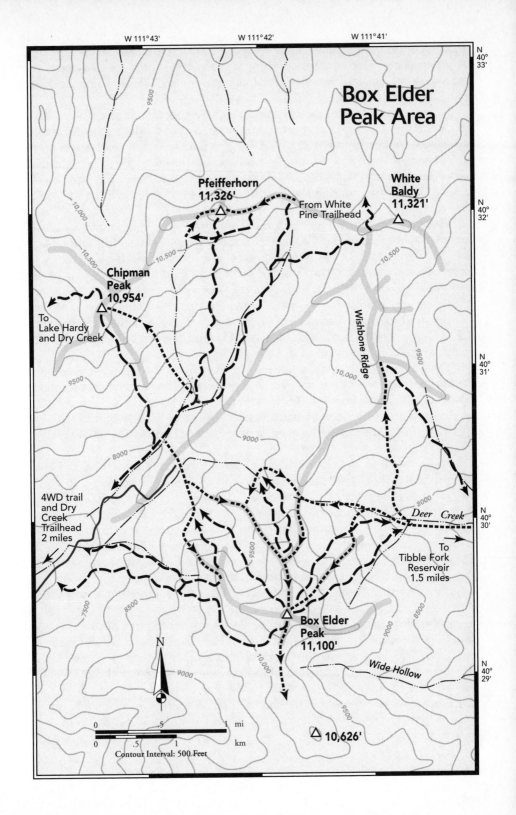

Pfeifferhorn
11,326'

From White
Pine Trailhead

White
Baldy
11,321'

Chipman
Peak
10,954'

To
Lake Hardy
and Dry Creek

Wishbone Ridge

4WD trail
and Dry
Creek
Trailhead
2 miles

Deer Creek

To
Tibble Fork
Reservoir
1.5 miles

N

Box Elder
Peak
11,100'

Wide Hollow

10,626'

9500

10,000

10,500

9500

10,500

10,000

9500

9000

8000

9500

7500

8500

10,000

8500

9000

9000

9500

8000

9000

0   .5   1 mi
0   .5   1 km
Contour Interval: 500 Feet

W 111°43'   W 111°42'   W 111°41'

N
40°
33'

N
40°
32'

N
40°
31'

N
40°
30'

N
40°
29'

10,300 feet and are actually deep erosion gullies. The better skiing is in the well-spaced north-facing trees adjacent to the gullies. These steep woods are also the safest option if weather prohibits a summit bid. They can be reached from Tibble just as easily.

If favorable conditions prevail, the summit is a spectacular spot with skiable options to the southwest, northwest, northeast, and east. The southwest is relatively low angle and can be skied en route to the west face, which starts from 10,500 feet. It can also be used as the access route to Peak 10,626, the unnamed and rarely visited southern counterpart to Box Elder. This peak has a spectacular northeast-facing slide path dropping into Wide Hollow and Tibble Fork Reservoir.

The east face of Box Elder becomes very steep in the middle and is usually sun affected before enough avalanche stability exists to make it a safe objective. The northeast shot has huge exposure as it drops at 40 degrees from just north of the summit. At 10,200 feet, it splits into two distinct bowls. The more north-facing drop is steeper initially and continues through two gullies for a 2,700-foot run that can have great snow. The more easterly bowl is White Canyon, and it's aptly named. The open, low-angle bowl between 9,800 and 8,200 feet is a huge snowfield. Below 8,200 feet, the run continues through sparse avalanche regrowth to Deer Creek.

The northwest cirque is the prize line on Box Elder. A wide-open bowl with impressive limestone cliffs forming its western wall, it catches the late-afternoon light and lures skiers from the Pfeifferhorn area. It's a continuous drop of 2,700 feet beginning at 35 degrees and breaking over to 40 degrees through two short, parallel chutes before a giant, low-angle bowl and finally an avalanche runout.

Steep, north-facing chutes fall from the northwest buttress of Box Elder (point 10,280). These are accessed by skinning up the northwest ridge. This trail also accesses the west face, a moderate run that falls from 10,500 feet and spreads out like a fan before funneling into two dangerous erosion gullies. These were formed after overgrazing and a nasty cloudburst caused a wall of water to gush down the face in the 1950s. Terracing efforts by the Forest Service have stabilized the terrain and are visible when snowpack is thin. Passing the erosion zone at the bottom of these gullies is the crux of skiing the west face. Your best option is to stay skier's left of the southern gully and intersect the Dry Creek Trail at 6,600 feet.

Tibble Fork Reservoir is the best access for skiing the immense northeast shots. Follow Silver Creek Road past Granite Flat Campground before heading west at 7,000 feet where the road switchbacks east toward Silver Creek Reservoir. Above here, follow the old four-wheel-drive road or the creek, but stay north of the marshy flats. Ascend to the obvious saddle dividing Deer and Dry Creeks. Ascend the northeast spur of the north ridge, and then follow the main ridge to the summit. Alternatively, cross Deer Creek at 7,800 feet and ascend through protective woods to the northeast ridge. Unlike the continuously protruding northwest ridge, this ridge fades into a headwall at 10,000 feet. Visit the northeast face of Box Elder only when the snowpack is strong.

The White Pine Trailhead is an appealing access route to Box Elder when good corn-snow skiing exists on the south face of Dry Creek. Start early. Ascend to the south side of the Pfeifferhorn (as described in Tour 31, Little Cottonwood Canyon South) and ski the south face to 8,800 feet. Traverse south (skier's left) and drop to the base of the northwest spur of Box Elder's north ridge. A vehicle should be cached at the Dry Creek Trailhead to facilitate a descent of the west face or northwest cirque, as described above.

Mighty Mount Timpanogos

Rating: Easy to difficult.

Gear: Skis or split-board with skins; ice ax and crampons for summit bids.

Tour 44

Summary: The mammoth west face of "Timp" stretches 5 miles wide and falls more than 5,000 feet to the Happy Valley and Provo Lake. Few ski peaks in the lower forty-eight—and none in Utah—exceed the 11,750-foot "Sleeping Maiden" for sheer volume of uplifted terrain. Mount Nebo is a close second, and many Uinta, La Sal, and Tushar summits are higher, but the ridge that extends from American Fork Canyon to Provo Canyon rises 4,000 feet above the surrounding land for 4 amazing miles of ski terrain. Although the lofty summit is an all-day challenge, less ambitious recreationists can revel in the unmatched beauty of the Aspen Grove and Woolly Hole areas on shorter outings. Utah's mightiest massif offers skiing for all levels, but avalanche danger can be extreme. Cross-country skiing is possible on Timpooneke Road.

Maps: USGS 7.5-minute Timpanogos Cave, Aspen Grove; 1:100,000 Provo.

Trailheads: Mutual Dell, Timpooneke Campground, Aspen Grove.

Distance: 2.5 miles to the north summit; 3 miles to the south summit.

Starting altitude: Mutual Dell, 6,500 feet; Timpooneke, 7,260 feet; Aspen Grove, 6,900 feet.

High points: Mount Timpanogos; North Summit, 11,383 feet; South Summit, 11,722 feet.

Access: For Mutual Dell and Timpooneke Campground, go east on Utah State Route 92 from Alpine into American Fork Canyon. Continue east as it becomes the Alpine Loop Highway, passing the junction with UT 44. Look for the Mutual Dell private holding on your right. Park along the highway. Timpooneke Campground is about 2 miles farther, past a switchback where winter maintenance usually ends. A snowmobile in winter or bicycle in spring can eliminate 2 to 3 miles of road slogging above here.

For Aspen Grove, go north from U.S. Highway 189 on Alpine Loop Road past Sundance Ski Resort. Park at the well-established trailhead.

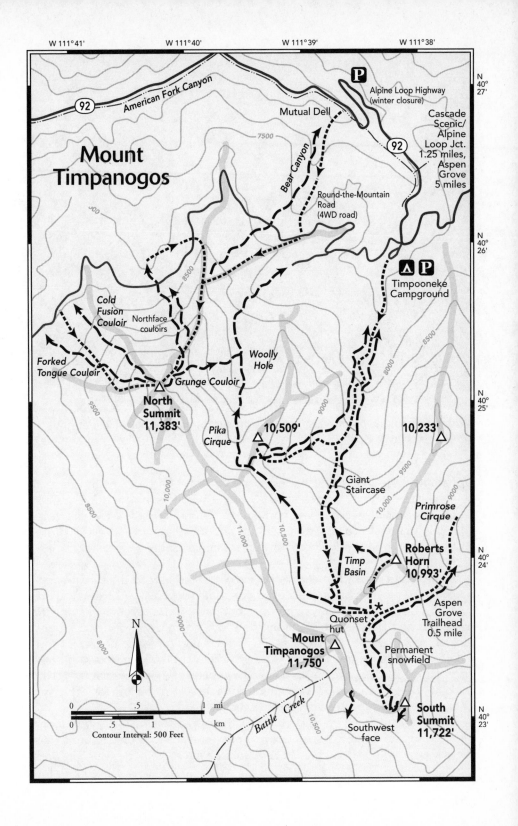

W 111°41' W 111°40' W 111°39' W 111°38'

Mount Timpanogos

American Fork Canyon

92

Mutual Dell

Bear Canyon

Round-the-Mountain Road (4WD road)

Alpine Loop Highway (winter closure)

P

Cascade Scenic/ Alpine Loop Jct. 1.25 miles, Aspen Grove 5 miles

92

N 40° 27'

N 40° 26'

Timpooneke Campground

Cold Fusion Couloir
Northface couloirs

Forked Tongue Couloir

Grunge Couloir

Woolly Hole

△ **North Summit 11,383'**

Pika Cirque

10,509' △

10,233' △

N 40° 25'

Giant Staircase

Primrose Cirque

△ **Roberts Horn 10,993'**

Timp Basin

N 40° 24'

Quonset hut

*

Aspen Grove Trailhead 0.5 mile

△ **Mount Timpanogos 11,750'**

Permanent snowfield

N

0   .5   1 mi
0   .5   1   km
Contour Interval: 500 Feet

Battle Creek

Southwest face

△ **South Summit 11,722'**

N 40° 23'

Mount Timpanogos; northeast view. North summit and Woolly Hole at right; Timpooneke area at left.

Description: Aspen Grove is the highest year-round trailhead. From this small community of summer homes above Sundance Ski Resort, climb 2,600 steep and highly avalanche-prone feet up Primrose Cirque to reach a hanging valley containing Emerald Lake, a quonset hut, and a year-round snowfield. Glisse-starved skiers have been known to carve summer snow here in August and September!

Carry on to the saddle above the snowfield and ascend the summit ridge northwest to the main summit or east to the south summit, 11,722 feet. The true summit is marginally skiable on the west, but traversing is necessary around the numerous rock bands up high. From the south summit, one of Utah's biggest runs drops 3,000 to 5,000 feet into Dry Canyon and on to the neighborhoods of Orem. Pick up the trail below 7,000 feet and follow it for a mile or two to the water tank in Lindon, where a car should have been cached. Alternatively, climb back to the saddle on the prominent ridge north of the canyon. This was Brimhall and Hardy's 1916 first winter ascent route.

The descent from the saddle along the approach route in north-facing Primrose Cirque down to Aspen Grove is also an epic 4,000 feet. Roberts Horn is easily climbed from the Emerald Lake area via the south ridge. The northwest shot drops into Timpanogos Basin and can also be accessed from (or skied to) Timpooneke, making a great loop route. The north-facing bowl below the main summit's 1,000-foot cliffs is a more moderate entrance into Timp Basin. Traverse the basin northwest to Pika Cirque for an even more scenic loop descent route via Woolly Hole or the east-facing bowl below point 10,509.

Aspen Grove is also the departure point for tours to Elk Point and Peak 10,791. Head south from the parking area and switchback through the woods, working southwest up an indistinct ridge. South of this ridge is the open northeast face, which makes an excellent steep run for a short tour. Peak 10,791 is accessible by continuing above Elk Point on the northeast ridge. This spectacular east buttress of Timp is skiable on the southeast for a quick 4,000-foot drop to Sundance Ski Resort. The east and northeast shots are 45 degrees in steepness with cliff bands in all but the deepest snowpacks, but in those years they are awesome steep descents.

Timpooneke Campground is the standard summer trailhead for summit bids, but in spring the Alpine Loop Highway usually remains closed until June, so the access road provides a gentle and utterly spectacular cross-country ski tour in itself. It can be skied west from the campground below the north face (given avalanche stability) or east all the way to Aspen Grove or Cascade Springs. Safe and gentle touring also exists near the road in the vicinity of the junction with Cascade Scenic Drive (Forest Road 144) at 8,000 feet.

The summer summit route can be used in winter and leads due south from the campground up the Giant Staircase into Timpanogos Basin. Series of rock bands present problems and can be passed on the west. The best ski terrain is in the east-facing bowl below point 10,509. Ascending above this avalanche-prone, 35- to 40-degree bowl is also the easiest way to reach and ski off the main summit ridge from Timpooneke. Avoid this route, and all others on the upper Timpanogos massif, in any but very stable avalanche conditions.

For the north summit and Woolly Hole before the road is plowed to Timpooneke, use Mutual Dell, a private camp and lodge. Nestled in shadowy American Fork Canyon directly under Timpanogos's ominous north summit, it feels like a low and uninspiring start. Nonetheless, the trail beginning here is the fastest, most efficient route (save snowmobile-assisted access). Simply head south up Bear Canyon—which has a faint trail and isn't *too* densely wooded. Cross the summer four-wheel-drive road (where 'bilers can start) at 7,900 feet and continue south to the low-angle northeast ridge. Good skiing in aspens and pines exists north and east of this spur below 9,000 feet.

Woolly Hole, an attractive northeast-facing bowl offering acres of good (but avalanche-prone) skiing, becomes visible from here. Ski it from point 10,400, where the ridge becomes steep. A cliff band below Woolly Hole can be passed on the west in most years. Ski mountaineers can thread the needle from Woolly Hole south into seldom-visited Pika Cirque, a hanging snowfield rimmed by inhospitable limestone cliffs. It communicates into the west bowl of Timp Basin, making a loop route to Giant Staircase, as outlined above.

The north face is also accessible from the northeast spur ridge. Although the direct north aspect off the 11,383-foot north buttress is an unskiable mélange of horizontal cliffs and supersteep snowfields, ski routes exist on the east and west flanks. Above Woolly Hole, the northeast ridge becomes steep and indistinct, with rotten snow between nearly vertical cliff bands. It's easier (although more avalanche-prone) to traverse into the Grunge Couloir and boot up it.

Named long before Nirvana or Pearl Jam hit the charts, this classic gully is enclosed through the "choke" by 200-foot walls and holds snow into summer, when mountaineers have most often climbed it. At this time, the crumbling cliffs coat its snowy surface with a layer of stone and gravel, making it appear gray and grungy, hence the name. Wear a helmet and proceed rapidly.

The crux of the Grunge Couloir is the often overhanging cornice formed at its top from prevailing westerly winds. Chop through it in a small part (maybe only 2 feet of overhang), or tunnel through as if you were in the Himalayas or Alaska. Adding to the drama is the slope angle of the upper couloir, measured by Andrew McLean at 62 degrees!

Those who relish this type of couloir skiing will want to hang a hard left upon emerging at the bottom of the 1,200-foot Grunge Couloir and traverse to a pair of north-facing chutes, the Pinball Alleys. They run through the north-facing cliff bands and spill onto the sublime aprons below. These can also be skied from the top of Woolly Hole. The return to Mutual Dell is pretty much survival skiing through the woods, so you can reduce the "average cost" of big-peak skiing by returning to the summit on the already established trail and skiing one of the two northwest chutes as well.

From the summit, wander northwest looking for one of the two inauspicious breakovers that lead to 3,000-foot slide paths. Skier's left (west) is the Forked Tongue; skier's right is Cold Fusion. The two parallel shots diverge slightly as they widen out. At the bottom, find the jeep road (likely buried under tons of accumulated avalanche debris) and contour back under the north face to find the Mutual Dell trail and follow it wearily down to your car, probably by headlamp the last mile! The northwest couloirs are only 35 to 40 degrees in steepness, despite their intimidating appearance from I–15 around the point of the mountains. The standard approach to these chutes is directly up the west branch of the Forked Tongue and the northwest ridge from the summer jeep road.

South Fork, Provo River

Rating: Easy to difficult.

Gear: Skis or split-board and skins.

Summary: This beautiful, rugged area has difficult access, but rewarding bowls and headwalls that see little ski-touring traffic. Heli-skiing occurs in February and March, when the snowpack can be comparable to the Central Wasatch. In other winters it remains much shallower and more dangerous. Water Hollow offers shorter approaches to excellent skiing in safer, smaller-scale terrain, but Trefoil Ranch Girl Scout Camp actively blocks access from the base of Water Hollow and Shingle Mill Canyons. Cross-country skiing is possible in canyon bottoms.

Tour 45

Map: USGS 7.5-minute Bridal Veil Falls.

Trailheads: Bunnells Fork or Big Springs.

Distance: 3.5 miles to Lightning Peak or Cascade Mountain; 4 miles to the head of Shingle Mill.

Starting altitude: Bunnells Fork, 5,450 feet; Big Springs, 5,800 feet.

High points: Cascade Mountain, 10,908 feet; Lightning Peak, 10,056 feet; unnamed point, 10,006 feet.

Access: From U.S. Highway 189 in Provo Canyon, go south at Vivian Park (1 mile west of Sundance Road) on South Fork Road. South Fork Park, 1.8 miles south, is the trailhead for Bunnells Fork. The Big Springs Trailhead turnoff is 3.4 miles south of Provo Canyon and is a large, well-maintained parking area. It's the highest available start for tours to Big Springs, Shingle Mill, and Water Hollow.

Description: Bunnells Fork is steep, avalanche-prone, and brushy, making it unpopular as an ascent route. But it is a feasible outrun for shots off the incredible east face of Cascade Mountain, the head of Davis Canyon, and lower, north-facing drops off the divide between Bunnells and Big Springs drainages.

Big Springs Hollow provides the highest and most direct access point in the South Fork watershed. Low-angle tours suitable for cross-country skis with wax or fish scales begin here and go up the broad canyon floor for 700 vertical feet over 1.5 miles. Alternatively, make a loop by turning south out of Bunnells at

South Fork, Provo River

Water Hollow

Windy Pass

Holes of Hobble Canyon

Dry Canyon

First Hole

Second Hole

Third Hole

Lightning Peak
10,056'

Big Springs Trailhead
1.5 miles

Shingle Mill Canyon

9,139'

Big Springs Trailhead
approx. 1 mile

10,006'

Big Springs Hollow

Dry Fork
of Rock Canyon

Highly
avalanche-prone
cirques

10,125'

10,760'

Upper Bunnells Fork

Cascade Mountain
10,908'

N

1 mi

km

Contour Interval: 500 Feet

N 40° 19'

N 40° 18'

N 40° 17'

W 111°30'

W 111°31'

W 111°32'

W 111°33'

W 111°34'

W 111°35'

7000

8000

9000

8500

8000

7000

7500

9500

8500

9000

7500

7000

8000

9000

9000

9500

9000

8500

10,000

9000

6,150 feet on a jeep road. Follow it toward Shingle Mill Canyon until it crosses a big field above the creek, and return by skiing north across the meadows for 0.5 mile back to the parking area.

Ski tourers with skins use Big Springs to approach the shots into Bunnells Fork as well as the three major basins at its head. Stay in the north branch where the canyon splits at 6,500 feet, and climb the first prominent ridge on the north to ski the midlevel north-facing slide paths into Bunnells Fork. There is no safe route to Cascade Mountain, but the most reasonable is to stay north in Big Springs through its many splits and gain the ridge between Big Springs and Bunnells at a saddle west of point 9,016. Boot up the steep, narrow, and sometimes rocky ridge. All this terrain is subject to avalanches, including the canyon floor, so make a conservative assessment.

At 6,500 feet, the South Fork of Big Springs splits off and rises more steeply past a northwest-facing gulch that offers good skiing. The safest approach for this gulch is along the well-defined east ridge, leading to point 9,139. Use the trail a second time and ski back to the trailhead via 2,000-foot slide paths in a

Big Springs Hollow and Cascade Mountain (right); east view.

north-facing subcanyon falling from point 9,139.

Big Springs Hollow splits again at 7,700 feet; more reasonable access and skiing exist in the southern branch. The easiest approach to the Cascade divide from here is to stay north of the canyon floor above 8,200 feet. A col at 9,500 feet provides good north-facing runs into Big Springs and access into Dry Fork above Rock Canyon. One-thousand- to 2,500-foot south-facing corn shots fall off the Cascade divide from here and to the west. Return to Big Springs by ascending Dry Fork to 9,300 feet and contouring north up to the divide—but venture into this area only in stable avalanche conditions.

Drop into upper Shingle Mill Canyon from high on the traverse out of Dry Fork or by traveling south along the divide from Big Springs. There's an even lower pass west of point 9,622 on the ridge between Shingle and Big Springs. Climb south from 8,200 feet in the South Fork of Big Springs to a wooded saddle, and ski or traverse south into Shingle Mill. This is the north cirque of Shingle, where a moderate bowl at the head makes for spectacular runs.

The south ridge of this bowl can be climbed to point 10,006 on the Cascade divide, and from here an even larger bowl stretches to the south toward the rugged north face of Shingle Mill Peak. There are very steep chutes dropping from the north ridge of this 10,700-foot summit. A hanging, low-angle basin dominates the east cirque of Shingle Mill, and a pair of cliffs must be passed in the middle or on the far east to travel between here and the relatively narrow main canyon. From this hanging basin, a minimal climb to the south accesses Third Hole and east-facing skiing into upper Dry Canyon, a tributary of Hobble Creek. There's plenty of vertical to be enjoyed here, but it's wise to cut skier's left (north) at 8,700 feet and traverse into Second Hole and First Hole in order to return to the South Fork over Windy Pass at the head of Water Hollow.

Shingle Mill is a less viable ascent canyon than Big Springs due to its narrow V-shape, which increases avalanche danger, and because the canyon mouth is private property. It's not bad as an exit, however, because the duration of exposure is much shorter. Water Hollow, the next major drainage east of Shingle, is a safer and shorter ascent to the high country, but it too can only be approached from the Big Springs Trailhead.

Cross a large, low-angle field south of the parking area, contour above 6,200 feet into Shingle Mill, and cross it to Water Hollow. You can mitigate avalanche exposure in Water Hollow by ascending through the woods west of the canyon bottom above 6,800 feet. Windy Pass isn't hard to reach and provides access to the east ridge of Lightning Peak and the west ridge of Peak 9,474 (Water Hollow). Lightning has a very steep northeast face but offers more moderate drops on the wooded north (back toward the South Fork) and east (into First Hole).

Mount Nebo Area

Rating: Difficult.

Gear: Skis or split-board with skins; ice ax and crampons may be useful in late season.

Summary: Following a two-hour drive from Salt Lake City and continuously ascending approach up a four-wheel-drive road, dense woods, and slide paths, you may have this entire massif to yourself. There are spectacular views of central and western Utah. This rewarding climb to the highest summit in the Wasatch Range is recommended as an extremely long single-day or long two-day adventure.

Tour 46

Map: USGS 7.5-minute Mona.

Trailhead: Mona Pole Road.

Distance: 6 miles (one way).

Starting altitude: 6,000 to 6,500 feet.

High point: Mount Nebo, 11,928 feet.

Access: Approach Mount Nebo by driving 90 miles south of Salt Lake City on I–15 to the hamlet of Mona. Turn north at the "city center" and continue for 2 miles. Turn east onto Mona Pole Road and follow it under I–15. At a junction near the gravel pit, take a right and begin climbing southeast toward the narrow canyon mouth. Mona Pole Road climbs steeply up Pole Canyon and is essentially impassable above 6,000 feet. To attempt four-wheeling on it, you must obtain a permit from the Forest Service. Alternate winter approaches do exist; they are discussed below. Others become available in late spring, but no matter where you start, it's a long way to the top. I've chosen the northwestern approach from Mona despite its 6,000-foot ascent because of its climbing efficiency and quality of skiing.

Description: From the base of Pole Canyon, follow the switchbacking jeep road to about 7,500 feet, where it bends north across a relatively flat basin below some visible avalanche slide paths. Pick a route through the white fir and aspen that leads up and southeast to a forested gully and finally reaches a plateau below the massive northwest basin of Nebo's north summit. Camp

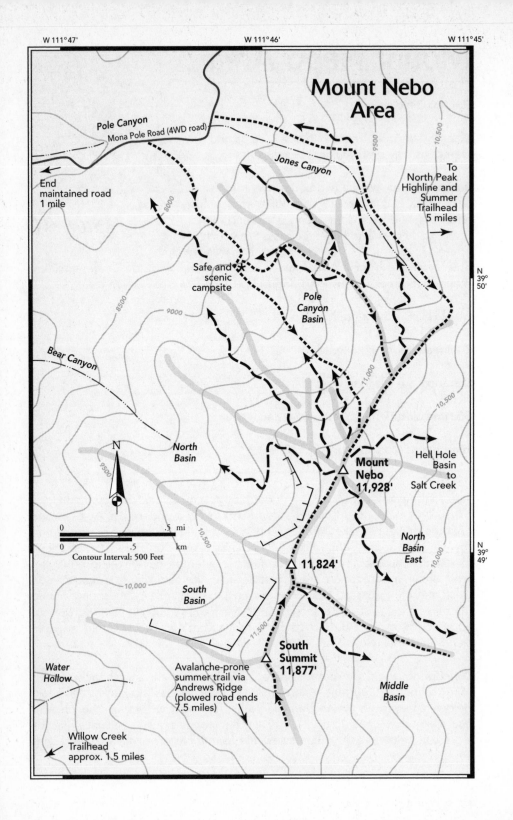

Mount Nebo Area

Pole Canyon
Mona Pole Road (4WD road)

Jones Canyon

To
North Peak
Highline and
Summer
Trailhead
5 miles

End
maintained road
1 mile

Safe and
scenic
campsite

Pole
Canyon
Basin

N
39°
50'

Bear Canyon

N

North
Basin

Hell Hole
Basin
to
Salt Creek

Mount
Nebo
11,928'

North
Basin
East

N
39°
49'

0　　　　　.5 mi
0　　　　　.5 km
Contour Interval: 500 Feet

11,824'

South
Basin

10,000

Water
Hollow

South
Summit
11,877'

Avalanche-prone
summer trail via
Andrews Ridge
(plowed road ends
7.5 miles)

Middle
Basin

Willow Creek
Trailhead
approx. 1.5 miles

8000

8500

9000

9500

9500

10,500

10,500

11,000

11,500

10,500

10,000

10,000

here (at about 9,200 feet) if you're on an overnight trip, being sure to choose a site well back from the maximum avalanche runout zone, as indicated by trim lines.

Several decent possibilities exist for routes on the upper mountain. In low avalanche danger (which is the only safe time to be on Mount Nebo), skin up the northwest basin and boot up the northwest couloirs. It has two branches; the left one is much easier, since it leads to the main north–south summit ridge just 50 feet below the north peak. The right (west) couloir terminates 200 feet below the summit on the wind-scoured talus on the west ridge. Crampons may be useful in the couloir. Climbing it also enables you to preview the descent route and conditions.

Another option is a narrow couloir that leads due south through a very narrow passage and gains the summit ridge about 500 vertical feet and 0.5 mile below the top. This "pinball alley" is an aesthetic climb with views to the valley floor and, from the summit ridge, glimpses of the east face and east-central Utah.

In times of slightly higher avalanche danger, it's marginally safer to skin up the northwest ridge directly from Pole Canyon Basin and gain the summit ridge above Wolf Pass at 11,300 feet. Follow the spectacular ridge to the north peak. All routes must be continued south along the summit ridge for another 300 feet to reach the actual high point, 11,928 feet. From here, you can also see south into the giant North Basin, which is lined by stacks of off-fall-line couloirs along its west ridge. It's skiable in some years by dropping southwest off the summit. Farther to the south is yet another big cirque, South Basin. Nebo has these three matching cirques on its west aspect and a similar number of high basins on the east. Any of them would provide days of uncrowded skiing in spectacular scenery, but the two more southerly west-facing basins lack a reasonable access route.

Descend the northwest couloir or the northwest ridge, or make a loop by dropping down the east face and using a preplaced car shuttle at Salt Creek. If you're returning to Mona Pole Road, however, it's advisable to stay farther south than you did on your approach once you're below the tree line (about 9,000 feet), linking up a series of more open slide paths with aspens and small pines. From the base of these, just drop down the fall line through the old-growth woods and intersect Mona Pole Road.

The standard summer approach is from the southeast up Andrews Ridge from the Salt Creek Canyon Trailhead at 6,450 feet. Unfortunately, the road isn't plowed to the trailhead in winter, and the trail leaves Andrews Ridge and traverses avalanche-prone basins at midslope before intersecting the high divide. Epic descents of the enticing east-facing basins—Hell Hole, North, Middle, and South—have been accomplished, but the avalanche danger becomes more severe down low, because the lines all funnel into gullies. Eventually, they all terminate at Salt Creek, which conveniently parallels the summit ridge and can be descended on an old road back to the west branch of Nebo Scenic Loop Road.

East face of Mount Nebo with Salt Creek at base.

This road offers access from the northeast at the Highline Trailhead, 9,253 feet. This route climbs up and over North Peak (11,174 feet) en route to Wolf Pass and Nebo. It's not available until July in most years and provides more expedient access to Bald Mountain and North Peak than to Nebo. Yet another access option is from the south and Willow Creek. Drive south from Mona, heading east after 1 mile past the cemetery and over the freeway. The terrain in Water Hollow above the trailhead at 6,700 feet is wooded and slightly safer from an avalanche standpoint than Andrews Ridge on the southeast.

VII

La Sal Mountains

Skiing over Slickrock

Giant white peaks etched against a backdrop of red rock and blue sky beckon every skier who has ever hiked, biked, or climbed in the Moab area, and getting to them isn't that difficult. The easily accessible central La Sal Mountains offer incredible ski touring—but proceed with caution when touring this high range in midwinter. The peaks, despite their enticing availability, are notoriously unstable from an avalanche standpoint. The convex shape alone renders them dangerous, but once you add in steep temperature gradients (resulting in weak underlying snow) and copious wind (creating slabs above), you have nearly chronic instability in the alpine terrain until spring.

Yet winter touring is often good in the wooded, protected midaltitude areas near Geyser and La Sal Passes. The road to Geyser Pass is now being plowed year-round to the 9,600-foot level! This means hard-core skiers can even ski the aspen glades between the switchbacks and use car shuttles to make runs. Why mope in Moab on a snowy winter day when one of the highest trailheads in Utah is just forty-five minutes away? Corkscrew Glades are a good full- or half-day destination for advanced tourers, as are many drops off the aptly named Laurel Highway, a ridge leading safely and efficiently into the high country from the Geyser Pass snow park and winter trailhead.

Multiday tours based out of shelters in the Dark Canyon, Mount Tomasaki, and La Sal Pass areas can be arranged through Tag-A-Long Adventures, with transport by snowcat to the conveniently located huts. Keep in mind, however, that proximity to the base of the high peaks should not breed complacency. Midwinter ski descents off the summits have had grave results. Use the huts in spring to get early starts for corn runs off the peaks.

Allow a period of warm, stable weather to melt and refreeze the snowpack into a consolidated mass, and then travel easily over the supportable crust to ski perhaps the finest alpine terrain in Utah off Tukuhnikivatz, Peale, Mellenthin, Tomasaki, Manns, and Waas. These and numerous other unnamed 12,000-foot rubble piles are more Colorado-esque than Wasatch-like, and travel on skins and crampons is far more efficient and friendly than on loose summer talus. The high altitude and stable weather patterns often make it possible to ski excellent corn late into the day, but get to safe terrain before the snow becomes break-able slush, and be wary of afternoon thundershowers. Many adventurers prefer another feasible option: morning skiing and afternoon biking or rock-climbing.

The La Sals are generally divided into three groups: north, middle, and south. The north group includes everything north of Geyser Pass, and the south is south of La Sal Pass (basically, just South Mountain). The popular middle group includes the three highest peaks and is the most easily accessible, but the south gets the most snow, and the north has the longest north-facing runs. The descriptions of tours given here build on themselves, starting with the closer-in places and working out to the farther and more obscure destinations.

La Sal Information

La Sal Avalanche Forecast Center, (435) 259–SNOW (7669)

Manti–La Sal National Forest, Moab Ranger District, (435) 259–7155

Tag-A-Long Adventures, (435) 259–8946 or (800) 453–3292

Moab Desert Adventures, (435) 260–2404

Laurel Highway and Gold Basin

Rating: Easy to difficult.

Gear: Skis or split-board and skins; waxed or scaled skis on roads.

Summary: This is the easiest, shortest, and safest approach to the heart of the La Sals. Touring possibilities range from flat-tracking to 50 degrees and durations from two hours to a long day. This makes a good approach route for Mounts Mellenthin, Laurel, and Peale.

Tour 47

Map: USGS 7.5-minute Mounts Tukuhnikivatz and Peale.

Trailhead: Geyser Pass snow park.

Distance: 2.5 miles to Pre-Laurel Peak.

Starting altitude: 9,600 feet.

High points: Pre-Laurel Peak, 11,705 feet; Laurel Mountain, 12,271 feet; Mount Peale, 12,721 feet.

Access: Drive south out of Moab on U.S. Highway 191 to the well-signed turnoff to Ken's Lake and La Sal Loop Road. The loop road splits right within a few miles and climbs above the Moab Valley to a junction with Geyser Pass Road. Turn right onto a switchbacking gravel two-wheel-drive road. Skiing between the upper switchbacks is popular for ski-resort-deprived locals. The parking area is plowed and has a toilet. Given dry roads, the drive from Moab takes forty minutes.

Description: From the parking area, take Geyser Pass Road to Gold Basin Road and follow it back to the southeast. Or you can take a shortcut by leaving the Geyser Road after about 0.5 mile where it crosses a gully and makes a sharp left turn. Climb up the fall line through evergreens from here, or any previous point along the road that looks reasonable, and you'll intercept Gold Basin Road. Short runs in these semispaced old-growth Engelmann spruce can be made, especially from point 10,235 on the southwest end of the woods. From this high point, it's also possible to ski a corn-snow meadow facing west-southwest back to the highest 180-degree bend in Geyser Pass Road.

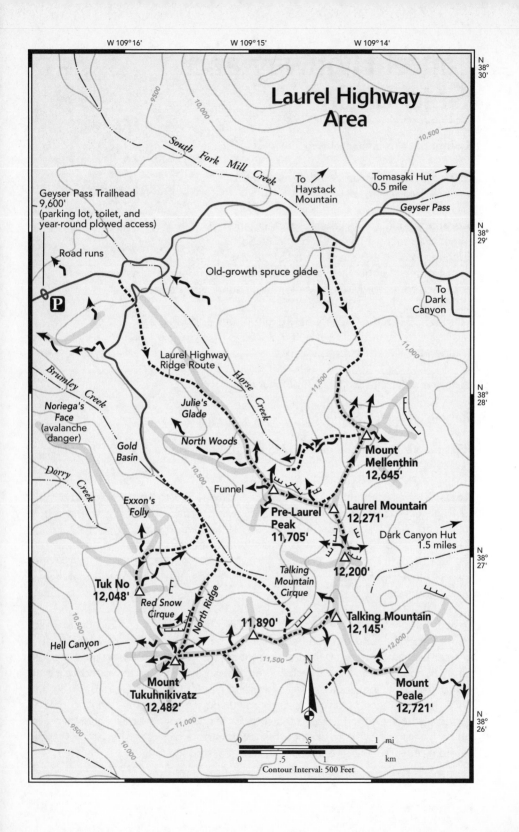

Pre-Laurel Peak (left), Laurel Highway (left), Gold Basin (center), and Tukuhniki-vatz (right); west view.

The route to Laurel Ridge (locally known as the Laurel Highway) crosses (or leaves) Gold Basin Road above the spruce glade and continues in similar terrain and foliage. For Gold Basin tours, it's perhaps quicker to follow the road directly into the basin, but if your destination is high in the basin, it's safer and more fun to climb Laurel Highway and ski in from Pre-Laurel Peak. Gold Basin Road makes a fine cross-country ski tour for waxed or scaled skis. Make a rising traverse south above the road and cross a series of southwest-facing meadows that offer spectacular views of the Tukuhnikivatz peaks and Gold Basin. These meadows are also good skiing in their own right and can be skied down to the road for a short, moderate run.

Laurel Highway narrows above the meadows, and the route is on the edge of the steep woods falling northwest into Horse Creek. These woods are pretty tight and avalanche-prone due to their steepness, although higher up the angle becomes more reasonable until finally an avalanche chute cuts through. This is a nice run, when it's stable. Above here, Laurel Highway breaks out of the trees, and many a seasoned ski tourer has become disoriented along the wide, rounded ridge during whiteouts.

At 11,400 feet, good, intermediate powder-type runs drop northwest in the North Woods and Julie's Glade. Although not immune to the La Sal snowpack problems, these woods are well anchored and have a relatively shallow angle. The drop is 1,400 feet to Gold Basin Road and Brumley Creek.

Three hundred feet higher the ridge flattens out; a weather station is situated at a high point known as Pre-Laurel Peak. Good skiing options from here include southwest into the Funnel, southeast into upper Gold Basin, and northeast into Horse Creek. The Funnel is wide and open at the top but becomes a narrow, yet skier-friendly, gully below. It ranges from west through south in aspect and falls for 1,600 feet to Gold Basin Road and the base of many long runs from Tukuhnikivatz (Tuk) and Tuk No (the northern satellite summit).

The southeast drop off Pre-Laurel, known as Goldminer's, is wide open and moderately steep. It provides an excellent 900-foot run into the glorious upper cirques of Gold Basin. The north face of Laurel Ridge is more aggressive terrain. The runs are up to 45 degrees in steepness, but the breakovers of that angle are partway down, making ski cuts ineffective for avalanche testing. You must be confident of both your skiing ability and the snow stability to ski this side.

The most benign ski route into upper Horse Creek is from the saddle just east of Pre-Laurel's weather station. Look for wind-eroded snow that may be described as "pressed" powder—but be alert for wind slabs. Back toward the Pre-Laurel weather station and below it, the shots are steeper, with cliff bands in the middle. A good chute falls directly from the station, but after 200 feet you must traverse slightly skier's right to avoid rocks. Any of these shots into upper Horse Creek provide an efficient approach to Mount Mellenthin's south face.

Farther up Laurel Highway are gully runs off Laurel Mountain and its west shoulder, wrapping either side of a cliff. The very summit of Laurel, 12,271 feet, is often wind scoured on the west down to the gray diorite talus. The proud line on Laurel is the northeast face, however, which falls steeply and unbroken for 1,000-plus feet into upper Dark Canyon. Ski mountaineers bound for Mellenthin or Peale can traverse below the summit of Laurel on either the west or south, since both are only moderately steep faces and usually hold little snow. Mellenthin is described in detail in Tour 49, Mount Mellenthin.

Mount Peale, the highest point in the La Sals, unfortunately has relatively little snow (due to its lee position east of the La Sal divide), hard access, and many cliff bands. The best run is the east face, and skiers do reach it from Laurel Highway when ridge travel is fast and stable. This shot is about 2,700 feet long, and it's better accessed from the La Sal Pass area on the southeast side of the range. The Beaver Lake Hut makes a good base camp for the early start necessary to ski corn on the south and east aspects (see Tour 51, La Sal Pass Area). Peale's north face is excellent skiing for 1,200 feet, but then a sizable cliff band blocks all passage, except for one ribbon of snow on the far east in certain conditions.

Returning from Laurel Highway tours is as user-friendly as the approach. From Horse Creek, simply follow the drainage to Geyser Pass Road and go left. Gold Basin Road is also easy to find and follow, but unfortunately it includes a lengthy section of flats, where many people elect to skin up on the way home. In some wintry cases this can be avoided by staying low along Brumley Creek down to a four-wheel-drive road at 9,200 feet, just below a cliff on the north. Contour out of the canyon back to the Geyser Pass Road switchbacks, well below the parking lot, and hitchhike back up.

Mount Tukuhnikivatz

See map on page 190.

Rating: Moderate to difficult.

Gear: Skis or split-board with skins; ice ax and crampons in spring.

Summary: The signature La Sal ski peak, Tuk's southwest couloir(s) feature a mind-boggling 3,500 feet of steep fall-line skiing. The north ridge is a classic alpine climb, and steep chutes and moderate basins form four major skiable cirques in Gold Basin.

Tour 48

Map: USGS 7.5-minute Mounts Tukuhnikivatz and Peale.

Trailheads: Geyser Pass snow park; La Sal Pass Road; Hell Canyon Road.

Distance: 3 miles to the summit from Geyser Pass snow park; 1.5 miles from La Sal Pass; 1–2 miles from Hell Canyon.

Starting altitude: Geyser Pass, 9,600 feet; La Sal Pass Road, 7,000 to 9,000 feet; Hell Canyon Road, 8,000 to 9,000 feet.

High points: Pre-Laurel Peak, 11,705 feet; Tuk No, 12,048 feet; Mount Tukuhnikivatz, 12,482 feet; Talking Mountain, 12,145 feet.

Access: Drive south out of Moab on U.S. Highway 191 to the well-signed turnoff to Ken's Lake and La Sal Loop Road. The loop road splits right within a few miles and climbs above the Moab Valley to a junction with Geyser Pass Road. Turn right onto a switchbacking gravel two-wheel-drive road and ascend to the plowed trailhead at 9,600 feet.

Another option is to approach from or leave a car (or bike) in Hell Canyon below the southwest chutes. Take Pack Creek Road (south) off La Sal Loop Road before any switchbacks. Drive 3 miles to the picnic area and find a four-wheel-drive road into Hell Canyon. It's unmarked, begins at a parking area and drops immediately down to cross Pack Creek. It climbs into upper Hell Canyon and usually becomes snow covered at 8,700 feet, where it crosses Hell Creek at an abandoned mine. Leave a vehicle here for the south chute or, for the southwest or west line, park 0.5 mile west of here at the unmarked Dorry Creek Trailhead (the last creek before a long dry traverse into the bottom of Hell Canyon). The chutes can be climbed directly from Hell Canyon.

Yet another approach is over La Sal Pass from the Beaver Lake Hut.

South and west aspects, Mount Tukuhnikivatz. Hell Canyon–La Sal Pass Road at base; Mount Mellenthin behind left; southwest view.

Description: The most efficient approach for the southwest chutes is probably from Hell Canyon, but if you want to do some skiing in the Gold Basin or on Tuk No, the northwest satellite peak of Tukuhnikivatz, Geyser Pass is closer. Some skiers even do a car shuttle from Geyser Pass to Hell Canyon. The best approach for the south face is from the east over La Sal Pass.

From Geyser Pass, a good option is to climb Laurel Highway and ski the southeast (Goldminer's) shot off Pre-Laurel Peak to reach upper Gold Basin and the north ridge of Tuk. Otherwise, reach Gold Basin Road by cutting east through the woods 0.5 mile above the Geyser Pass parking lot. Follow the road into Gold Basin. Some like to cut off the first switchback by heading due east where the road bends south in a saddle and meadow at 10,100 feet.

Directly in front of you as you contour into Gold Basin is a slide path falling north off Tuk No called Exxon's Folly, because Exxon drilled for oil at its base in the late 1970s. It's a clean shot (thanks to countless avalanches) and shouldn't be skied unless snow is stable.

The best access to Tuk No is via the northeast ridge, which can be gained from just above the drill site and the end of the road. The initial trees are pretty steep; it may be easier to climb slightly past the ridge and switchback to it. The northeast face of Tuk No is perhaps the most aesthetic line in the entire La Sal Range. An absolutely perfect chute, delineated by parallel rock ribs, falls from the exact summit and continues fall line for 1,500 feet. At the top it's wide enough for one set of tracks only. The east face is also skiable into the Red Snow Cirque, but it breaks over to 50 degrees in the middle where it passes through cliffs.

From Gold Basin Mount Tukuhnikivatz is best climbed by its north ridge, which frames Red Snow Cirque on the east. Desert sand often blows onto this face through the pass between Tuk and Tuk No, hence the name. I once skied it in alpenglow at 7:00 P.M., at which time the snow also had a red hue, but not from sand. The narrow north ridge of Tuk is an alpinist's dream, flanked by what I call the "Makalu" cliffs on the west. The ridge protrudes enough to be avalanche-safe until 12,000 feet, where it becomes less sharp. Assess avalanche stability as you go.

The Red Snow Cirque, between Tuk and Tuk No, is steeper than 50 degrees in the middle where it's cut by the cliffs. Ski from the summit to just above these cliffs, then traverse left to ski the west face into Hell Canyon. Another option would be to climb to Tuk No after traversing left from upper Red Snow Cirque. In a huge-snow year, or with a little bit of "air" or a rope, you could undoubtedly find a way through the cliffs to make a 2,100-foot run in the cirque. It's usually feasible to end-run the cliffs on the west.

The northeast face of Tuk is free of cliffs and angled at 40 degrees off the top, gradually easing as it descends for 2,000 feet through Tuk Cirque and finally into upper Gold Basin. An unnamed ridge east of Tuk separates Tuk Cirque from Talking Mountain Cirque. This ridge features some well-protected powder skiing, including the Cleaver Couloirs, a pair of narrow, classic ski lines enclosed between spectacular rock cleavers.

Talking Mountain is the locals' name for point 12,145 between Tuk and Peale. El Pinche is the couloir dropping northwest from the summit into upper Gold Basin. Otherwise, there is more moderate skiing from the pass just west of the summit. This, however, is the site of a fatal avalanche accident in the early 1990s. Three experienced skiers, including the National Forest avalanche forecaster for the La Sal Mountains, were buried by a massive slab avalanche while approaching this pass. Beware the depth-hoar snowpack!

North of Talking Mountain is the Laurel Cirque, below Laurel Mountain. A classic couloir falls west of point 12,200, Talking Laurel Peak, cutting through a rock band and into the cirque. A matching shot splits cliffs on the east side into Dark Canyon. Talking Mountain also has skiing on its south aspect toward La Sal Pass. A well-defined gulch goes almost due south (see Tour 51, La Sal Pass Area).

From La Sal Pass, approach Mount Tukuhnikivatz via point 11,841, a buttress east and south of the summit. It has a superb corn run on its triangular southeast face, which rises from just east of the pass. Climb it and continue over

Dave Medara skiing above the Moab Desert, north group, La Sal Mountains.

the buttress to the east ridge of Tuk. It's often easier to boot (or crampon) than skin along the slightly exposed cockscomb that leads to the summit.

The southeast face of Tuk drops for 2,500 feet to La Sal Pass Road just 0.5 mile west of the pass. But this is small potatoes compared to the three distinct lines going south and west off the mighty Tuk, each named for the degree it faces on the compass. First is 210 degrees (3,200 feet). It jogs slightly skier's left after the top and then goes fall-line forever to a convenient four-wheel-drive spur off Hell Canyon–La Sal Pass Road. Simply follow the road back over the pass if you've come from the east. Go west and down if your vehicle is in Hell Canyon, but for this particular line, the pass approach is more efficient.

The next line to the west is the longest fall line and is very prominent from Moab and points south along US 191. It faces 260 degrees and goes fall-line to 8,800 feet, but the better finish is to cut skier's right (west) at the bottom of the final avalanche chute (9,700 feet) to find another snowy apron going slightly north of west to the Dorry Canyon pack trail.

The west face (actually 300 degrees) can be skied from the top (if it's not wind scoured) or from the Red Snow Cirque headwall. It drops cleanly into a narrow avalanche chute. Where this gully terminates in a thicket of avalanche-smashed aspens, traverse west to open meadows and finish on the Dorry Canyon pack trail to a stashed car at Hell Canyon.

From Hell Canyon, simply follow the old four-wheel-drive road as it switch-backs south of the hellish ravine and then follows the creek to La Sal Pass. Climb Tuk from the pass as described above. Of course, it's also possible to boot straight up one of the southwest couloirs, 210 degrees being the most feasible. A branch of the road leads directly to its base.

Mount Mellenthin

See map on page 190.

Rating: Moderate to difficult.

Gear: Skis or split-board with skins; ice ax and crampons in spring.

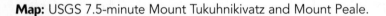

Summary: The easiest major peak in the La Sals to reach and to ski, Mount Mellenthin's north face is truly a classic line; the southwest face isn't bad either in a good snow year. The lower west slopes offer easily accessed, low-angle terrain for short, safe outings.

Map: USGS 7.5-minute Mount Tukuhnikivatz and Mount Peale.

Trailhead: Geyser Pass snow park.

Distance: 4 miles to the summit via Geyser Pass; 3 miles via Laurel Highway or Horse Creek.

Starting altitude: 9,600 feet.

High point: Mount Mellenthin, 12,645 feet.

Access: Drive south out of Moab on U.S. Highway 191 to the well-signed turnoff to Ken's Lake and La Sal Loop Road. The loop road splits right within a few miles and climbs above the Moab Valley to a junction with Geyser Pass Road. Turn right onto a switchbacking gravel two-wheel-drive road. In late spring it may be possible to drive all the way to Geyser Pass and still find skiable snow on the north face of Mellenthin.

Description: From the parking area, follow Geyser Pass Road east-northeast for about 3 miles to the pass. Alternatively, it may save time to leave the road at a switchback in a gully at 10,300 feet, about 0.5 mile below the pass. In either case, travel south-southeast up the fall line toward the north ridge of Mellenthin. The moss-draped giant Engelmann spruce forest gives way to open talus fields at 11,000 feet. Gain the prominent north ridge and follow it to the summit. From Tomasaki Hut, simply skin up the Forest Service spur road leading to the hut from Geyser Pass, and then proceed up to the north ridge.

In very stable avalanche conditions, a more direct approach can be made up the west or southwest face. The base of the southwest face can be reached from Pre-Laurel Peak and its north-facing chute; a faster approach would be straight up Horse Creek. Crampons may be useful on the supportable (hopefully) snow of the southwest face. It's really a pair of gullies linked by a bowl in which the climber must traverse right. I skied this line at midday on a cool, breezy April day, then returned to the summit in my existing track and skied the north face.

Yet another approach is to follow Laurel Highway past the weather station and over Laurel Mountain. Either ski the northeast face and climb back to the saddle between Laurel and Mellenthin, or descend directly to the saddle. Climb the south ridge, staying west to avoid the cliffy southeast aspect.

The north face of Mellenthin is a broad squarish face, obviously designed with skiers in mind. It's split into a series of separate "lanes" between slightly protruding rock lines (unless these are all covered, as they were in April 2001). All runs lead to the rolling moraines 1,200 feet below. The upper 500 feet of skiing is an invigorating 40 to 45 degrees in steepness. The east side of Mellenthin is mostly bisected by cliff bands, although there's one route into Dark Canyon due east. This is a ribbon of snow that cuts between rock bands at 11,600 feet.

The west flanks of Mellenthin harbor some avalanche-safe winter powder terrain, although it's all low angle. It can also be nice for a mellow afternoon corn tour. Leave Geyser Pass Road at an obvious meadow just 300 yards north of Gold Basin Road. Ascend to 11,000 feet through woods interspersed with open glades. Ski back along the approach trail, or drop north and find another nice open shot dropping northwest. Yet another shot falls due north in a shallow gully to intersect Geyser Pass Road at 10,000 feet where the Haystack approach takes off to the north. If you're returning to the Geyser Pass Trailhead, simply kick, glide, and herringbone your way down (and up) the undulating road.

Corkscrew Glades

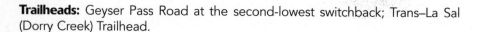

Rating: Easy to moderate.

Gear: Skis or split-board and skins.

Summary: Enjoy a short approach (especially from Moab) to this low-altitude, midwinter powder-oriented tour. Tree and meadow skiing with *relatively* low avalanche hazard is available here, possibly as a half-day outing.

Tour 50

Map: USGS 7.5-minute Mount Tukuhnikivatz.

Trailheads: Geyser Pass Road at the second-lowest switchback; Trans–La Sal (Dorry Creek) Trailhead.

Distance: 2 miles to point 10,974.

Starting altitude: 9,000 feet.

High points: Noriegas Peak, 10,597 feet; unnamed point, 10,974 feet.

Access: Drive south out of Moab on U.S. Highway 191 to the well-signed turnoff to Ken's Lake and La Sal Loop Road. The loop road splits right within a few miles and climbs above the Moab Valley to a junction with Geyser Pass Road. Turn right onto a switchbacking gravel two-wheel-drive road. Park at the first switchback (it's a 180-degree bend) on the south.

Description: Drop slightly and contour into Brumley Canyon. Cross the creek at about 8,800 feet, then contour out of the narrow canyon bottom. All this can be done on the Trans–La Sal summer pack trail—which may not be visible under good snow coverage. The skiing is on two blunt ridges falling from the Tuk No massif. For the low-angle shots off Noriegas Peak (10,597 feet), start skinning up the fall line immediately. The terrain steepens gradually; return runs can be made at any point. The triangular west-facing glade narrows down and becomes unvegetated above 10,300 feet. Dropping north off Peak 10,597 is the open, convex Noriegas Face (ugly to an avalanche forecaster's eye). This "facet garden" talus field has been the site of huge avalanches and is not recommended.

The steeper, longer, and more avalanche-prone forest south of Dorry Creek and directly northwest of Tuk No is the Corkscrew Glades—a series of circular meadows that line the south edge of the northwest-facing, 1,000-foot

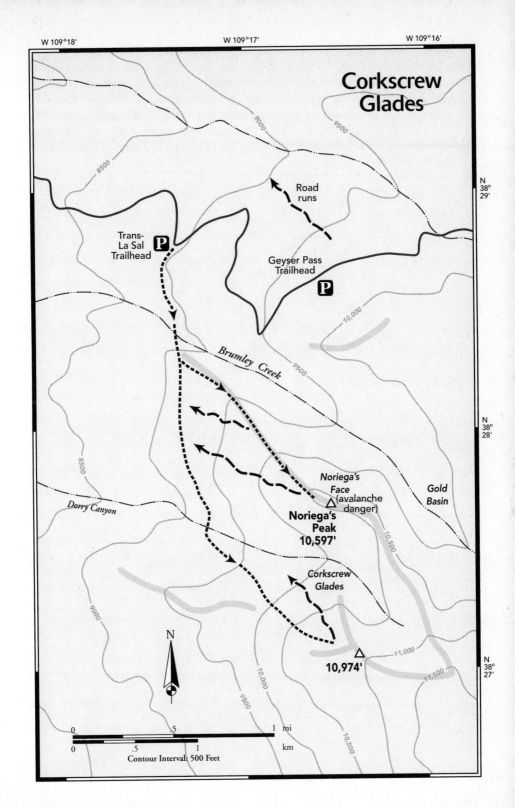

Corkscrew Glades

W 109°18' W 109°17' W 109°16'

N 38° 29'

N 38° 28'

N 38° 27'

Road runs

Trans-La Sal Trailhead

P

Geyser Pass Trailhead

P

Brumley Creek

Noriega's Face (avalanche danger)

Noriega's Peak 10,597'

Dorry Canyon

Corkscrew Glades

Gold Basin

10,974'

N

0 .5 1 mi

0 .5 1 km

Contour Interval: 500 Feet

slope. They are a good bet for powder, although La Sal winds can damage even the most protected spots. Simply contour at a slightly rising incline to the southeast and cross Dorry Creek. Climb above some meadows and switchback up through the woods to a forested, flat crest above 10,900 feet. Ski back along the track or anywhere in the glade. The west- and southwest-facing shots are steeper, especially down low, but just after storms they can also have good snow. Due north from point 10,974 isn't recommended: It's steep and avalanche-prone.

La Sal Pass Area

Rating: Easy to difficult.

Gear: Skis or split-board with skins.

Summary: La Sal Pass is the gateway to three major ski-mountaineering peaks, including Mount Tukuhnikivatz, with its truly epic southwest chutes; Mount Peale, the highest La Sal summit; and South Mountain—oddly enough, the snowiest peak in the La Sals. Beaver Lake Hut is located east of the pass near good terrain for low-angle corn runs and winter powder tours.

Tour 51

Map: USGS 7.5-minute Mount Tukuhnikivatz and Mount Peale.

Trailhead: La Sal Pass Road, as high as you can drive.

Distance: South Mountain, 5 to 6 miles; Mount Peale, 4 to 5 miles.

Starting altitude: 7,000 to 9,000 feet.

High points: Unnamed point, 11,124 feet; unnamed point, 11,290 feet; South Mountain, 11,817 feet; Mount Tukuhnikivatz, 12,482 feet; Mount Peale 12,721 feet.

Access: Drive south out of Moab on U.S. Highway 191 to La Sal Junction and head east on Utah State Highway 46 toward Colorado. Once you're 3.5 miles past the town of La Sal, turn left onto Twomile Road toward La Sal Pass, Dark Canyon Lake, and Buckeye Reservoir. Either go left again on La Sal Pass Road after 1.5 miles and drive as high as you can get toward the pass (the crux is a four-wheel-drive creek ford), or continue for another 3.5 miles and turn left onto Forest Road 129 for another 3.5 miles to the Dark Canyon/Beaver Lake Trailhead, where plowing typically ends. It's possible to hire a snowcat shuttle for gear to Beaver Lake Hut from this trailhead.

Description: Your approach will vary a little, depending upon how high you can drive. In midwinter a popular area is the South Mountain Glades—forested, northeast-facing slopes below point 11,124, which is an unnamed summit east of South Mountain above La Sal Creek. These glades can be reached from La Sal Pass Road by picking a route along La Sal Creek after the road crosses it at about 8,250 feet. A 600-foot slide path crosses the creek at 8,600 feet; skirt this to the north, then cross the creek at 8,800 feet and climb west past point 9,574,

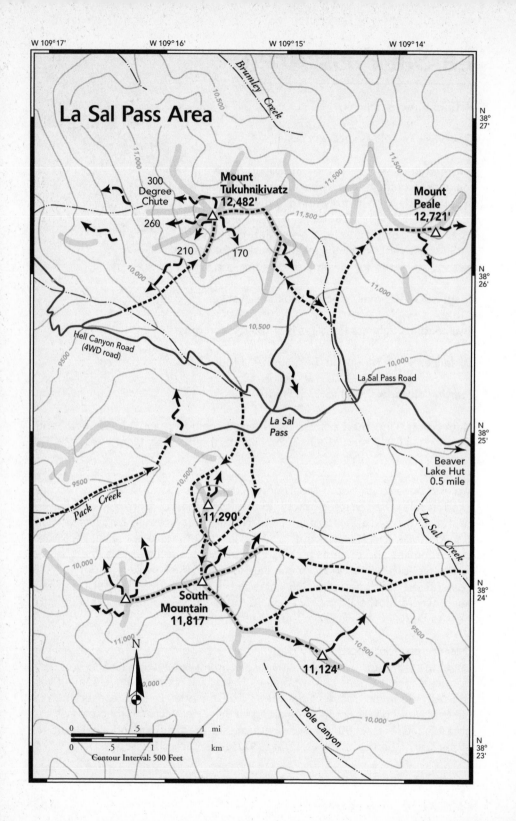

La Sal Pass Area

300 Degree Chute

260

210   170

Mount Tukuhnikivatz
12,482'

Mount Peale
12,721'

10,500

11,000

11,500

11,500

11,500

11,000

10,500

10,000

Hell Canyon Road
(4WD road)

9500

La Sal Pass Road

La Sal Pass

Beaver Lake Hut
0.5 mile

9500

Pack Creek

La Sal Creek

10,500

11,290'

10,000

9500

South Mountain
11,817'

10,500

11,124'

N

11,000

10,000

10,000

Pole Canyon

0   .5   1 mi
0   .5   km

Contour Interval: 500 Feet

W 109°17'   W 109°16'   W 109°15'   W 109°14'

N 38°27'

N 38°26'

N 38°25'

N 38°24'

N 38°23'

Brumley Creek

a small buttress in the woods, and then south through glades to the summit. Many drops of 2,000 feet can be earned on this subpeak of South Mountain, but you may prefer to yo-yo the open meadows with the best snow and least avalanche potential. These meadows are directly north of point 11,124 and can be reached from the Beaver Lake Hut by skiing a short shot due south to La Sal Creek and then ascending from 8,800 feet as described above.

Another popular area for powder seekers when a moderate avalanche potential exists is off the north and west aspects of South Mountain's north buttress, Point 11,290, but don't put too much stock in the generally dense forest—avalanches run here, too. Ascend to La Sal Pass along the summer road, then take a spur road southwest along the northern base of the peak. Switchback south through the woods from this road to the summit, staying west of a steep, open slide path near the summit. The north face of point 11,290 is about a 1,000-foot drop, and the west aspect falls for 1,700 feet. After skiing west, climb along Pack Creek east and north until you reach a low-angle south-facing meadow. Climb this to the saddle east of point 10,398 and the road back to La Sal Pass. From the north face, just intercept the road and return on the approach route.

Climbing South Mountain from the east is safest via the southeast ridge. It rises from the pass west of point 11,124, the winter powder stash. The north-east ridge is a more rugged and direct alternative, and it accesses the J-chute, an initially steep, 700-foot north-facing gully that may warrant a run before continuing up. It's one of the few places in the area where a well-placed ski cut can actually clean out instability in a run. The prize line on South Mountain is the northeast basin, a 1,300-foot run of 30 to 45 degrees falling directly from the (often corniced) summit. It holds perhaps the deepest snow in the entire La Sal Range (an indication of greater strength), but it could be highly avalanche-prone after a southwest wind or new snow.

On a day when the northeast basin is *stable,* it may be much easier to skin directly up it, as I did during a long April high-pressure period. Slightly north and lower than the main summit are several imposing chutes, falling almost due north from a rocky buttress. Although shorter than the main shot, they're steeper and perhaps more aesthetic. They end up in the vast northeast basin as well. If skiing these chutes is your goal, a faster approach would be from La Sal Pass, either right over the top of point 11,290 (which involves an undulation of 200 feet) or by making a rising traverse around the west side of point 11,290 and hitting the South Mountain summit ridge at the pass (11,078 feet). Do not attempt to traverse around point 11,290 below the summit on the east: It becomes very steep and cliffy.

The view south from South Mountain's summit is a desert lover's dream. Red bluffs and tan petrified dunes stretch to the Abajo Mountains near Monticello. Looking east, you may see the huge San Juan Range of southwestern Colorado, with Lone Cone standing sentinel before it. The vast Canyonlands is on the west. To the north is the south aspect of the middle group.

Skiing northwest off the summit is often impossible due to wind-scoured rock bands. Drop down along the summit ridge toward the west summit, however, and good ski lines beckon. The cleanest is the main north shot, a 2,000-foot deforested slide path to Pack Creek. Ski northwest from the same summit and you'll encounter steep avalanche gullies—the Crow's Feet—that eventually converge into one deeply gouged erosion gully. It's a 2,700-foot run to Pack Creek. To return, simply skin east along the base of South Mountain following Pack Creek as described for the west face of point 11,290.

Mount Tukuhnikivatz from La Sal Pass is a reasonable objective, especially if your goal is to ski southeast or southwest (210 degrees) from the peak into upper Hell Canyon (see Tour 48, Mount Tukuhnikivatz). The west shots (260 and 300 degrees) make more efficient ways to ski back to a vehicle on Pack Creek Road.

Mount Peale is the granddaddy of La Sal peaks, but in terms of snowfall it languishes in the shadow of Tuk and South Mountain. The cleanest and longest ski lines are on the east and southeast and can sometimes be skied for 3,300 feet, right to the Beaver Lake Hut. Both runs start off moderately steep, then break over in classic La Sal fashion for a stimulating 1,000 feet before backing off into aprons. The approach of choice is to angle northwest from the hut along the La Sal Pass summer road until a short branch of it goes north at 10,000 feet. Follow this route for 0.4 mile, then continue along a small creek drainage as it bends east and rises steeply. Where the creekbed becomes a gully above timberline and falls more from the north, leave it and continue climbing northeast to the summit ridge. Follow it for 0.25 mile to the summit.

Excellent low-angle corn-snow terrain is abundant in the meadows below 11,000 feet along the route to Mount Peale. Another great gentle meadow sits above La Sal Pass Road just west of the Peale cutoff above Medicine Lakes. From the top of this meadow, another open run falls southwest into Hell Canyon. For 0.5 mile in every direction around La Sal Pass is safe, low-angle terrain ideal for cross-country or beginner telemark skiing.

Geyser Pass and Mount Tomasaki

Tour 52

Rating: Easy to difficult.

Gear: Skis or split-board with skins; scaled or waxed skis are effective to the hut and environs. You'll want an ice ax and crampons for climbing the high peaks in firm spring conditions.

Summary: Despite its location in a flat meadow, the Tomasaki Hut offers great access to both the north and middle La Sal groups. Beginner meadows surround the structure, and intermediate powder terrain exists in Tomasaki Basin and around the flanks of Mount Mellenthin. In corn season this is the ideal starting point for ascents of Tomasaki, Haystack, Manns, and Mellenthin. Route descriptions here are valid regardless of whether you're using the Tomasaki Hut or coming from Geyser Pass.

Maps: USGS 7.5-minute Mount Waas, Mount Tukuhnikivatz and Mount Peale.

Trailhead: Geyser Pass snow park.

Distance: 4 miles to the hut; from there, it's 1 mile to Mount Tomasaki, 2 miles to Manns, and 2.5 miles to Haystack or Mellenthin.

Starting altitude: 9,600 feet.

High points: Haystack Mountain, 11,640 feet; Mount Tomasaki, 12,239 feet; Manns Peak, 12,272 feet; Mount Mellenthin, 12,645 feet.

Access: Drive south out of Moab on U.S. Highway 191, turning east onto the well-signed La Sal Loop Road. The loop road splits right within a few miles and climbs above the Moab Valley to a junction with Geyser Pass Road. Turn right onto a switchbacking gravel two-wheel-drive road with wicked washboards and follow it to its terminus.

Description: From the parking area, follow the undulating Geyser Pass Road east-northeast for about 3 miles to the pass at 10,500 feet. Take off your skins here and kick and glide on the left fork of the road marked FOREST SERVICE BOUNDARY 2 MILES. Stay right at the next fork and glide gently downhill through the woods. Continue on flat terrain into a huge meadow. Look for the hut at 10,000 feet after reentering sparse woods on the east end.

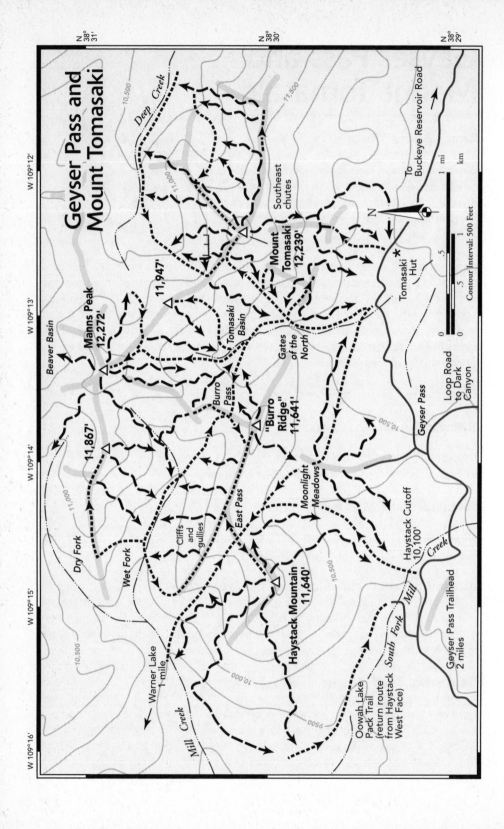

Geyser Pass and Mount Tomasaki

If the hulking blob of Haystack Mountain (and its awesome north bowl) is your goal, and you aren't visiting the hut, cut off from Geyser Pass Road at 10,120 feet where it makes a sharp turn to the south. The toe of Moonlight Meadows, below Haystack's southeast flanks, is visible here, as is the peak. Climb these meadows to the pass east of Haystack, staying well east of the runout zone for potential avalanches off Haystack's southeast face.

From the hut, head west and slightly north along the base of an unnamed ridge to the north; I call it "Burro Ridge" for the pass on its north side. A very gradual climb leads to a 10,800-foot saddle. Stay skier's right above this and be careful of the avalanche potential as you cross above Moonlight Meadows to the obvious pass east of Haystack Mountain. These low-angle slopes will be your return route but can also be the goal in themselves, especially if the high peaks are unsafe or unappealing due to weather.

From the pass between Haystack and Burro Ridge, there's no entirely avalanche-safe route to the summit. Conditions must be stable to ascend the broad, convex east flank above the pass. After 200 feet, however, the angle decreases; a mellow cruise along the gentle summit ridge offers incredible views of Castle Valley, Moab, slickrock trails, and beyond.

The proud line off Haystack's 11,640-foot summit is the north face, a half-mile-wide bowl dropping at 35 degrees for 1,000-plus feet. This is decidedly avalanche-prone terrain. The return to the east pass is easy. Just skin up the sparsely treed, shallow gully feature northeast of the bowl. Ski back along the ascent route to the hut or down the Moonlight Meadows to Geyser Pass Road.

Mount Tomasaki, 12,239 feet, is one of the steeper of the major La Sal summits, especially on its north face. It's easily accessible from the hut to its south, but from the Geyser Pass Trailhead it's a 5-mile slog. From the trailhead, proceed toward the hut as described above, but leave the Forest Service road 0.5 mile west of the hut and head north toward the Gates of the North—the narrow entrance into Tomasaki Basin.

After passing the canyon entrance, begin climbing east onto the steep west aspect of Tomasaki. Stay in the timber if an avalanche hazard is present or if you're looking for powder skiing on the west flank. Otherwise, it's very efficient to climb directly up the west gully of Tomasaki. Before 10:00 A.M. this is a safe and shady approach, possibly warranting the use of crampons. This is also an excellent corn-snow run after the sun softens it, but the area doesn't usually hold snow up high due to its sun- and wind-affected southwest exposure.

Climb to the 11,600-foot saddle northwest of Tomasaki and follow the northwest ridge to the summit. The talus here isn't terribly steep or loose, but if snow is your preferred medium, wrap around to the northeast side of the ridge where a ribbon of it is usually found. The summit itself is large and flat, but the north face drops at 40 degrees and breaks over to 45 degrees as cliffs develop. To ski through the rock bands, stay skier's right and enter a couloir at 11,500 feet. The pitch soon moderates as the aprons of upper Deep Creek Basin are reached. Escape this basin by climbing west to the Tomasaki saddle. This is open country with avalanche potential. Alternatively, ski the north face

Haystack Mountain (right) flanked by Burro Ridge and Pass. Mount Mellenthin is behind with Geyser Pass in between; northwest view.

to above the cliffs at 11,500 feet, cut skier's left back to the approach saddle, and return down the west basin to the gates.

Another good ski line off Tomasaki is the east-northeast face, which falls at a 35-degree angle for 1,500 feet before entering trees and continuing to Deep Creek. A pair of fine snow ribbons fall from the peak 0.75 mile east of Tomasaki into the same canyon. It's advisable to return to the summit after skiing these lines via the northeast or east ridge of Tomasaki, since Deep Creek leads east away from access roads.

The most continuously steep shot, and a direct return to the hut, is via the southeast couloirs. Three snow-filled gullies drop from Tomasaki and just east of the summit for 2,000 feet at 35 to 40 degrees. Ski all the way to the flats and skate west to the hut, or traverse skier's right at 10,800 feet through a small col north of a forested knob, then drop south again directly to the hut.

Manns Peak, 12,272 feet, stands at the north end of Tomasaki Basin, directly north of Burro Pass. The moderately steep south aspect provides straightforward access and a great return run, especially in corn conditions. Simply stick close to the creek as it flows from the west and later the north directly from Manns Peak. The northeast and northwest faces of Manns are amazing drops into Beaver Basin and the Dry Fork of Mill Creek, respectively, but these runs will be discussed in Tour 53, North Group, La Sals.

The southwest line off Manns falls into the Wet Fork of Mill Creek from just northwest of the true summit. It's a steeper line than the south (maybe 30 degrees) but still moderate. Return to Tomasaki Basin and the hut or Geyser Pass by climbing along the summer pack trail up to Burro Pass. Stay north along the creek, away from the steep, highly avalanche-prone north face of Burro Ridge.

Finally, the southeast drop off Manns is a fine line going at 30 to 35 degrees for 800 feet. Ski it into Deep Creek Basin and return to Tomasaki Pass as described above, or traverse skier's right after 500 feet and come back into Tomasaki Basin via the saddle south of Manns and north of point 11,947.

Mount Mellenthin, 12,645 feet, is the second highest in the La Sals, and its north face is an outstanding run. See Tour 49, Mount Mellenthin, for details on skiing it from Geyser Pass or the Tomasaki Hut.

Tomasaki Basin is a good place to poke around on stormy or avalanche-prone days. The upper reaches of the Wet Fork of Mill Creek also offer protected, avalanche-safe terrain. Burro Pass itself is dangerous to cross when snow stability is iffy, because of its proximity to the very steep north face of Burro Ridge, the long east–west ridge feature south of the pass. In stable conditions the short chutes east of the pass and the longer ones to the west offer 40- to 50-degree skiing.

Other good stashes near the cabin are on the three wooded knolls below the south face of Tomasaki. In particular, the one that forms the eastern pillar of the Gates of the North has good, protected northerly facing drops of up to 500 feet. The other two more easterly knolls have mostly south-facing terrain, but it's wooded and well anchored.

North Group, La Sals

Tour 53

Rating: Difficult.

Gear: Skis or split-board and skins; ice ax and crampons in spring.

Summary: The huge, spectacular terrain of the north group sees only a fraction of the skiers the south and middle groups do because of its remoteness from trailheads, but a traverse of these impressive summits is a tremendous experience during stable weather and snow conditions. A solid melt-freeze crust is almost mandatory to allow easy travel over the great distances. One day is enough for a fit party to go from Geyser Pass to Willow Basin, but if you carry light camp gear, a day in Beaver or Miner's Basins could yield some rewarding skiing. These two canyons offer alternative access to (or egress from) the area.

Maps: USGS 7.5-minute Mount Waas, Warner Lake (for Miner's Basin).

Trailhead: Geyser Pass snow park; stash a vehicle for one-way traverse at Willow Basin or as high as possible on the four-wheel-drive approach roads to Beaver or Miner's Basins.

Distance: About 12 miles from Geyser Pass to Willow Basin (distance varies with alternate routes).

Starting altitude: 9,600 feet.

High points: Manns Peak, 12,272 feet; Mount Waas, 12,331 feet; unnamed point, 12,044 feet; Green Mountain, 12,163 feet; Castle Peak, 12,001 feet. (The vertical gain is 6,000 feet for the main highline route.)

Access: Drive south out of Moab on U.S. Highway 191 to the well-signed turnoff to Ken's Lake and La Sal Loop Road. The loop road splits right within a few miles and climbs above the Moab Valley to a junction with Geyser Pass Road. Turn right onto a switchbacking gravel two-wheel-drive road with wicked washboards and follow to its terminus at a plowed parking area (with a toilet).

Description: Follow Geyser Pass Road to the pass (3 miles of nearly flat track). Remove your skins and glide down the north-trending Forest Service spur road that leads to Tomasaki Hut. It's marked by a sign stating FOREST SERVICE BOUNDARY 2 MILES. Glide to a huge, open meadow and cross it to the north before

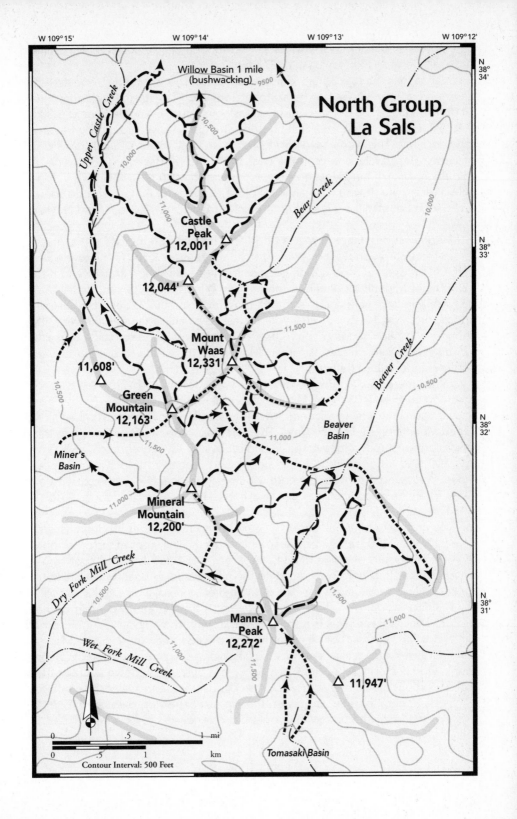

W 109°15'   W 109°14'   W 109°13'   W 109°12'

N 38°34'

Willow Basin 1 mile
(bushwacking)

Upper Castle Creek

Bear Creek

North Group,
La Sals

9500
10,500
10,000
11,000

Castle
Peak
12,001'

12,044'

Beaver Creek

10,000

N 38°33'

11,500

Mount
Waas
12,331'

11,608'

Green
Mountain
12,163'

10,500

Beaver
Basin

10,500

N 38°32'

Miner's
Basin

11,500

11,000

Mineral
Mountain
12,200'

11,000

Dry Fork Mill Creek

10,500

11,500

Manns
Peak
12,272'

N 38°31'

11,000

11,000

Wet Fork Mill Creek

11,500

11,947'

N

0   .5   1 mi
0   .5   1   km
Contour Interval: 500 Feet

Tomasaki Basin

putting your skins back on for the ascent up through the Gates of the North and Tomasaki Basin to Manns Peak, 12,272 feet.

Manns has fine ski lines on five aspects. The southerly aspects are described in Tour 52, Geyser Pass/Mount Tomasaki. The northeast is a beautiful drop starting at 35 degrees and decreasing gradually in angle over its 1,800 feet. Ski it all the way to the flats; do not attempt to save ground by traversing skier's left. This won't save effort or time and will mean midline traversing of some steep, avalanche-prone slopes. This is Beaver Basin, a giant drainage with many forks. It holds lots of snow and was studied in the 1970s as a potential ski resort site. It would be an ideal place to camp for a night and do some skiing, or it could make a fine alternate finish to the one-way tour from Geyser Pass.

Northwest off Manns is also a good line, and later in the day it may have firmer, more stable snow. It goes at 30 to 35 degrees for 1,100 feet into the Dry Fork of Mill Creek. Climb northeast back to the La Sal divide and ascend it to 12,200-foot Mineral Mountain at the head of Miner's Basin. Ski northeast into Beaver Basin from here and join the eastern traverse route as described below, or drop west into Miner's Basin if you've stashed a vehicle there. Otherwise, it's a long climb back out, and you're better off staying along the divide to point 12,163 (unofficially known as Green Mountain). It has fine drops north and northwest, described below.

Climb the upper northwest fork of Beaver Basin to its head, then ascend northeast to the 12,331-foot Mount Waas. Many other appealing ski lines in Beaver Basin may lure an adventurous skier, including those falling southeast off Green Mountain just west of Waas. The northeast drop off Waas goes into the lower northwest fork of Beaver Basin and drops at a 40-degree pitch for 800 of its 1,200 feet. It's a hard one to pass up, being probably the proudest line on Mount Waas, and the exit to the north would be reasonable over the col west of Waas. There's a good shot into Bear Basin from this pass, as well as from point 11,841 to the east.

The north line off Waas begins as a ridge and then falls at 30 degrees into Bear Basin for 1,100 feet. A northwest variation of the line stops at the pass north of Waas and south of point 12,044, which has a spectacular 2,200-foot semi-extreme shot off its northwest face into the headwaters of Castle Creek. Under stable avalanche conditions, it's one of the more impressive runs in the La Sals.

A similar run into Castle Creek drops north from Green Mountain at the head of Miner's Basin. This is a steep headwall with snow ribbons cutting past cliff bands for 1,000 feet of skiing in the 35- to 40-degree range. Green Mountain's northwest face is also a good steep shot, dropping into the head of Castle Creek. Descending Castle Creek can become a bushwhack down low, but the higher portions are usually snowy and free of bushes due to avalanche strafing. It may be easier, however, to stay on the high La Sal divide past point 12,044 and ski off the northernmost major peak on the divide, Castle Peak, 12,001 feet.

Climb this peak from Bear Basin via its often snow-free but moderately angled southwest ridge. The views of Castleton and Fisher Towers are unrivaled. Skiing options off the top are many. The northeast face drops for 2,000 feet before it becomes a forested gully. It holds plenty of snow. Other shots fall from the north end of Castle Peak's summit ridge. One great line falls northwest for 2,500 feet to Castle Creek. It's wind scoured and thin initially, but stay skier's left and it becomes more north facing and splits into several rock-lined gullies for 800 feet of 35- to 40-degree skiing. It then moderates and follows the narrowing canyon.

Another shot drops northeast off Castle Peak's north ridge. It divides at 11,200 feet. Continue down the fall line into a north-facing subdrainage and stay skier's right of the creek to enjoy open meadow skiing. This is probably the least avalanche-prone descent route off the north end of the La Sals. You can make a longer open shot, however, by traversing skier's left at 11,200 feet and making a few short drops to the northeast before regaining the high ground at 11,000 feet where another open face falls north. This line drops uninterrupted to 9,000 feet, making it a 3,000-foot run from Castle Peak.

From the base of all these drops, the skiing becomes sporadic at best. Look for open country, since the woods are generally dense. All the creeks lead to Willow Basin, so it's impossible to miss it. Just crash through the woods and keep an eye out for the rooftops of the private homes in the basin. From upper Castle Creek, the best exit route is to contour skier's right out of the creek bottom and find a series of meadows that lead down to 8,800 feet, where the going is undeniably a bushwhack. Alternatively, it may be possible in thin snow conditions to pick up the summer pack trail where it parallels Willow Creek above 9,600 feet. Unfortunately, it stays on the snowier northeast aspect as it drops west of the creek. It continues all the way to Castleton/Gateway Road at Bachelor Basin, 7,200 feet.

The preferred option for this traverse at 8,200 feet is to stash a vehicle in Willow Basin. Look for a well-maintained two-wheel-drive road taking off to the east from Castleton/Gateway Road at 7,500 feet. The main road makes a sharp bend to the north here. Climb steeply on this road and take the right-hand fork where a private home is located at 8,100 feet. This branch becomes a little rougher as it descends into a beautiful ponderosa meadow and climbs steeply out the other side. At this point, private property owners have gated the access. This is Willow Basin. Park at a pullout.

Other one-way traverse tours could finish at Miner's Basin west of the range or at Beaver Basin on the east. Miner's Basin Road (four-wheel-drive) climbs steeply east from La Sal Loop Road above Pinhook and Castle Valleys. The snow line is low here, and some winter powder seekers with a high tolerance for avalanche hazard come here for quick access to north-facing slide path runs. The headwaters of Pinhook Creek offer some outstanding west-facing skiing (as described above) off Green Mountain and the unnamed point 12,200.

Beaver Basin can be reached from the northeast via Don's Lake Road (Forest Road 669) off Castleton/Gateway Road, but the snow line is low and the approach is pretty long. Drive as far as possible on this muddy four-wheel-drive road.

VIII

Abajo Range
Treasure of Southeast Utah

Looking to escape the heat of Canyonlands in spring or dodge ski crowds on a powder day? Try a powder-oriented tour from the old Blue Mountain Ski Resort in winter or a north–south or east–west traverse of the Abajos in spring. Easy access, plenty of excellent terrain, and a complete lack of other skiers make this unknown range a winner. Situated in the southeast corner of Utah outside the agricultural community of Monticello is this compact, skier-friendly range also known as the Blue Mountains. Presumably this is because of the evergreen forests that make the peaks appear blue compared to the surrounding redrock desert terrain and barren gray-brown of the high La Sal Mountains to the north. These forests are predominantly composed of Engelmann spruce but also include Douglas and subalpine fir, ponderosa, piñon, limber pine, juniper, and cedar. Mule deer and wild turkeys are common in the Colorado Plateau country below the high peaks.

Geologically speaking, the Abajos are similar to the Henry, La Sal, and Navajo Peak Ranges. All are laccolith mountains, or frustrated volcanoes; that is, molten magma was forced up but did not reach the earth's surface. Instead, it pushed up other formations; later erosion left the intrusive rock exposed. The upshot is that these "island ranges" jut up impressively from the surrounding sea of red desert terrain. The views are truly amazing, especially from the peripheral summits such as South Peak.

The skiing here is mostly in the intermediate range of steepness (35 degrees and less) with little exposure to cliffs, but good avalanche assessment skills are necessary because there's no public information source about the Abajo snowpack, aside from what you can extrapolate from the La Sal Avalanche Forecast Center's information. Historical snowfall information is sketchy at best, but indications are that favored locations receive 200 to 300 inches of snow annually, creating a viable touring snowpack down to the 8,000- or 9,000-foot level by February and lasting through April in a normal year. The presence of four-wheel-drive roads climbing to the high peaks means that summer skiing may also be feasible in big-snow years.

Although spring corn-snow conditions are the safest and most user-friendly for traveling in the Abajos, much of the terrain is also conducive to midwinter powder tours, and the access is reasonable for this, especially at the old Blue Mountain Ski Resort and above the North Creek Road in North Canyon. The peaks are not as high or convex in shape as the La Sals, thus they're inherently less avalanche-prone. Add to this the presence of trees for anchors right to the highest summits, and the result is safer and more protected winter touring potential. Access, although lower in altitude than in the La Sals, is relatively short and easy from Monticello, where the altitude is already 7,000 feet.

Aside from the three primary trailheads outlined (North Canyon, old Blue Mountain Resort, and North Fork Verdure Canyon), several other feasible starting points exist. Most notably, Mount Linnaeus, the western high point of the range, can be approached from Gooseberry Road (Forest Road 095). It starts north out of Blanding as Johnson Creek or Abajo Loop Road. It's typically drivable by early spring to 8,500 feet in Allen Canyon on the west flank of Linnaeus. Jackson Ridge, which extends from Linnaeus east to Cooley Pass, offers ski shots all along but especially on the west end. Points 10,998 and 11,014, roughly 0.5 mile northeast of Linnaeus, have attractive southeast-facing meadows. This ridge would make a good east-to-west high traverse route.

Other secondary trailheads of interest are Spring Creek and Buckboard Flat Campground. Both are located along the main Blue Mountain/Harts Draw Loop Road running west out of Monticello, about 7 and 8 miles from town, respectively. Although not officially maintained, this road typically remains drivable at least to North Creek all winter, owing to its popularity with Monticello snowmobilers, except right after significant new snow.

Abajo Information

Manti–La Sal National Forest, Monticello Ranger District, (435) 587–2041

La Sal Avalanche Forecast Center, Moab, (435) 259–SNOW (7669)

North Creek

Rating: Easy to difficult.

Gear: Skis or split-board with skins, or scaled or waxed skis on the road.

Summary: Easily accessible from Monticello all winter, North Canyon offers cross-country skiing along the summer road or impressive bowl skiing off Horsehead Peak. The area is very popular with snowmobilers.

Tour 54

Map: USGS 7.5-minute Abajo Peak.

Trailhead: North Canyon.

Distance: 2.5 miles to North Creek Pass; 3 miles to Horsehead or Abajo Peak.

Starting altitude: 8,500 feet.

High points: Abajo Peak, 11,360 feet; Horsehead Peak, 11,212 feet.

Access: From Monticello on U.S. Highway 191 in southeastern Utah, go 2 blocks south of the junction with US 666 and turn west onto Blue Mountain/Harts Draw Loop, also called North Creek Road. Follow this wide, straight, well-maintained "highway" for roughly 5 miles to a parking area on your right just below the junction of the North Creek summer road, which goes all the way over the range.

Description: Skin up the gradually rising road as it switchbacks into North Canyon and follow it to 10,200 feet. (Or use a snowmobile to cover the 2.5 miles in a fraction of the time.) Here the road leaves the creek and climbs an open east-facing slope to North Creek Pass and continues into the head of Indian Creek. Good beginner terrain surrounds the pass area. To reach Cooley Pass and moderate, north-facing tree skiing, follow the creek south where the road doubles back to the north.

To gain Abajo Peak or its southwestern counterpart, point 11,285, ascend southeast along the Abajo divide from Cooley Pass. Northerly facing trees offer cold snow skiing all along the high ridge here, with steepness increasing toward Abajo Peak. Northwest-facing tree shots into lower North Canyon are less popular with snowmobilers than the open east-facing runs near the pass. There is one open shot off point 10,837 on the east rim of North Canyon.

Abajo Mountains

W 109°28' W 109°27' W 109°26'

Main North Creek Road
3 miles

North Creek Road
1 mile

Buckboard
Flat

North Canyon

Horsehead
Peak
11,212'

Old Blue
Mountain
Ski Resort

Old lift
line

10,755'

N 37° 52'

N 37° 51'

Indian Creek

North Creek
Pass

Jackson
Ridge
10,995'

Johnson Creek

Abajo Peak
11,360'

N 37° 50'

N

Summer
road to
Abajo
Peak

Gold Queen
Gulch

0   .5   1 mi

0   .5   1 km

Contour Interval: 500 Feet

Cooley
Gulch

10,831'

Dickson Gulch

Dickson Pass

Old
4WD
track

Terraced
terrain

10,988'

North Verdure Canyon

brushy

Monticello
9 miles

N 37° 49'

To South
Fork Road
2.5 miles

South Peak
11,122'

South
Fork
Road

Horsehead Peak and its tremendous, wide-open northeast bowl are best accessed by leaving the road where it crosses North Creek for the first time at 9,400 feet. Climb into the side canyon just south of the peak and work up through the evergreens to the west rim of North Canyon at the saddle south of Horsehead. Follow the ridge north to the 11,212-foot summit. Make a conservative avalanche decision about this huge bowl, which terminates in a narrow gully. When exiting the bowl, it's wise to stay skier's right above the brush that chokes the gully bottom below 9,600 feet.

Another good option after skiing Horsehead Bowl is to climb north to another big bowl above Buckboard Flat. Ski this comparable 1,000-foot shot, Buckboard Bowl, and work down through brushy avalanche regrowth to North Creek. Cross and climb 150 feet east to intersect the road before it traverses east out of North Canyon.

It may be possible to make a loop by descending northwest off Horsehead Peak or north from the top of Buckboard Bowl and skiing back to the main road via Spring Creek or Buckboard Campground. Other ski terrain accessible from North Canyon is off Jackson Ridge into the head of Indian Creek. These woods contain many glades and drop for 1,600 feet. To return, simply follow the low-angle creek bottom back to North Creek Pass.

Old Blue Mountain Ski Resort

See map on page 220.

Rating: Easy to difficult.

Gear: Skis or split-board with skins.

Summary: Before the ski resort closed down due to lack of business, this was the primary access to the range. The road is no longer maintained, but it still offers the shortest route to Abajo Peak—and the shortest access to ski terrain in the Abajos.

Tour 55

Map: USGS 7.5-minute Abajo Peak.

Trailhead: Old Blue Mountain Ski Resort.

Distance: 2.5 miles (one way).

Starting altitude: 8,300 to 8,800 feet (depending on snow along the road).

High point: Unnamed point, 10,755 feet.

Access: From Monticello on U.S. Highway 191 in southeastern Utah, go 2 blocks south of the junction with US 666 and turn west onto Blue Mountain/Harts Draw Loop, also called North Creek Road. Follow this wide, straight, well-maintained "highway" for roughly 4 miles to the unmarked junction of Blue Mountain Road at 8,300 feet. Drive to the end of this road or as high as possible given snowbanks.

Description: Ascend the old cat tracks south of the main cut run or climb directly up the run. Ski a shot here, then come back up and climb along the ridge above the resort as it trends southwest. It becomes less defined above 10,200 feet in open, avalanche-prone terrain. Another cut run falls northeast from here and can be skied en route back to the resort.

Continue up to the ridgetop at 10,755 feet. East-facing meadows present themselves. Skiing here is avalanche-prone, but it's potentially good powder terrain. After skiing 1,000 feet, cut skier's left into the woods and climb or contour back to the ascent ridge.

Climb Abajo Peak by following the broad, undulating ridge above the east-facing shots. The peak has good skiing on the south, especially in corn season,

Abajo Range; northeast view.

and on the north into North Canyon. Dropping down North Canyon makes a good loop route. Gold Queen Gulch, below the corn shots, is tough to get out of. It's best to come back up to the ridge and return to the resort along the up route, or drop into North Canyon.

South Peak

See map on page 220.

Rating: Difficult.

Gear: Skis or split-board with skins.

Summary: This is a very efficient tour to steep, north-facing terrain. An understanding of ava-lanche conditions and route finding is essential. This is also a starting point for the traverse to North Creek.

Tour 56

Map: USGS 7.5-minute Abajo Peak.

Trailhead: South Mountain Road (as high as snow allows).

Distance: 1.5 miles to the summit from the 8,600-foot level on the access road.

Starting altitude: 8,600 feet (lower in midwinter if snow blocks the road).

High point: South Peak, 11,122 feet; unnamed point, 10,988 feet; unnamed point, 10,831.

Access: From Monticello on U.S. Highway 191 in southeastern Utah, go 2 blocks south of the junction with US 666 and turn west on Blue Mountain/Harts Draw Loop, also called North Creek Road. At the edge of town, the road crosses Montezuma Creek, and South Creek Road splits to the south. The recreation sign says LLOYD'S LAKE 2 MILES. It's a good gravel road to at least 8,600 feet, where snowbanks often block it. Above this point, the road contours south and trav-erses the south face of South Peak. If it's drivable this far, continue into Recapture Creek Canyon and begin touring from there.

Otherwise, park where snowbanks block the road and follow it to 8,700 feet, where it crosses the North Fork of Verdure Creek.

Description: From the North Verdure Creek crossing (which isn't always appar-ent), leave the road and ascend west-northwest toward the narrow mouth of the canyon, staying south of the creek where snow is deeper. The safest and least brushy route in this trailless canyon is on the south ridge. It can be gained via an open talus field beginning at 9,000 feet. Switchback up the 25-degree slope and continue into steeper evergreen woods above. Angle southward and avoid the open, east-facing slide paths if any avalanche hazard exists. The initially blunt ridge becomes more obvious above 10,000 feet.

Ski runs can be made through the ascent woods or on the east-facing slide track. Otherwise, continue along the summit ridge to South Peak, 11,122 feet. A steep and appealing northeast-facing ski line falls from 10,900 feet just east of the summit to the canyon bottom. It's a slide path but has sparse trees up high; it can be effectively ski cut. At 10,500 feet, a shorter path splits off to skier's left and drops due north.

Off the summit of South Peak, a consistent 35-degree run drops northwest to Recapture Creek for 1,500 feet after crossing the summer road at 10,000 feet. The slope is mostly wooded, with ample spacing for excellent skiing and many small glades. Far skier's left is an open line (a slide path). The skier's-right lines funnel into a lower-angle west-facing gully. This draw can be climbed back to the pass north of South Peak. A good open, northeast-facing run drops east from this pass.

Low-angle south-facing shots exist at the head of Recapture Creek. These can be reached by following the creek or the summer road as it continues toward Abajo Peak. The slightly steeper shots farther west, like many open slopes in the range, are crosscut by terraces dating from the Civilian Conservation Corps era. Be wary of the west-facing avalanche-prone slope below point 10,988 that the road crosses en route to Dickson Pass. The safer ascent route is west of Recapture Creek.

Above Dickson Pass to the southeast is a beautiful, moderately steep meadow falling from the Abajo divide just north of point 10,988. From the same point, a 1,500-foot slide path offers excellent skiing into Dickson Gulch, the next drainage north of North Verdure Creek. The ridge between these two draws is also a good ascent route, being low angle enough to skin directly up sans switchbacks. The top of the ridge is point 10,988. A good run, especially in corn conditions, falls east-southeast for 1,200 feet from here into North Verdure Canyon.

The north fork of Dickson Gulch also has good skiing, either from Dickson Pass or from the divide north of point 10,831. Reach the latter shots by following the summer road as it contours into Cooley Gulch, then doubling back to the broad divide. Appealing west-facing shots also fall into Cooley Gulch from the road. Ski these runs with respect for the avalanche potential, and climb back up in the woods to the south if any hazard is present.

If stable (corn) conditions exist, a traverse from South Peak to North Canyon is very feasible. Either follow the road, follow the divide ridge, or ski a series of west-facing shots into the Recapture, Cooley, and Johnson drainages, climbing out each canyon to the north. At the head of Johnson Creek is Cooley Pass; below it is 20-degree tree skiing to North Canyon Road, which can be easily followed to the main road. The traverse could alternatively include a climb along the summer road to Abajo Peak or a steeper tree shot into North Canyon (see Tour 55, Old Blue Mountain Ski Resort).

The lower creek bottom of North Verdure Creek below South Peak is a dense nightmare of postavalanche regrowth. Avoid this as you return to the starting point on South Creek Road by one of two primary options. From the bottom of the runs off South Peak, the pass north of it, or point 10,988, contour skier's right through the woods above the gully bottom and intersect a slide path that drops to the canyon floor from point 9,800. Ski it, then descend along the ascent route after crossing the talus slope above 9,000 feet near the canyon mouth.

The second option is from Dickson Gulch. Ski the gully until it becomes brushy. Then stay skier's right in evergreen woods until they terminate in a meadow at 8,900 feet. Look for a four-wheel-drive track cutting south into North Verdure Canyon from here. It intersects South Creek Road at 8,700 feet after descending a usually dry south-facing Gambel oak slope, where the road is highly beneficial.

IX

Henry Mountains
The Island Range

In the heart of canyon country, visible from practically everywhere in south-central Utah, the remote Henry Mountains burst out of the rugged, colorful low-lands. This is a laccolith range of "wannabe volcanoes," and the last mountain range in the lower forty-eight states to be explored and mapped. The range is home to a bison herd planted in 1941 and is the stuff of Wild West legends. Butch Cassidy and the Sundance Kid hid out in Robert's Roost Canyon to the northeast. The summits offer good ski terrain (when there's enough snow) with incomparable views. Skiing here is most feasible in spring or during extended periods of winter high pressure, but avoid negotiating the long and rugged access roads during or just after storms—they become slick and dangerous.

Mount Ellen, the highest peak, offers by far the most accessible and friendly skiing. Pennell and Hillers are wooded to their summits, in contrast to the wide-open snowfields of Ellen's distinct north and south massifs. The east face of Pennell and the north buttresses of Hillers hold snow into spring, when access becomes reasonable via four-wheel-drive roads, but I prefer to concentrate my efforts on Mount Ellen. The Horn, a purple granite dome just north of Mount Pennell, is becoming a popular rock-climbing area, making the Henrys an attractive option for a multisport day or weekend.

Mount Ellen is composed of the North Summit Ridge and the South Summit Ridge, each about 2 miles in north-to-south length and separated by 10,485-foot Bull Creek Pass, which can be used as a base camp to explore both. Driving to the pass isn't possible until after most of the snow is melted on the runs, however, so camp must be carried in, most expediently from McMillan Spring Campground on the west side. Alternatively, you can use this campground as a starting point for one-day ski forays onto the south massif. The north massif and highest point is more easily accessible from Lonesome Beaver Campground and Dandelion Picnic Site on the east.

Henry Mountains Information

Bureau of Land Management, Henry Mountain Field Station, (435) 542–3461

North Summit Ridge, Mount Ellen

Rating: Intermediate to difficult.

Gear: Skis or split-board with skins; ice ax and crampons may be useful in spring.

Summary: The shortest drive, most efficient climb, and longest, most consistently filled-in ski shots in the Henrys are located here on the east side of the north peak of Mount Ellen.

Tour 57

Map: USGS 7.5-minute Mount Ellen.

Trailhead: Sawmill Basin's Dandelion Flat.

Distance: 2.5 miles (one way).

Starting altitude: 8,100 feet.

High point: Unnamed point, 11,522 feet.

Access: Turn south from the post office onto 100 East in Hanksville, following this road as it rises out of the red sand, past the purple granite of Bull Mountain, and into the ponderosa forests of Sawmill Basin (22 miles). It's a rough, steep, two-wheel-drive or comfortable four-wheel-drive road, but it can be wild just after a snowstorm.

Description: A trail that was once a four-wheel-drive road leaves from the idyllic picnic site at Dandelion Flat, where there's a toilet and a sign reading LOG FLAT 1, EAST SADDLE 4. Half a mile farther up the road is the lovely Lonesome Beaver Campground. Leave the auto road at Dandelion Flat and skin or hike along East Pass Road as it immediately crosses Bull Creek. It can be hard to find at Dandelion Flat, but it parallels the main road west of a tributary creek until a divide. The left fork goes to Lonesome Beaver Campground. Ignore it and go right; if you're on the right trail, it will begin to switchback steeply up to the west.

Within 0.5 mile you'll reach the tall ponderosas of Log Flat. Above here, you'll catch glimpses of snow slopes and couloirs falling from the southern end of the North Summit Ridge of Mount Ellen. The drops above Log Flat are some of the most sustained lines and hold snow late into spring, due to their favorable northeast exposure. Given the rubble-pile nature of the high Henrys, spring is probably easier than summer to climb them.

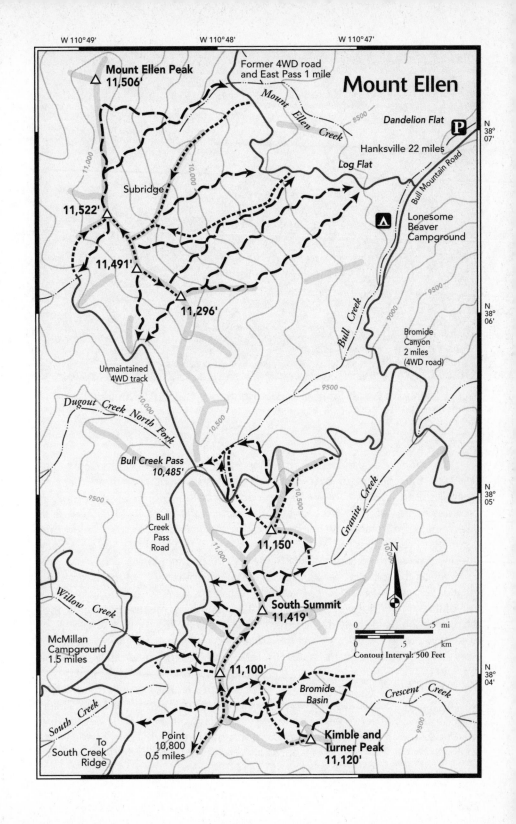

Mount Ellen Peak
△ 11,506'

Former 4WD road
and East Pass 1 mile

Mount Ellen

Mount Ellen Creek

8500

Dandelion Flat 🅿

N
38°
07'

Hanksville 22 miles

Log Flat

Subridge

Bull Mountain Road

11,522'
△

10,000

11,000

Lonesome
Beaver
Campground

11,491'
△

9500

11,296'
△

Bull Creek

9000

N
38°
06'

Bromide
Canyon
2 miles
(4WD road)

Unmaintained
4WD track

10,000

Dugout Creek North Fork

9500

Bull Creek Pass
10,485'

10,500

Granite Creek

N
38°
05'

9500

Bull
Creek
Pass
Road

10,500

10,000

11,150'
△

N

Willow Creek

11,000

South Summit
△ 11,419'

0   .5 mi

McMillan
Campground
1.5 miles

0   .5 km
Contour Interval: 500 Feet

11,100'
△

Bromide
Basin

Crescent Creek

N
38°
04'

South Creek

To
South Creek
Ridge

Point
10,800
0.5 miles

9500

Kimble and
Turner Peak
△ 11,120'

Mount Ellen with North Summit Ridge (right), Bull Creek Pass (middle), and Dandelion Flat (foreground); east view.

If there's any avalanche risk, it may be wise to continue on the East Pass Trail past the couloirs to East Pass and climb to Mount Ellen from there. A steeper subridge comes down to the road just before Mount Ellen Creek and provides a less safe but more direct approach to the summit ridge. The most direct line, given stable avalanche conditions, is to leave the road before the first major creek crossing, just 0.25 mile above Log Flat. Look for a sparsely treed, subtle ridge feature directly below the longest couloir.

Stay on the more open southeast-facing "micro-aspect" of the deepening gully until steeper terrain forces you into it. It leads directly to the highest section of the summit ridge and accesses half a dozen runs, mostly slide paths, that drop from the ridge between points 11,522 and 11,296. There is also a more east-facing drop from lower on the same ridge where it falls away from the Henry divide. The drops are steep for 2,000 to 2,500 feet and can be skied all the way to Log Flat if enough snow is present.

A large bowl north of point 11,522 offers moderately steep, open skiing with a little more east in the aspect. It's easiest to reach from the Mount Ellen Creek subridge. There's also plenty of open skiing off the high divide on the west side. The best shot falls from just north of point 11,522 and heads west-southwest for 1,800 feet in a decent snow year. A wind-scoured ridge just north of the run provides a safe and efficient return route to the summit. The panorama from point 11,522 includes Capitol Reef's Waterpocket Fold immediately to the west, Aquarius Plateau (Boulder Mountain) farther west, the Tushar Mountains beyond that, Thousand Lake Mountain to the northwest, San Rafael Reef and the buttes around Goblin Valley to the north, the La Sal Mountains and Canyonlands to the east, Glen Canyon and the Abajo Mountains to the southeast, and Navajo Mountain over Lake Powell to the southwest. It's a glorious 360-degree view of Utah's desert wilderness from the ultimate "island range." It's well worth the effort—*and* you get to ski down!

South Summit, Mount Ellen

Tour 58

See map on page 229.

Rating: Moderate to difficult.

Gear: Skis or split-board with skins.

Summary: This standard western approach offers the best access to Bull Creek Pass, the South Summit Ridge, and Bromide Basin.

Map: USGS 7.5-minute Mount Ellen.

Trailhead: McMillan Campground.

Distance: 2.5 miles to the summit ridge and Bromide Basin; 3.25 miles to Bull Creek Pass.

Starting altitude: 8,500 feet.

High points: Unnamed point, 11,100 feet; South Summit, 11,419 feet; unnamed point, 11,150 feet.

Access: From Utah State Route 24 east of Capitol Reef National Park, turn south onto Notom Road. Turn left at the first prominent junction onto Bull Mountain Road, where a Forest Service sign gives mileage to the Henry Mountains and other specific destinations. Lock in your hubs, because the crux of the road is the first ford at Sandy Creek. After the second ford, make a left at an unmarked junction. (The right fork goes to Stevens Narrows.) A smooth section of two-wheel-drive road ensues before another unmarked junction. Go left and immediately ford South Creek. (The right fork goes to Penellen Pass and the Horn.) Now the left fork climbs in earnest to McMillan Campground and on up. Begin the tour by driving as high as possible toward Bull Creek Pass on this road.

Description: Depending on how high it's possible to drive, there may be some travel on the road to start your tour. Dry Lake and Nasty Flats are crossed at 9,000 and 9,500 feet, respectively, and usually hold snow even when the higher south-facing portion of the road doesn't. At Nasty Flat, a branch of the road splits off to the south and can be used to access the skiable bowls on the south end of the Mount Ellen ridge. Travel by auto will virtually always be blocked at

10,000 feet on the road to Bull Creek Pass. Leave the road here and ascend a blunt ridge, often blown free of snow, to the east for 1,100 feet to the South Summit Ridge. Just north of this ascent ridge is a 35-degree, northwest-facing slide path that continues for 1,500 feet along the headwaters of Dugout Creek.

East of this 11,100-foot point is Bromide Basin and its ramshackle old mining buildings. They have somehow survived at the base of an avalanche-prone bowl, perhaps because the slope angle is a friendly 25 degrees in this east-facing cirque. Kimble and Turner Peak, south of Bromide Basin, has a 1,500-foot tree shot on its northeast face into Crescent Creek. An old four-wheel-drive road leads back up past the mine shacks and makes an efficient return route to the summit ridge. Northwest off the west ridge of Kimble is a low-angle shot into the basin.

The highest spot on the south summit massif is Peak 11,419, with its communications tower. It stands north of Bromide Basin and can be reached by ascending northeast along the divide ridge. Good runs fall northwest along here. Returning to the McMillan area is straightforward along the road, but it isn't always visible on the upper west face of Mount Ellen's south ridge. From Peak 11,419, west- and east-facing shots fall from a point just north of the summit. The east bowl is good for 1,200 feet of open skiing before it funnels into Granite Creek, creating an avalanche terrain trap. Climb north out of this

Mount Ellen's south summit with South Creek Ridge at right; southwest view.

drainage to point 11,150, or the saddle west of it, and more runs fall northeast and north toward Bull Creek Pass.

A good traverse of the south massif can be made by going right (south) at the Nasty Flat Road junction; follow the road through the mellow upper basin of South Creek to the spot where it crosses the South Creek Ridge at 9,424 feet. Then ascend the initially gentle ridge east and south to point 10,800. There are fine west- and northwest-facing shots back into South Creek from here. To traverse, however, simply stick to the undulating divide, staying east of the crest where winds have blown the western side free of snow, and enjoy incredible views of the desert country. From the north end, drop toward Bull Creek Pass on the low-angle gully that is the source of Bull Creek, and contour skier's left to the pass. Glide back along the road as it contours west to Nasty Flat. A more ambitious traverse itinerary would involve skiing a series of shots into the east-facing cirques along the way or continuing to the North Peak.

X

The Tushars and Pine Valleys

The Terrific Tushar Range and Southwest Utah

Southwestern Utah's crowning glory (for a skier) are the 12,000-foot Tushar Mountains. This collection of high, windy peaks gathers an average of 400 inches of base-building snow per winter, and although the high country is often wind crusted in winter, there are plenty of protected powder shots on Lake Peak, around the Big John Flat Yurt, and in the City Creek Glades. These areas are all accessible from Elk Meadows Ski Resort or its access road, Upper Meadows Drive off Utah State Route 153. Unfortunately the ski area has been closed since 2001 because of financial backing troubles. Since this land is privately owned, skiing within the ski area boundaries is considered trespassing and should be avoided. Tushar Mountain Tours offers yurt-based skiing and guiding out of its Big John Flat shelter below Delano Peak and a second yurt near City Creek Peak and Puffer Lake.

Perhaps the greatest time to ski the Tushars is in spring and summer. This may be the easiest place in Utah to get twelve months of skiing, thanks to Marysvale Loop Road, a four-wheel-drive track that reaches nearly 12,000 feet on its rugged route across the range. Long before the road melts out for four-wheeling to the tops, the spring corn conditions become prime.

Start from below Elk Meadows Ski Resort and traverse to a stashed car in Kimberly, the historic ghost town south of I–70 on the north end of the range. April and May typically offer long high-pressure periods when such a traverse can be made. Be prepared for wind, however, because this range gets it! Take two days to cruise directly, or add a few nights and ski the sights along the way: Delano, Baldy, and Belknap Peaks. Baldy beckons from I–15 and I–70 with its enticing lines on all aspects. It's not easy to reach, but it's a gem of Utah skiing.

Shelly Baldy Peak and Circleville Mountain—as well as many other peripheral areas—undoubtedly offer good skiing, but they aren't detailed here. This chapter begins with descriptions of the easiest to access areas near Elk Meadows and builds out from there.

Tushar Information

Beaver Ranger District, (435) 438–2436
Tushar Mountain Tours, (435) 438–6191
Beaver County Search and Rescue, (435) 438–2862

Mount Holly

Rating: Easy to difficult.

Gear: Skis or split-board with skins.

Summary: Accessible from Puffer Lake or the Tushar Mountain Tours Yurt at Big John Flat, this peak offers gentle to moderate slopes on the south and west, and steeper, premium corn lines on the southeast. Mount Holly makes a good partial day tour.

Tour 59

Maps: USGS 7.5-minute Delano Peak, Shelly Baldy Peak.

Trailheads: Big John Flat Road or Puffer Lake.

Distance: 4 to 6 miles (one way).

Starting altitude: Big John Flat Road, 9,000 to 10,000 feet; Puffer Lake, 9,655 feet.

High point: Mount Holly, 11,985 feet.

Access: From Beaver on I–15 in south-central Utah, travel east for 20 miles on Utah State Route 153 to Forest Road 123 to Big John Flat. Park at the junction and begin skinning. Or you can ask Forest Service personnel in Beaver whether the road is open, then drive the increasingly steep and rough four-wheel-drive road as high as possible. The Tushar Mountain Tours Yurt is located in this drainage, and Holly can be climbed from the yurt.

To get to Puffer Lake from Beaver travel east for approximately 23 miles on Utah State Route 153, passing Elk Meadows Ski Resort. Park at the end of the plowing near the south shore of Puffer Lake. The road is paved the entire way.

Description: From the Big John Flat yurt climb and contour southeast along the summer Skyline Trail route. Cross a small ridge at 10,800 feet, and contour west into the Merchant Creek drainage. Cross the creek and head up the fall-line on the broad west aspect of the Great White Whale, a popular destination for powder turns off a bulbous west-facing ridge. From the large, flat, 11,526-foot summit, travel west to the Tushar divide and climb southeast to Mount Holly.

The east face is good for paragliding, but not recommended for skiers. One can dabble on its north or south peripheries, but the lines don't go through to Cottonwood Creek and the Piute Reservoir.

The west ramp drops down a very shallow and wide depression. It is maybe

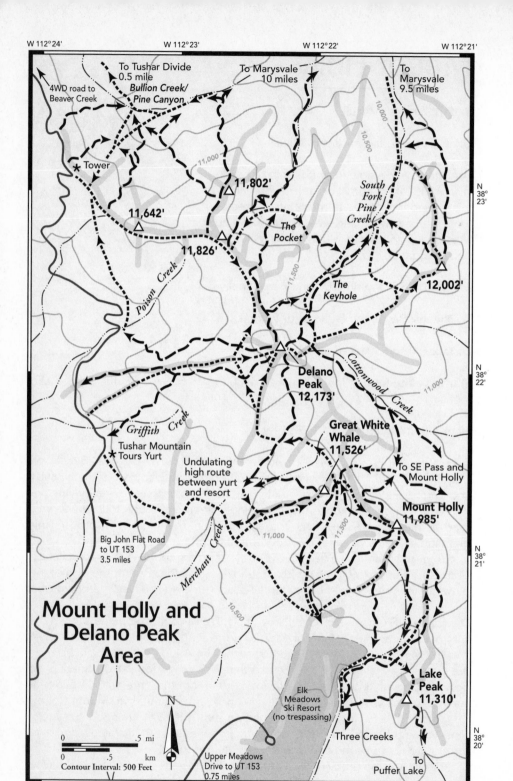

Mount Holly and Delano Peak Area

W 112°24'   W 112°23'   W 112°22'   W 112°21'

To Tushar Divide
0.5 mile
**Bullion Creek/
Pine Canyon**

To Marysvale
10 miles

To
Marysvale
9.5 miles

4WD road to
Beaver Creek

10,000

10,500

*Tower

11,000

11,802'

*South
Fork
Pine
Creek*

N
38°
23'

11,642'

11,826'

The Pocket

11,500

The
Keyhole

12,002'

Poison Creek

Delano
Peak
12,173'

Cottonwood Creek

11,000

N
38°
22'

**Great White
Whale
11,526'**

Griffith Creek

Tushar Mountain
*Tours Yurt

Undulating
high route
between yurt
and resort

To SE Pass and
Mount Holly

**Mount Holly
11,985'**

N
38°
21'

Big John Flat Road
to UT 153
3.5 miles

11,500

11,000

Merchant Creek

10,500

N
38°
20'

0   .5 mi

0   .5   km

Contour Interval: 500 Feet

N

Elk
Meadows
Ski Resort
(no trespassing)

**Lake
Peak
11,310'**

Three Creeks

Upper Meadows
Drive to UT 153
0.75 miles

To
Puffer Lake

30 degrees at the breakover point, and otherwise less steep. Traverse skier's left around the 11,000-foot level and ski southwest through the steeper "finger chutes." From the base of the west ramp simply contour northwest along the Skyline Trail back to the yurt. If you are heading for Delano Peak or Big John Flat, there is also a northwest-facing ramp that is only 15 degrees in steepness at the top and drops only a few hundred feet over the course of a half-mile or so. Its high point is typically the highest-reaching snow on Mount Holly.

From Puffer Lake, ascend the unnamed drainage north of the southern Tushar Mountain Tours yurt to the plateau east of Lake Peak, and then traverse left around the slopes of Lake Peak. Cross Three Creeksand climb to the gradual slope that leads to the summit of Mount Holly.

The south face is best reached from the southwest ridge and falls away at about 25 degrees from the south end of the summit plateau. It drops into the open basin between Mount Holly and Lake Peak. The southwest gully drops from the east end of Holly near the true summit. It is a moderately step line as well, but very aesthetic with up to 1,400 feet of fall-line skiing to the cabin on Three Creeks. To exit from these runs without trespassing on Elk Meadows land, ski east through the 11,052-foot saddle between Lake Peak and Holly. Kick and glide down the summer road along Lake Stream to Puffer Lake.

A steeper drop on the southeast is the premier corn line. It is over 30 degrees and has avalanche potential as it breaks over below the summit plateau. This route drops east of the Holly-Lake Peak pass into the Lake Stream drainage. Kick and glide down the road to Puffer Lake and the southern Tushar Mountain Tours yurt.

An east-facing line splits off from the southeast face and fades into Cottonwood Creek, creating the best access to the eastern basin below Holly. Return by climbing southwest up an obvious draw to 11,250 feet and traversing back to the Holly/Lake Peak saddle. You can also use this route to return from the steep couloirs dropping into Cottonwood Creek from the Tushar divide north of Holly. Skiing the west face of Lake Peak (the Canvas) is very feasible on the way back from the south or east side of Mount Holly.

Delano Peak

See map on page 238.

Rating: Easy to difficult.

Gear: Skis or split-board with skins.

Summary: The highest summit in the Tushar Range is accessible from Tushar Mountain Tours Yurt at Big John Flat. The skiing is moderate on the west, north, and east but steeper on the south. This is one of the friendliest 12,000-foot peaks in the state of Utah, yet expert terrain is also nearby. With a car shuttle, a 5,000-foot descent into Pine Canyon above Marysvale is quite feasible from this peak. The Pocket, just north of Delano, can be skied twelve months a year, and in summer a four-wheel-drive road goes all the way over the Tushar divide to make access easy.

Maps: USGS 7.5-minute Delano Peak, Shelly Baldy Peak, Mount Brigham, Mount Belknap.

Trailheads: Big John Flat Road.

Distance: 3 to 5 miles (one way).

Starting altitude: 9,000 to 10,000 feet.

High points: The Great White Whale, 11,526 feet; Delano Peak, 12,173 feet; unnamed point, 11,826 feet; unnamed point, 11,802 feet; unnamed point, 11,642 feet; unnamed peak, 12,002 feet.

Access: From Beaver on I-15 in south-central Utah, travel east for 20 miles on Utah State Route 153 to Forest Road 123 to Big John Flat about 2 miles before Elk Meadows Ski Resort. Park at the junction and begin skinning. During the late spring and early summer, inquire with the Forest Service in Beaver to determine whether the road is open, then drive the increasingly steep and rough four-wheel-drive road as high as possible. The Tushar Mountain Tours yurt is located in this drainage, and Delano Peak can be climbed from the yurt, or as a moderately long one-day push.

Description: Follow Big John Flat Road past the flats and the Tushar Mountain Tours yurt until it crosses Griffith Creek at 10,400 feet. Climb northeast to gain the broad west ridge of Delano Peak. Climb the moderate, open slopes on Delano's vast western aspect to the indistinct main summit. Strong winds often scour the west and south facing ridges as well as the entire high divide in this notoriously windy range. Hence the best routes are below ridges and in loaded gullies.

Southeast of the Big John Flats yurt is point 11,526, called the "Great White Whale," by local skiers. The Whale is a popular destination for powder turns off a bulbous west-facing ridge. Ascend southwest from the yurt along the Skyline Trail passing some appetizing west-facing meadow runs dropping to Big John Flat. Cross a small ridge at 10,800 feet, and contour west into the Merchant Creek drainage. Cross the creek and head up the fall-line on the broad west aspect of the Whale. Ski down along the ascent route for easier skiing or, to find steeper terrain, ski northwest off the top into the Merchant Creek valley.

Delano Peak commands a panoramic 360-degree view of the Marysvale

Delano Peak and Bullion Canyon; east view.

Valley and Piute Reservoir to the east, Richfield area to the northeast, Mount Belknap and Mount Baldy to the northwest, Beaver Valley to the west, and Mount Holly and Circleville Mountain to the south. If you decide to climb to the summit, there is a register tucked into the rocks. The safest run off the top is the west flank. It is long and moderately difficult, dropping at 15 to 20 degrees for over 1,600 feet to the edge of Big John Flat. There is virtually no avalanche hazard on this line.

Other good skiing options off Delano Peak include the south aspect into the Merchant Creek drainage and the east aspect into Cottonwood Creek. The north is a moderate drop into Poison Creek with an increasingly steep slope south of it. The ravine can be skied when avalanche hazard exists, as long as that north-facing south bank is given a wide berth. The Poison Creek ravine is similar in steepness to the west flank, but can be made steeper by traversing skier's left onto the south side of the drainage, and then skiing the fall-line again.

Further to the north is another cirque in upper Bullion Canyon called "The Pocket." It holds snow all year-round and can be skied from point 11,826 at the head of Poison Creek. Access it in mid-summer by driving Big John Flat Road to the Tushar Divide and walking southeast along the ridge to point 11,826. In good years it is possible to ski northeast-facing shots off the divide into Bullion Canyon from right where the road meets it, making this area the summer skiing capital of Utah!

Further north is point 11,802 and a fine north-facing drop into the north or main fork of Bullion Canyon. There is a more moderate entrance into this upper Pine Creek drainage and the Bullion Pasture area from the saddle west of point 11,826 toward point 11,642. Either climb back out of Bullion via this gully line, or camp in the pastures and continue north to make a classic, two- or three-day traverse of the Tushar Range (see Tour 63, Mount Belknap and North to Kimberly for a description of the entire traverse).

The south face of Delano is a wider and steeper couloir dropping from Delano's south summit at 30 to 40 degrees. The "Main South Chute" is popular in spring when the snow becomes supportable corn. It is hazardous during periods of moderate (or greater) avalanche danger. Drop as far as you like since the line wraps west down the headwaters of Merchant Creek before traversing skier's left (southwest) and contouring south to the climb for the Great White Whale (point 11,526) and Mount Holly.

The eastern aspect is perhaps the most intriguing, but it drops you into the south fork of Bullion Canyon, and you must climb back out, unless a vehicle has been cached in Bullion Canyon above Marysvale. Nonetheless, it is a huge bowl with 1,000-foot drops along a broad north-trending rim. The runs funnel into a narrow gap between cliffs called "The Keyhole." A reasonable return climb ascends south from the Keyhole to the broad east ridge of Delano Peak and follows it to the summit, which is often blown free of snow. You may choose to bypass the true top on the return from Bullion Canyon and descend instead from the south summit via the Main South Chute back into Merchant Creek.

It is feasible in low avalanche hazard conditions to ski through the Keyhole and emerge in a gigantic north-facing bowl between peak 12,002 and Delano Peak. This "South Bullion Bowl" has a half-dozen clean entrances via north-facing couloirs from the high south wall of Bullion Canyon. These lines are steeper than 40 degrees at the top, and drop for as much as 1,000 feet. The area typically holds patches of snow year-round and offers some incredible late-spring and summer skiing. It can also be accessed from Marysvale up Bullion Canyon's south fork.

City Creek Peak and Puffer Lake Area

Rating: Easy to moderate.

Gear: Skis or split-board with skins.

Summary: Extremely accessible from Elk Meadows, this peak offers gentle to moderate glades and tree shots on the northwest. It's a good area for powder tours in winter.

Tour 61

Maps: USGS 7.5-minute Delano Peak, Shelly Baldy Peak.

Trailhead: Puffer Lake, south end.

Distance: 1.5 miles (one way).

Starting altitude: 9,655 feet.

High point: City Creek Peak, 11,161 feet.

Access: From Beaver off I–15 in south-central Utah, travel east for approximately 23 miles on Utah State Route 153, passing Elk Meadows Ski Resort. Park at the end of plowing near the south shore of Puffer Lake. The road is paved the entire way.

Description: To reach the Puffer Lake Yurt, follow the summer road along the northwest shore of Puffer Lake for 1.4 miles. The yurt is located roughly 0.25 miles northeast of the lake on the east bank of Lake Stream. To climb City Creek Peak from the yurt, skin southeast up a low-angle drainage and cross the Puffer Lake Loop Road. Gain the ridge to the south and follow it to the summit ridge. Excellent tree skiing exists in this northwest-facing drainage and in the spruce glade east of the summit ridge. To reach the summit and the clear-cut skiing, climb southeast and stay just west of the rocky summit ridge.

To climb and ski City Creek Peak or the glades without visiting the yurt, follow UT 153 south from the trailhead for Puffer Lake for about a mile as it contours south to a junction with Puffer Lake Loop Road.

Go north on this road and leave it after 0.25 mile where it bends west. Climb moderate slopes for 300 feet, passing a small slide path to the south that can be skied. Go northeast along the undulating divide, and climb open slopes for the final 400 feet to City Creek Peak, 11,161 feet.

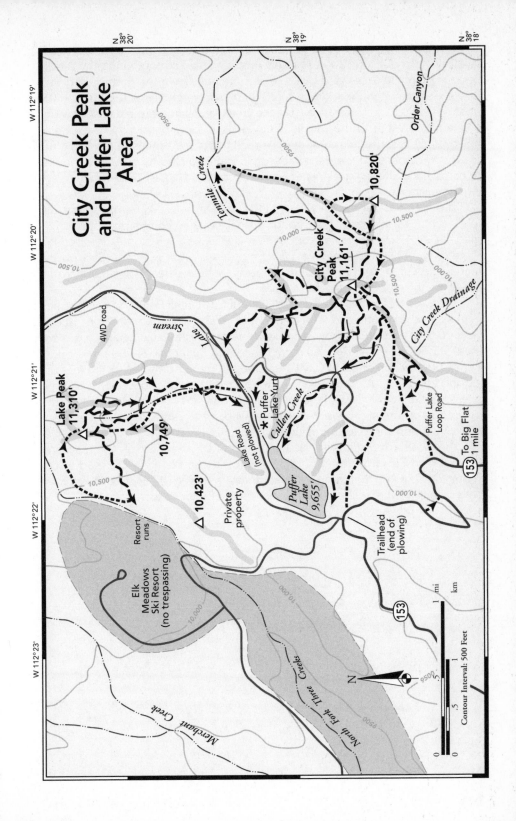

City Creek Peak and Puffer Lake Area

N 38° 20'
N 38° 19'
N 38° 18'

W 112°19'
W 112°20'
W 112°21'
W 112°22'
W 112°23'

Order Canyon

Tenmile Creek

△ 10,820'

City Creek Peak
11,161'

City Creek Drainage

10,500

10,000

9500

4WD road

Lake Stream

Lake Peak
11,310'
△

△
10,749'

△ 10,423'

Puffer Lake Yurt
★

Cullen Creek

Lake Road
(not plowed)

Private property

Puffer Lake
9,655'

Puffer Lake Loop Road

153
To Big Flat
1 mile

10,000

Trailhead
(end of plowing)

153

Elk Meadows Ski Resort
(no trespassing)

Resort runs

Merchant Creek

North Fork Three Creeks

10,000

9500

N

1 mi
1 km
.5

Contour Interval: 500 Feet

The low-angle south face can be skied when recent snow covers it, but it typically melts out soon after. The east face is a nice 750-foot run to the saddle between Tenmile Creek and City Creek. Continue down the north-facing Tenmile Creek drainage for another 1,200 feet if snow conditions are good in the trees. The terrain is moderate east of the creek, and a ridge to the east provides a safe return route to the saddle. Between the saddle and City Creek Peak, however, there's no safe route; this is a slide path. The aspens to the south are the best ascent route, but remember that they're a disaster species—the first to come back after an avalanche. Make a conservative assessment before skiing the east face.

The northeast face of City Creek Peak is tight trees. Ski northwest for 200 feet, then traverse skier's right through a small notch to enter a beautiful spruce glade falling northeast toward upper Tenmile Canyon. It becomes steeper and more of a confined gully with avalanche potential after 500 feet. Stay on the higher ground skier's right or left of the gully below here. Climb out to the divide via the woods north of the gully.

The west face is the obvious prize line of City Creek Peak and can be seen from everywhere north and west of the peak. The glades are more open due to clear-cutting, and good shots fall due west and northwest. The angle is moderate (25 degrees); the runs fall for 1,100 feet to Puffer Lake Loop Road.

A subpeak northwest of City Creek also has good northwest-facing tree skiing for 1,000 feet. A more open west-facing shot can be found by traversing skier's right at 10,500 feet to the north side of the small gulch. These shots funnel into Lake Stream above Puffer Lake, where you can follow the road back along the north shore to the trailhead.

The west-facing glades and clear-cuts can be skied across the road and down Cullen Creek to the north end of the lake. Or ski along the road to the south and gain 100 feet to a saddle southeast of point 10,184. Drop west from here directly to the trailhead at the south end of Puffer Lake.

Lake Peak

See map on page 245.

Rating: Easy to moderate.

Gear: Skis or split-board with skins.

Summary: Accessible from Puffer Lake, (and the Tushar Mountain Tours Yurt just east of the lake) or as a return route from Mount Holly, this peak offers gentle to moderate slopes on the north, south, and west. A user-friendly area suitable for a novice's first backcountry tour, it is very possible to enjoy it even on a partial-day tour.

Tour 62

Maps: USGS 7.5-minute Delano Peak, Shelly Baldy Peak.

Trailheads: Puffer Lake, south end.

Distance: 1.5 miles (one way).

Starting altitude: Puffer Lake, 9,655 feet.

High point: Lake Peak, 11,310 feet.

Access: From Beaver off I-15 in south-central Utah, travel east for approximately 23 miles on Utah State Route 153, passing Elk Meadows Ski Resort. Park at the end of the plowing near the south shore of Puffer Lake. The road is paved the entire way.

Description: Ascend the unnamed drainage north of the yurt to the plateau east of Lake Peak, and then climb west to the summit. From the north end of Lake Peak, "September Run" drops down for 600 feet to Three Forks Creek. It is a good bet for powder and smooth snow underneath for relatively safe early season turns (hence the name). Good skiing falls away from just below the rocky summit on the western shot called "The Canvas." The only clean ski line directly off the summit is a steep chute on the southwest. It bends west onto the Canvas.

The southeast aspect of Lake Peak (the ascent route from Puffer Lake) is a moderately steep shot and drops into a broad gully that leads down to Lake Stream above Puffer Lake. Alternatively, climb west from the tree line on the southeast shot and return to the Canvas.

Mount Holly and Lake Peak (front left); southeast view from City Creek Peak.

More excellent south-facing skiing near Lake Peak exists on an unnamed point 0.25 mile to the southeast, and in the broad, low angle draw between the two. A steep couloir falls directly south from the southwestern corner of the broad, flat 11,040-foot southeast knoll. There is also a good, moderate run falling southeast off this point. Both shots drop into the north fork of Lake Stream and can be skied down to Puffer Lake or climbed out to the west for a return run on the Canvas.

Mount Belknap and North to Kimberly

Rating: Difficult.

Gear: Skis or split-board with skins; ice ax and crampons optional in spring.

Tour 63

Summary: The second highest summit in the Tushars is easier to reach than Baldy, but it receives less snow than its southwesterly neighbor. High-quality shots drop only on the favored north through east aspects. Belknap is probably more realistic as a spring corn than a winter powder objective, given its high avalanche potential and remote location. Ski it as part of a south-to-north spring traverse of the Tushar Range. It's about equidistant from trailheads either north, south, or east.

Maps: USGS 7.5-minute Shelly Baldy Peak, Mount Belknap, Delano Peak.

Trailheads: Upper parking lot, Elk Meadows Ski Resort; the backcountry access gate at the top of Big Elk Triple Chairlift; or Big John Flat or Marysvale Loop Road, as high as you can drive.

Distance: 6 miles from Elk Meadows Ski Resort or 4–6 miles from Big John Flat Road (one way).

Starting altitude: Elk Meadows base, 10,355 feet; Big Elk Chair, 10,400 feet; Big John Flat, 9,000 to 10,000 feet; Marysvale Loop Road, 9,000 to 10,000 feet.

High points: Mount Belknap, 12,139 feet; Gold Mountain, 11,650 feet.

Access: From Beaver off I-15 in south-central Utah, travel east for 22 miles on Utah State Route 153 to Elk Meadows Ski Resort. Go left on Upper Meadows Road to Upper Meadows Lodge, where a rental shop is also located. These are paved roads. If you're skiing at the resort, ride Big Elk Triple Chairlift. Otherwise, simply skin up from the parking lot and climb 200 vertical feet over 0.25 mile to the lift top.

Alternatively, go left on Forest Road 123 to Big John Flat, about 2 miles below the ski resort off UT 153. Ask Forest Service personnel in Beaver whether the road is open, then drive the increasingly steep and rough four-wheel-drive road as high as possible. The Tushar Mountain Tours Yurt is located in this drainage.

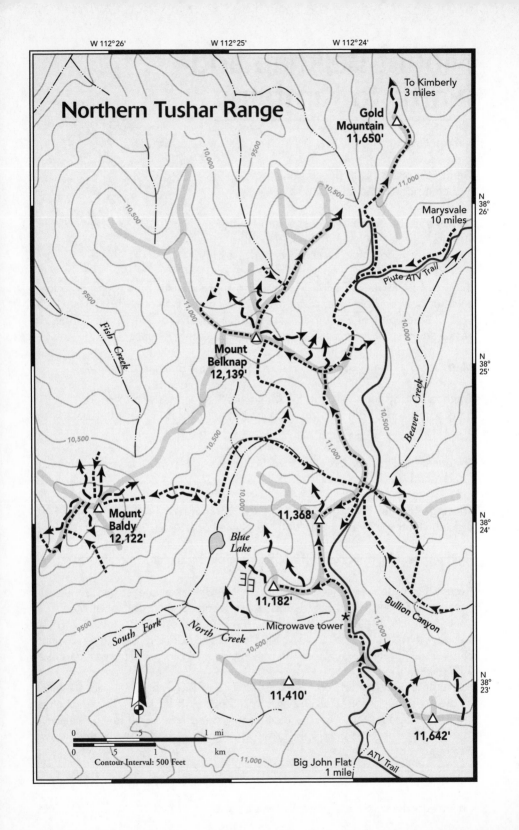

Northern Tushar Range

W 112°26' W 112°25' W 112°24'

To Kimberly
3 miles

Gold
Mountain
11,650'

Marysvale
10 miles

N 38° 26'

Piute ATV Trail

Fish Creek

Beaver Creek

Mount
Belknap
12,139'

N 38° 25'

10,000

10,500

11,000

9500

10,500

N 38° 24'

Mount
Baldy
12,122'

11,368'

Blue
Lake

Bullion Canyon

11,182'

South Fork

North Creek

Microwave tower *

9500

10,500

N
11,410'

N 38° 23'

0   .5   1 mi
0   .5   1   km

Contour Interval: 500 Feet

11,000

Big John Flat
1 mile

ATV Trail

11,642'

From Marysvale on U.S. Highway 89, go west on Marysvale Loop Road into Beaver Canyon, driving as close as possible to the base of Belknap's east face. The summer road goes practically to the summit, and midsummer skiing is often possible here.

Description: From the Elk Meadows Ski Resort, ascend to Delano Peak's western flank as described in Tour 61, Delano Peak. Traverse the moderate, open slopes on Delano's vast western aspect to the headwaters of Poison Creek.

Contour in and out of this shallow canyon, trending northwest without getting sucked down. Follow the crest of the ridge northwest past a microwave tower. You may encounter the summer four-wheel-drive road right along the divide. Hug the divide as it goes due north and then drops northeast to a three-way pass between the headwaters of Blue Lake Creek on the west, Beaver Creek on the northeast, and Pine Creek (Bullion Canyon) on the southeast. This pass is the last protected camping possibility before Belknap. The trip takes about five hours in supportable snow conditions.

From Big John Flat Road, simply follow the road from the highest drivable point past Mud Lake and intercept the divide near the microwave tower. From here, you'll be on the high route described above. Either route, however, has a viable alternative that involves more skiing and a more protected campsite possibly with running water available (especially after mid-April): Drop into upper Bullion Canyon from the south rim of Poison Creek. Excellent runs fall northwest through northeast as the cirque makes a semicircle from point 11,826 to the microwave tower.

Put your skins on after dropping 600 to 1,000 feet and follow Pine Creek as it bends north to the three-way pass mentioned above, or camp along the creek well below the pass.

To reach Belknap from the three-way pass, simply follow the divide over two humps, the second of which is nearly a 500-foot gain, and ascend the peak's southeast ridge, which holds snow late into spring. Avoid setting foot on the loose, southwest-facing talus of upper Belknap. At least one pair of climbers experienced a frightening phenomenon when the entire slope of flat, unconsolidated, unvegetated sedimentary rocks began to slide as they attempted to traverse below the summit. There is a trail up high on this face, but even this is prone to instability. Locals say the only thing that holds these rocks in place is the ceaseless westerly winds. Stay on snow whenever possible—it's your ally!

The northwest face of Belknap is a spectacular run, dropping at 35 to 40 degrees to a small choke at 11,600 feet, then widening again before another narrow passage at 11,200 feet. This crux becomes a rock band where a rappel is necessary later in the year. If you plan to ski this line, scope it out from I–70 beforehand, or simply stop skiing and hike back up from the second narrows.

There are several other shots on the northwest face and a drop from 11,600 feet on the north. The east face begins at 40 degrees and moderates for 900 feet before continuing at roly-poly low angles over buried old glacial moraines for another 600 feet into the woods. It's feasible to ski all the way down the

Dave Braun cuts up the afternoon slush on the northeast face of Mount Belknap.

gully to 10,300 feet, where the Marysvale Loop four-wheel-drive road intersects Big John Flat Road. Coming from Marysvale, this is the route of approach.

If you're doing a traverse, you can climb out of Beaver Canyon on a contouring road to the pass southwest of Gold Mountain. Still, there's a nice run off the northeast face of the unnamed point between Belknap and Gold. In order to ski it, stop at 10,800 feet after skiing the upper east face of Belknap and traverse north to join an old jeep road that contours across the southeast face to the northeast summit. The beautiful northeast face of this "Goldnap" peak ends right at the pass below Gold where an old cabin is falling apart. A spur of Marysvale Loop Road crosses this pass into the Fish Creek watershed.

To complete the traverse to Kimberly, the 1800s ghost town on the north end of the Tushars, stick to the top of the broad divide up and over Gold Mountain and, if you can resist the fine northeast-facing runs, carry on north to Signal Peak. Ski the wide north-facing cirque off Signal, and skate or flat-track northwest from its base. After 0.25 mile, work skier's left through sparse pines into a slide path that leads down to the Middle Fork of Mill Creek. Look for a road on the east side of the deepening creek gorge. Ignore several spurs that climb or contour east, and stick close to the gully. You will (hopefully) have cached a vehicle as high as possible on Forest Road 113, Kimberly-Marysvale Road. It leaves I–70 at Fremont Indian State Park.

Mount Baldy— Treasure of the Tushars

See map on page 250.

Rating: Difficult.

Tour 64

Gear: Skis or split-board with skins; ice ax and crampons in spring.

Summary: The most serious Tushar peak and a steep skier's dream, Baldy is seldom skied due to hard access. Incredibly proud lines fall from four aspects, three of them highly visible from Interstates 15 and 70. An overnight camp is necessary but worthwhile. Like Belknap, this is more of a spring corn than a winter powder skiing objective, given the high avalanche potential and remote location. Consider skiing Baldy as a side trip on a south-to-north spring traverse of the Tushar Range.

Maps: USGS 7.5-minute Shelly Baldy Peak, Mount Belknap, Delano Peak.

Trailheads: Upper parking lot, Elk Meadows Ski Resort; the backcountry access gate at the top of Big Elk Triple Chairlift; or Big John Flat Road, as high as possible.

Distance: 6 miles from Elk Meadows Ski Resort or 4 to 6 miles from Big John Flat Road (one way).

Starting altitude: Elk Meadows base, 10,355 feet; Big Elk Chair, 10,400 feet; Big John Flat, 9,000 to 10,000 feet.

High points: Unnamed peak, 11,182 feet; Mount Baldy, 12,122 feet.

Access: From Beaver off I–15 in south-central Utah, travel east for 22 miles on Utah State Route 153 to Elk Meadows Ski Resort. Turn left onto Upper Meadows Drive to the Upper Meadows Lodge, where a rental shop is also located. All roads are paved. If you're skiing at the resort, ride Big Elk Triple Chairlift. Otherwise, simply skin up from the parking lot and climb 200 vertical feet over 0.25 mile to the lift top.

Alternatively, go left on Forest Road 123 toward Big John Flat, about 2 miles below the ski resort on UT 153. Ask Forest Service personnel in Beaver whether the gate is locked, and drive this increasingly rough road as far as possible.

It's also possible to approach Baldy from the west or south, but considerably more vertical gain and lowland travel would be involved—that is, bushwhacking, sweating, and no ski runs along the way.

Description: Follow the route description in Tour 63, Mount Belknap and North to Kimberly, until you reach the microwave tower along the divide north of Delano Peak. Drop northwest into this drainage (the South Fork of North Creek) and cross to its north side. A ramp at 10,500 feet wraps around the southwest aspect of Peak 11,182 and joins the summer trail to Blue Lake. If it's safe, stay high along the lake's eastern shore, but be aware of avalanche potential from the west face of Peak 11,182. Camp at the north end of Blue Lake. The trip takes about six hours in favorable conditions.

Alternatively, rather than dropping down North Creek, better skiing can be found off Peak 11,182 and the ridge connecting it to the main Tushar divide. Simply continue northwest along the main divide until this ridge splits off and angles west, dropping off the divide and onto the subridge. A good route drops down from just west of the junction of these two ridges and funnels into a gully that leads directly to the north end of Blue Lake.

The classic run to Blue Lake, however, is off the summit of Peak 11,182 and falls northwest for 1,400 feet to the lake. It breaks over in the middle; you can either continue straight down or traverse left below some small cliff bands at about 10,500 feet to reach a wide-open, steeper west face. It terminates at the south end of Blue Lake.

From Big John Flat Road, simply follow the road from the highest drivable point until you reach Big John Flat. Leave the road and contour north at 10,000 feet to the West Fork of Merchant Creek and follow its northernmost tributary to 10,900 feet, staying right (east) of the creek gully itself. Traverse west away from the drainage here and go through the pass south of point 11,410 into an unnamed fork of North Creek's South Fork. Drop down the skier's-right side of the low-angle canyon until you can contour north at 10,200 feet and ski into North Creek proper. Cross it and contour north at 9,800 feet to Blue Lake. If Big John Flat Road is drivable for a few miles above UT 153, this is going to be a shorter, easier approach than the high line described above. It should take half a day, but to break it up, or to ski the open slopes of Shelly Baldy along the way, consider spending a night in the yurt above Big John Flat.

Now for Mount Baldy itself. The Blue Lake area seems to get as much snow as anywhere in the snowy Tushar Range, and the lake is often well above its normal height in spring. A meadow above the lake provides good camping, but it sits below an east-facing avalanche path off Baldy, so consider camping in the old-growth fir and spruce trees rather than in the 10-foot-high disaster species regrowth.

The above-mentioned slide path, if conditions are stable, is the easiest way

Mount Baldy (left), Mount Belknap (right), and Blue Lake; south view.

to escape the narrow depths of Blue Lake Canyon in the direction of Mount Baldy. It's possible to duck into bigger trees on climber's left after only 300 feet of ascent in the terrain-trap gully. Switchback up to the tree line below the wide, triangular east face of Baldy. Do not proceed any farther without high confidence in the snow stability.

Boot or switchback on skins up the east face and southeast ridge to the summit, and feast your eyes on the Tushar Range to the east and the western valleys far below. The skiing is outstanding on every major aspect. The north face has three distinct couloirs. The easternmost, which falls from the east summit, drops into a slightly different drainage, separated from the main north face by a wooded ridge. The main shot falls from the saddle between the east and west summits and is incredibly aesthetic. It goes for 1,200 feet at 35 degrees before gradually flattening out below a distinctive reddish cleaver. I call it the "Red Cleaver Couloir," and it's the finest line I've found in the Tushars. To regain the summit, simply switchback up the same gully or ascend to the northwest ridge and follow it back up. You'll be tempted by many similar gullies across the broad north face.

There are two primary runs on the west face. One falls from the northwest ridge, about 300 feet below the west summit. The other steeper line begins about the same distance down the southwest ridge (Baldy has amazing symmetry). Both routes become slide paths, cutting into the trees at approximately 10,800 feet. Climb directly back up or contour to one of the ridges and climb it. Potentially good north-facing tree shots fall from the south wall of North Creek, the canyon below the west face. A road initiating just east of Beaver climbs into this canyon, but it becomes a jeep trail and terminates at 7,800 feet. This would be the approach for a one-day, one-run visit to Baldy.

The south face is dominated by a 2,800-foot, 35-degree fall-line couloir. When conditions are "phat," this highly aesthetic line drops continuously to Blue Lake Creek about 0.5 mile below the lake. There's a choke in the middle where small cliffs enclose the gully. The lower entrances on the east and west of the line don't reach the central couloir without dodging rock bands. Ski it from the top!

The east face of Baldy is like a fan that spreads out as you descend. Only one line presents itself off the summit, but lower down there are exciting options between rock bands on both the north and south ends of the widening face. The kindly northeast shot can be reached by initially skiing the east or north faces off the east summit for 200 feet before traversing into it. It begins as a ridge but quickly becomes a face-type feature with an increasingly eastern orientation. The angle of incline exceeds 40 degrees much of the way. Ski it all the way into the trees that you ascended above Blue Lake, and then down the slide gully to camp. This is undoubtedly one of the finest ski peaks in Utah!

Return to Elk Meadows or Big John Flat by using the approach route for the latter up the unnamed southerly fork of North Creek. To reach the Upper Meadows parking lot, make a descending traverse skier's left to Poison Creek, then skin back to the hogback as described in Tour 61, Delano Peak.

A better option is to return to the Tushar divide and continue north to Kimberly, skiing Mount Belknap along the way. To do this, skin north from Blue Lake and follow the creek as it bends west then south to the three-way pass above Bullion Canyon and Beaver Creek. A more direct but steeper option is to climb directly to Belknap by turning north at the second tributary gully along Blue Lake Creek. Ascend to the southeast ridge and follow it to the summit as described in Tour 63.

Leeds Couloirs, Pine Valley Mountains

Rating: Difficult.

Gear: Skis or split-board with skins; light hiker approach shoes; ice ax and crampons optional in spring.

Tour 65

Summary: Off the beaten track for skiers, this extremely scenic area commands a great view of Zion National Park and the St. George area. The numerous couloirs that split the rugged southeast escarpment of the Pine Valley Mountains are visible from I–15. Take a good look from here to determine which one you want and for some recognizable features near its top. Although it's the closest steep skiing to St. George, it's a rugged adventure, not a user-friendly ski tour.

Map: USGS 7.5-minute Signal Peak.

Trailhead: Oak Grove Campground.

Distance: 3 miles (one way).

Starting altitude: 6,526 feet.

High points: About 10,000 feet. Below unnamed point, 10, 217 feet; Trail Peak, 8,527 feet; Signal Peak, 10,365 feet.

Access: From Leeds on I–15 just north of St. George in southwestern Utah, drive west from the northern freeway interchange (exit 23) on Silver Reef Road. Above the plush homes of this bedroom community, the road splits. Go right where the sign reads OAK GROVE CG, 8 MILES. It will split again after about a mile. Stay right and follow the well-maintained two-wheel-drive gravel road to Oak Grove Campground, where camping is now prohibited.

Description: Oak Grove has many beautiful old-growth ponderosa pines as well as Gambel oaks, and it's full of ferns and tall grass—truly a desert oasis. It's a very popular escape for overheated southern Utahns. Park at the well-marked trailhead where a sign reads SUMMIT TRAIL, 3; THREE PINES CREEK, 1. Follow the trail (if possible) past the junction with the Highline Trail, which leads to Three Pines Creek and points south along the base of the cliffs. Instead, take the right trail

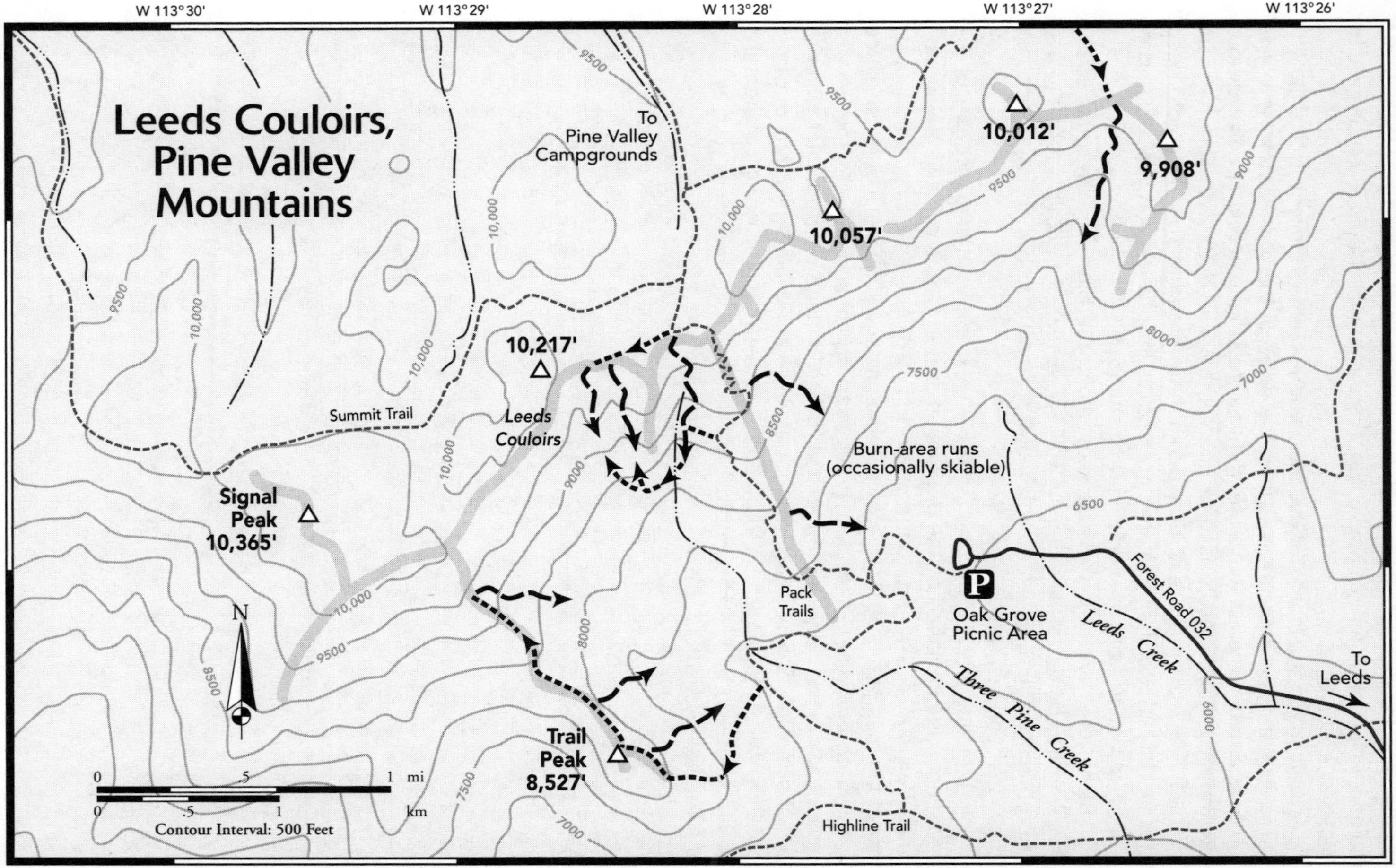

Leeds Couloirs, Pine Valley Mountains

N 37° 20'
N 37° 19'

W 113° 26'
W 113° 27'
W 113° 28'
W 113° 29'
W 113° 30'

To Leeds

Forest Road 032

Leeds Creek

6000

6500

Oak Grove Picnic Area

P

Three Pine Creek

Burn-area runs (occasionally skiable)

7000

7500

8000

8500

Pack Trails

Highline Trail

9000

9500

10,000

9,908'

10,012'

10,057'

10,217'

Leeds Couloirs

To Pine Valley Campgrounds

Summit Trail

Signal Peak 10,365'

Trail Peak 8,527'

7000

7500

8500

9500

N

Contour Interval: 500 Feet

1 mi
km
1
.5
.5
1
0
0

as it climbs through Gambel oak, mountain mahogany, and manzanita on a southerly aspect. A fine campsite with a great granite boulder (but no water) exists at 7,950 feet.

Continue up the trail to 10,000 feet, where it enters the woods and flattens out. Leave the trail and traverse along the edge of the cliffs southwest to one of three nearby couloirs that all feed into Three Pines Creek. The first drop is flanked by a huge granite face on the south (skier's left). The other two are about 0.3 and 0.4 mile west. They begin in trees and narrow down into deep granite defiles. Look for the many desert pines, including 4,000-year-old bristle-cones, sprouting from the vertical tawny stone.

Many other appealing couloirs exist along the bluff. The presence of the Highline Trail below and the Summit Trail above makes it possible to get to and from these exotic runs with a minimum of desert bushwhacking—especially those that end in Three Pines Creek.

In big-snow years it may be possible to ski the burn area just east of the indistinct ridge, followed by the pack trail between Oak Grove and the Summit Trail. Trail Peak's east- and northeast-facing pine glades also offer potential for skiing in times of heavy snow. Hike south along the Highline Trail to the Three Pines Creek crossing. Just past here, head south and up into the woods. Switchback to the ridge and on to Trail Peak. Continue over the peak to reach a higher couloir, Signal Peak. This ridge climb is spectacular—it juts out from the Pine Valley Bluffs near the formation's southern tip. The domes of Zion, the red rock around St. George, and endless desert landscape greet your eyes to the south and east.

Appendix A

Additional Resources

Avalanche Education

Fredston, Jill, and Doug Fesler. *Snow Sense,* 3rd ed. Anchorage: Alaska Mountain Safety Center, Inc., 1988.

McClung, David, and Peter Schaerer. *Avalanche Handbook.* Seattle: Mountaineers Books, 1993.

Tremper, Bruce. *Staying Alive in Avalanche Terrain.* Seattle: Mountaineers Books, 2001.

————.*Winning the Avalanche Game,* videocassette. Ketchum, Idaho: Forest Service National Avalanche Center, 1989.

Williams, K. *Snowy Torrents.* Jackson, Wyo.: Teton Bookshop Publishing Company, 1981.

Other Touring Books

Kelner, Alexis, and David Hanscom. *Wasatch Tours*, Vols. I, II, and III. Park City, Utah: Wasatch Tours Publishing, 1998.

McLean, Andrew. *Chuting Gallery.* Park City, Utah: Paw Prince Press, 1998.

Touring Maps

All of the following maps are available from Alpentech, 2871 South 2870 East, Salt Lake City, UT 84109.

Wasatch Touring Map 1—South Central

Wasatch Touring Map 2—North Central

Wasatch Touring Map 3—Ogden Mountains

Stansbury Ski Touring Map

Appendix B

Glossary

Many backcountry skiing and mountaineering terms are smattered throughout the text of this guidebook and may be confusing to unfamiliar readers. Here is a partial list of key words and contextual definitions.

alpine: The terrain above the timberline.

apron: An alluvial fan below a gully or headwall; usually offers moderate skiing.

aspect or exposure: The compass direction a run or mountain feature faces toward; often used to label terrain, e.g., southeast chutes, west buttress. (All aerial photo captions include the aspect from which the terrain is viewed.)

breakover: The point(s) often part-way down a run where the slope angle becomes significantly steeper; typical fracture point for a slab avalanche.

bushwhacking: To travel where no trail or road exists and/or dense vegetation is likely to be encountered.

choke: A narrow point of a gully or couloir.

cirque: An alpine bowl or drainage usually steeper at the top; often glacier-carved.

clean line: A ski run that is not interrupted by cliffs, traverses, or dense trees; can be skied without stopping.

climber's right or left: From the perspective of one facing generally uphill.

contour (v): To travel sideways, rather than up or down the fall line, usually staying at nearly the same altitude (often above or below a rock band or other parallel terrain feature).

corn snow: large, granular clusters of snow crystals at the snowpack surface created by the melt-freeze cycle of warm days and clear, cold nights. Early in the day, when it supports the weight of a skier, corn snow provides avalanche stability and a soft surface for carving.

couloir: A steep mountainside gully, often enclosed on both sides by rock.

cross-country skiing or flat-tracking: Skiing along snow-covered roads or across meadows where terrain is flat enough that climbing skins are not needed for traction; wax or (pattern-base) fishscales may be employed for minimal uphill purchase.

crux: The most difficult part of a particular route or run.

divide: The crest of a range or ridge between canyons from which separate watersheds drain in opposing directions.

drainage: The terrain area, usually a canyon or system of gulches, from which water flows into one stream; watershed.

erosion gully: A depression formed by water rushing down; typically loose, steep dirt or gravelly sides that make it a hazard to cross or travel in.

faceted: Loose, sugary grains of snow that have squared off sides or faces. They are metamorphosed from rounded or stellar grains by vapor rising through the snow as a result of a temperature gradient; faceted grains are often the shearing layer in cold snow avalanches; 3 millimeter or larger grains at or near the ground may be called "depth hoar."

fall line: The route a ball would take downhill; the direction of gravity's pull.

glisse: The generic term for sliding on snow in any mode (skiing, snowboarding, sledding, boot sliding, etc.).

massif: The entire mass of uplifted terrain associated with a particular summit or range.

melt-freeze crust (corn snow): A surface crust developed by warm days followed by clear nights; when mature, it supports the weight of a skier (or climber).

protruding terrain feature: A ridge, hogback, or other higher ground that usually isn't impacted by avalanches.

rock (or cliff) band: A horizontal cliff or series of rocks; usually with very few or no skiable ways through; may be referred to by rock type such as quartzite, limestone, granite, or sandstone.

scoured: A wind-blown area with firm or no snow; often on the upwind side of a ridge.

skier's right or left: From the perspective of one facing downhill.

slab: A smooth, less-than-vertical rock.

slab avalanche: A slide involving a patch of snow that releases at once and moves downhill, at least initially, as one connected chunk; very dangerous.

slogging: Travel that is tedious and/or physically demanding; as in "slogging up a featureless slope through waist-deep snow."

slope angle: The steepness of a run; low angle implies less than 20 degrees; moderate equals 20 to 35 degrees; and steep means 35 degrees plus.

snowfield: A snow-covered slope; as in "a steep snowfield between cliff bands."

snowpack: The accumulated snow cover on the ground; it usually includes many layers associated with the season's prior weather events (snow and wind storms, warm spells, etc.).

strong pack: Defined as having no significant weaknesses anywhere in the snowpack.

talus: Broken up boulders or loose rock; often an area for weak snow to develop; as in a facet garden.

temperature gradient (t-g): A difference in temperature, as between layers in the snowpack. In cold weather snow closer to the ground tends to be warmer than snow higher in the snow pack. A gradient of 10 degrees celsius over a meter of snow is enough to cause the formation or growth of faceted grains.

terrain trap: The area that catches snow sliding from above, such as a gully, couloir, or basin.

traverse: Usually a sideways section between portions of a run or route where relatively little gain or loss of altitude is involved.

traversing tour: A tour that goes from one point to another, usually crossing passes or peaks along the way. (South-to-north tours following on or near the crest of ranges are highly recommended in the La Sals, Tushars, and Abajos and have been done in the entire Wasatch. The Uintas offer a great west-to-east traverse.)

trailhead: The point where hiking or skiing begins for a particular tour or set of tours.

undulating: Going up and down rather than continuously rising or falling; as along a ridge.

weak pack: Defined as having known underlying weaknesses (e.g., faceted shearing layers) and is therefore relatively prone to avalanche.

windslab: A patch of snow that has become dense and connected by wind.

Appendix C

Aerial Photograph Index

Index

West Porter Fork, 103
West Tooele Cirque, 139
Wet Fork (Mill Creek), 211
White Baldy, 122, 126
White Canyon, 172
White Pine Canyon, 23, 91, 120, 139, 140–41
White Pine Creek, 22, 23, 123
White Pine Flat, 141
White Pine Gulch, 123, 125, 126
White Pine Knob, 21, 22
White Pine Lake, 23, 121
White Pine ridge, 120
White Pine Trail, 120, 121
White Pine Trailhead, 117, 120, 170
Wide Hollow, 172
Willard Peak, 54, 56–57
Willow Basin, 215
Willow Basin Trailhead, 212
Willow Creek, 98–99, 186
Willow Creek Trailhead, 99

Willow Heights, 99
Wilson Fork, 102
Windy Pass, 182
Wishbone Ridge, 126
Wolf Creek, 52
Wolf Pass, 185, 186
Wolverine Cirque, 91, 115
Wolverine Peak, 116
Wood Camp, 34
Wood Camp Cirque, 31, 38
Wood Camp High Country, 35–38
Wood Camp Hollow, 35
Wood Camp Trailhead, 35
Woolly Hole, 177, 178

Y

Y Chute, 53
Y Couloir, 128
Yellow Pine Canyon, 76
Y-Not, 128

About the Author

Backcountry skiing is Tyson Bradley's passion, and he has been exploring Utah's backcountry since 1984. Mountain guiding in Utah, Wyoming, Oregon, and Alaska has been his primary career since 1994. He guides skiing for Wasatch Powderbird Guides and Exum Utah Mountain Adventures. He also does avalanche control work at Alta Ski Resort and teaches avalanche courses.

Tyson has organized and led first ski-descent expeditions to Denali's Wickersham Wall, Mount Foraker's Sultana Ridge, and Mounts Fairweather and St. Elias. His lust for adventure has resulted in four Himalayan journeys, including ski descents of China's Muztagh Ata and Kyrgyzstan's Pik Pobeda. He has also been skiing and trekking in India, Pakistan, and Nepal and bicycling in China. He has traveled to South America's Andes twice, skiing Huascaran in Peru and smaller summits in Chile and Argentina.

Tyson writes regularly for the Salt Lake City–based *Sports Guide* monthly magazine. His articles have also appeared in *Couloir Magazine*, *American Alpine Journal*, and *Rock & Ice Magazine*.

To support his writing and guiding careers, Tyson is a commercial fisherman, formerly in Alaska's Bering Sea and currently on Utah's Great Salt Lake. He lives in Salt Lake City with his wife and climbing and skiing partner, Julie Faure, and their son, Roman.